Answers To Questions About

# OLD JEWELRY

## "1840 TO 1950"

by Jeanenne Bell

# 2nd Edition

ISBN 0-89689-053-8

BOOKS AMERICANA
INC

**Dedicated to:**
The One from Whom all good things cometh
and
my parents
Anne Lee Hopper Noblitt
and
Aaron Belton Noblitt
with love.

# TABLE OF CONTENTS

## Section III Is It Real?

**Special thanks to:**
  I. Dan Alexander, President of Books Americana for his friendship and positive motivation.
 II. G.I.A. and its President Richard I. Liddicoat, Jr. for allowing us to reprint illustrations from their course on colored gems.
III. Gem Media, a division of The Gemological Institute of America for providing photographs for The "Is It Real?" section.
IV. William Doyle Galleries, 175 East 875h St., New York, New York and Wendy Corhart for supplying photographs, descriptions and prices, and for granting permission for their use in this book.
 VI. Phillips, Blenstock House, 7 Blenhein St., New Bond St., London W1YOAS and Mr. John Condrop and Mr. A. Spice for their assistance and permission to use photographs, descriptions and prices from auction catalogues.
VII. Sothebys, 1334 York Ave., New York, and Jacqueline Fay for granting us permission to use photographs, descriptions and prices from their auction catalogue.
VIII. Sotheby & Co. Bloomfield Place, Off Bond Street London WIA 2AA., Mr. David Bemmett F.G.A. Head of Jewelry Dept. and his secretary, Joan Marchant, for permission to use auction photographs, descriptions and realised prices and for their assistance in supplying this information.
 IX. Mr. T. Roe of Jowsey & Roe #7 Sandgate, Whitby, North Yorkshire, England, for allowing me to photograph the jet jewelry in his shop and for sharing his memories of the history of the Whitby jet industry.
  X. Norm Williams and King Features Syndicate, N.Y., for permission to use illustrations from their 1949-50 pattern book.
 XI. Camille Grace, "Stuff" dealer, K.C. Mo. for allowing me to take her jewelry across the country to be photographed.

XII. Wayne Baldwin, Peggy Carlson, Mary Holloway, Anne Noblitt, A.B. Noblitt, Lela Reed, Margaret Sorrell and Mignon Stufflebam for sharing pieces from their collections.

XIII. Lucule and Sam Mundorff of "The Old 'n You Antiques Mart Inc.," K.C. Mo. for allowing us to photograph some of their pieces.

XIV. Edward J. Tripp, Blue Ridge, Texas for sharing his knowledge of ivory.

XV. Marilyn Roos, "Natural Amber," St. Louis, Mo. for an informative interview on amber.

XVI. Bob P. Holloway, K.C., Mo. artist, for the excellent Hallmark example in the "What is This Metal?" section.

XVII. Amanda Bell for her able assistance on the microfilm machine.

XVII-
I. And last but certainly not least, Don L. Bell, for his encouragement, love and help in typing the manuscript.

## A NOTE FROM THE AUTHOR

Most people are aware of the "gold rush" of 1980. When gold reached an all time high, many fine pieces of jewelry were sold for scrap. This affected jewelry collectors and dealers in two ways. First, many old pieces were melted, forever denying someone the pleasure of owning and wearing them. Secondly, because some gold dealers were wise enough not to melt good, old pieces, there is more jewelry on the market now than ever before. In my opinion, this is a passing surge. Once the overflow has been assimilated into collections, good antique jewelry will be more scarce than ever. Consequently, now is the time to buy.

A piece of antique jewelry, like any collectable, is worth what someone is willing to pay. Supply and demand play a major part in determining price. A few years ago stick pins were very fashionable. Many were sold, and the prices increased. Today Art Nouveau and Art Decco pieces are in demand. Consequently, prices reflect this. Always keep in mind that the price of antique jewelry cannot depend on the amount of gold involved anymore than an oil painting can be priced by the cost of the frame and canvas.

This book reflects the value of jewelry by what it is selling for in antique shops and antique shows. Over 80% of the jewelry in this book was for sale at the time it was photographed. These prices are for these particular pieces in their particular condition. Prices also vary in different parts of the country.

My advice is to collect jewelry you like and enjoy wearing. Then if it happens to appreciate in value (and it probably will) that is all the more reason to treasure it.

Buying, selling, and collecting antique jewelry has brought me many hours of happiness over the years. It has been a pleasure to share this information with you. My permanent mailing address is listed below. If you have any questions or if there are any pieces that you need more information about, do not hesitate to drop me a note. Please include a self addressed stamped envelope.

## A NOTE FROM THE AUTHOR
## SECOND EDITION

The first edition of this book was written with the person in mind who was curious about old jewelry. Whether it was someone who had pieces that had been passed down in the family or simply someone who had become fascinated with old jewelry and wanted to know more about it.

The original book was compiled on the premise that if one had jewelry worth thousands of dollars, they probably were aware of its value, but that one could well have a piece worth hundreds of dollars and have no idea of its worth.

I was very pleased with the reception the book received from the jewelry industry. Obviously, there was a real need for more of this researched information about old jewelry.

With this in mind, I strove to make this a more well rounded book. One that would be both interesting to the layman and a reference tool for the professional. To accomplish this, many expensive pieces have been added.

Pieces with the prices realized at auction are an important addition. Included are pieces auctioned in the United States at Phillips, Sotheby's and Wm. Doyle Galleries. In order to show the trends in England I included many pieces that have been auctioned there and the prices realized in pounds and dollars. The exchange rate of the dollar was about $1.45 to the pound.

An important fact to keep in mind when observing auction prices is that approximately 70% of these buying at auction are dealers. *Consequently many of the prices reflect what dealers are paying and do not include a retail mark-up.*

Since the designers and the makers have such an impact on the value of jewelry, I have included pieces by designers such as Costellini, Carlo Guiliano and Lalique. Jewelry retailed by firms such as Tiffanys, Cartier and Liberty & Co. is also included.

A glossary of terms used in this book is an addition that I hope will be most welcome.

I am grateful for the opportunity to add to your knowledge of old jewelry. It is a fascinating subject and I hope it brings to you the joy of discovery that it has brought to me.

Sincerely,
Jeanenne Bell
P.O. Box 282
Fairfield, Ala. 35064

# INTRODUCTION

Almost everyone is curious about old jewelry. Maybe it's because most people have a piece or two tucked away somewhere. It could be a locket that belonged to grandmother or a pin that has been handed down in the family.

Along with most jewelry comes unanswered questions—"How old is it? Is it valuable? What is the material?" Whether you are a serious collector or a curious owner, this book will help answer these questions.

Section I deals with jewelry styles from 1840-1950. To make looking at each style easier, they are divided into the following time periods.

| | |
|---|---|
| 1840-1860 | Victoria and Albert |
| 1861-1889 | Victoria |
| 1890-1915 | Edwardian; Art Nouveau |
| 1920-1930's | Art Deco |
| 1940-1950's | Modern |

Jewelry has always had definite period styles. These were reflected in jewelry motifs in much the same manner as they were reflected in furniture. Consequently, if you can identify a piece of Art Nouveau furniture you can probably recognize a piece of jewelry from that same period.

Period styles have a way of overlapping. Changes happened gradually. A style that was waning in England in 1860 could still be in its peak of popularity in the United States. As communications improved and travel made the world seem smaller, these changes took place more rapidly. This will be more evident as the later periods are examined.

A study of jewelry is incomplete unless it includes information about the lives and times of the people who wore it. How they lived and what they experienced was reflected in their clothes and accessories. For this reason each period begins with a short synopsis of the times.

Since jewelry was used to complement clothing, it is impossible to fully understand jewelry styles without relating them to the fashions they accessorized. Fashion plates are included in each time period to make real the clothing of the period. Many quotes from publications of the day are included, not only to supply information on the styles but also to provide a "flavor" of the times.

In each period certain pieces and materials were in vogue. These were determined by many things: the neckline, the hemline, the hairstyles, and even the economy.

The historical information, the magazines quotes, and the many photographs included in Section I should help provide answers to the questions: "When was it made?" and "What is its value?"

Section II deals with the different types of metal used in jewelry making. Gold, silver, pinchbeck, gold filled, gold plate, and platinum are some of the topics discussed. Many questions concerning a piece of jewelry can be answered by learning to identify its metal content.

Section III will help answer the question, "Is it real?" It contains simple tests to determine the authenticity of such material as amber, ivory, gutta-percha, and jet. Various methods of identifying stones are discussed.

Finding answers to questions about old jewelry is an interesting hobby. It can be an adventure into the past that can be a big investment in the future. Happy hunting and remember: stay curious!

# SECTION I

## When Was It Made?
## What Is Its Value?

### 1840-1860
### THE TIMES

The years from 1840 to 1860 were exciting times in which to be alive. The fruits of the Industrial Revolution were bringing about new social and economic conditions. Changes were taking place at a rapid pace.

The American spirit of creativity was boundless. These were the years in which Horace Greely founded the New York Tribune (1841), Goodyear patented his rubber making process (1844), Howe invented the sewing machine (1846), Tiffany opened his first store (1849), and Gail Borden patented his process for condensing milk (1856).

On January 24, 1848, gold was discovered in California. As the eyes of the world turned toward Sutter's Mill, people headed in that direction. They went by wagon, by horse, and by foot, seeking their fortune. This migration led to new towns all across the country. California's population increased 2,550% in one year.

Railroads were expanding. In 1840 there was 3,000 miles of track. By 1860 the total had grown to 30,000. Railroads were definitely on the move, bringing with them economic success.

Fortunes were being made. In 1845 New York had twenty-one millionaires; many more would be added to the list before 1861. The showman P.T. Barnum made his fortune promoting amusements. He sponsored Jenny Lind's American debut in 1850. The editor of Godey's Lady's Magazine had this to say about the trend it set:

*Of course now that Jenny Lind is more widely known to the American Public, shopkeepers lose no time in making the most out of the popular tasts for novelties. Jenny Lind bandeaux, were the only things extensively copied among us, until she had absolutely arrived and then the*

*furore commenced. At Stewarts', Beck's and Levy's there was no dif-*
*ference, but in the Bowery, Canal Street, or Eight and Second Streets,*
*in Philadelphia, Jenny Lind plaids, combs, slides, ear rings, work*
*baskets, bonnets, and even hair-pins were advertized and recom-*
*mended. Now, these had no legitimate claim to the title inasmuch as*
*we do not believe Mademoiselle Lind had ever seen, much less worn,*
*the articles in question. It was a barefaced shopkeeping ruse but*
*nevertheless it succeeded; and half the American public are now wip-*
*ing their heated brows with Jenny Lind pocket—hankerchiefs, or*
*dressing their hair with Jenny Lind's combs.*

For the first time the average person was allowed the luxury of leisure time activities. Baseball clubs sprang up in
towns across the country. In 1858 the National Association of
Baseball Players was formed. Trotting races, boxing, and
even football games were popular. Of course these activities
were 'for men only'.

In England these years were also filled with changes.
These were the years in which Britain became known as a
nation immersed in both industry and the arts. Already the
undisputed leader in steam navigation and railway construction, by staging the first International Exposition of Arts and
Industry in 1851, she became known as a patron of the arts.

With the exception of the years 1842 and 1848 when there
was a depression, the nation flourished with unprecedented
economic success. Cottage industries were becoming a thing
of the past. More and more people went to work in factories.
Factory made goods were cheaper and more plentiful than
their hand made predecessors, and most people had the
money to buy them.

Social conditions were improving. The Shaftesbury Act of
1842 made it illegal for the mines to hire children under ten
years of age. In 1847 the Fielden Act made it against the law
for a child to work more than ten hours a day.

No longer was a person destined to stay in the social class
to which he had been born. Victorians were beginning to
believe that with education, hard work, and the proper fear
of God, a person's opportunities were unlimited. Even the
young aristocrats were going into trade and industry.

Religion was an important element in Victorian life. On
'Census Sunday' in 1851, it was estimated that five out of
every twelve people attended a worship service. Most Sun-
days were spent attending church, reading the Bible, and

refraining from 'worldly' activities.

Quite often when things are changing too fast, society looks to the past for inspiration. This was the case with the Victorians. They looked back to the middle ages and were enchanted by knights in shining armor, fair maidens, and chivalry. They wanted to emulate these romantic ideals for their generation. Medieval Balls became the highlight of the social circle, giving everyone an opportunity to don the costume of that period. There was even talk of having a Medieval Ball as part of the Queen's coronation, but the idea was dropped because of the enormous expense involved.

Queen Victoria's exemplary lifestyle gave the country an opportunity to once again experience pride in its Royal Family. With her stable influence and the guidance of superb prime ministers, Britain expanded its imperialistic power and became a great nation. With the exception of the Crimean War (1854-56) this was a time of peace and prosperity.

## Victoria

Queen Victoria was born on May 24, 1819 at Kensington Palace. Her father was the Duke of Kent, the fourth son of George III. At birth there seemed to be little prospect of her ever becoming Queen of England, but fate would have it otherwise.

Victoria led a very sheltered life. Her father died when she was a baby. Her German mother, Victoria Maria Louisia, raised her in England, anticipating the day when she would inherit the crown. Victoria was never allowed time to herself. Someone was with her at all times. She even slept in the room with her mother. Always protected, she was never left alone.

It is little wonder that Victoria's first request, after being crowned Queen in 1938, was to spend time alone. Her request was granted. Later her bed was moved to a room of her own. She was the Queen, and it was exhilerating!

The people of England were anxious for the young Queen to marry and have children to insure the throne. Victoria, happy with her first taste of freedom, was totally against the idea until her cousin came to visit. She had met Albert a few years earlier when he and his brother came for a two week stay. At that time she had been impressed with his blue eyes and engaging smile. When she saw him again all her reservations vanished. She was in love.

The marriage was a happy one. The children, a total of nine, came one after another. Holidays were spent on the sea shore at Osborne or in their Balmoral House in Scotland. Victoria was a loving, giving person, who placed a high regard on sentiment. Her life centered around her God, her God given duties as Queen, her beloved Albert, and her children.

## Albert

Prince Albert should share equal "billing" with Queen Victoria in this time period. He was very instrumental in the impact England had on the world during these years.

Francis Charles Augustus Albert Emmanuel was born on August 26, 1819 in Colburg, Germany. His father was the Duke of Saxe-Coburg-Gotha. His aunt was Victoria Maria Louise of Saxe-Coburg, the mother of Queen Victoria. From early childhood he had been groomed as a possible husband for his cousin.

After the marriage, Albert worked as an aid and advisor to Victoria. Although some people worried about the Queen taking advice from someone who was not English, the nation grew to love and respect him.

He was as sentimental as his wife in many respects. The engagement ring he gave her was in the form of a serpent (an ancient symbol of good fortune). For their sixth anniversary he presented her with a wreath for her hair made of porcelian and enamaled gold. He had designed it himself. The orange blossom wreath had four enamaled oranges, each representing one of their children. He also designed a brooch the Queen presented to Florence Nightengale commemorating her services in the Crimean War.

Albert loved art, and one of his favorite ways to spend an afternoon was to browse through art studios and museums. This interest led to his appointment as head of a Commission to encourage art in England.

In 1844 he became president of "A Society For Improving The Conditions Of The Working Classes." He was very concerned and often personally inspected sites that needed improving or were in the process of being improved.

Albert was a firm believer in the importance of education. In 1847 he was elected Chancellor of Cambridge University. Many of his ideas were incorporated into the Universities' programs. Some of these ideas were even imitated by Oxford University.

One of the most exciting contributions Albert made to the Victorian era was his part in the Great International Exposition of 1851. There had been other expositions, but this was the first of international scope. The Crystal Palace Exhibitions Illustrated Catalogue speaks glowingly of his help.

> If, therefor, the merit of having originated exhibitions of her own manufacture belongs to France, it is to his Royal Highness Prince Albert that the more noble and disinterested plan of throwing open an institution of this description to all the competetion of the whole world, is exclusively due; and his suggestion has been carried out in a spirit every way worthy its grandeur and generosity.

Further into the history we find these words:

> But indeed, for his (Prince Albert) indefategable perserverance, his courageous difiance of all risks of failure, his remarkable sagacity in matters of business, and the influence which attached to his support the whole project, notwithstanding the great exertions which had been made to secure its realisation, must have fallen to the ground.

Lest we think these kind words were given because Albert was the Queen's husband, the article makes it very plain that this was not the case:

> It is difficult to assign to Prince Albert the degree of praise which is really due on this occasion without incurring the suspicions of being in some degree influenced by the exalted position he holds in the country ... Rather than incur the imputation of sycophancy, his admirers have sometimes been led to do less than justice to the very prominent part he has taken in this project, and to the consummate skill with which he has smoothed down all opposition to it. In a word, for the World's Exposition, the world is entirely indebted to the Prince Consort.

## THE GREAT EXHIBITION

The purpose of the Great Exhibition of the Industry of all Nations was to provide an arena for the celebration of the arts and industry of man. Each country displayed its newest and best in the four divisions: raw materials, machinery and mechanical inventions, manufactures, sculpture and plastic art. Prizes were awarded in each category.

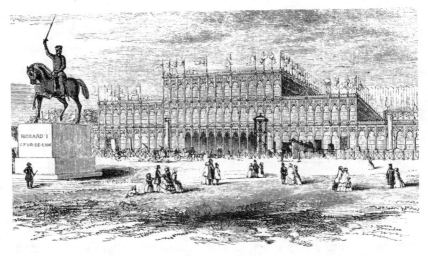

WESTERN ENTRANCE TO THE GREAT EXHIBITION.

**Courtesy Art-Journal Illustrated Catalogue**

The exhibition was housed in a building designed by Joseph Paxton and built by the firm of Fox and Henderson. Its glass and iron construction made it look like a gigantic greenhouse. Dubbed "the Crystal Palace," it was truly a wonder to behold. Built in the shape of a parallelogram, it had an enclosed area of 772,284 square feet (about nineteen acres). The construction utilized 9,000,000 feet of glass, 550 tons of wrought iron, and 3,500 tons of cast iron. But the building had such a light and airy look that people were concerned about its safety. After several tests proved the strength and safety of the design, the public could hardly contain their excitement until opening day.

The Queen and her husband presided a the official opening on May 1, 1851. The Archbishop of Canterbury gave the invocation and a hugh, combined choir sang the Hallelujah Chorus. The procession was regal. Clearly this was the event of the decade. Only season ticket holders were allowed to attend this ceremony. An estimated 25,000 people were present.

After opening day, the general public came. Using England's excellent railroads they flocked from all over to see the Crystal Palace and its contents. It was the place to see and be seen. Many days were required to view the exhibition properly. There were literally miles of things to see. For a small fee the average working man or woman could see sights normally reserved for royalty.

The largest section in the building housed machinery. Machines for making rope, lace, silk, flax, and furniture could be seen in operation. Steam hammers, hydraulic presses, and fire engines were on display. Power for the machinery was furnished by an engine house built one hundred and fifty five feet from the main building. Its five boilers produced enough steam power to serve the entire exhibition.

Each country had a section in which to show the best of its machinery, inventions, art, and products. There were musical instruments, furniture, carpets, vases, china, laces, clocks, watches, toys, stained glass, and much much more. The jewelry and precious stones attracted much attention. The two hundred and eighty (280) carat "Kah-i-Norr" diamond and Adrian Hop's one hundred seventy seven (177) carat diamond were on display along with such everday items as chantelaines and brooches.

A.W.N. Pugin, an Englishman, designed the Medieval Court section of the exhibition. Here he displayed the jewelry collection he had designed using Gothic motifs. There were bracelets, brooches, ear-rings, and necklaces featuring lovely blue and green enameling. They were enchrusted with pearls, turquoise and cabachon garnets (Cabachon was a popular cut for stones set in medieval style.) These ecclesiastical, medieval designs appealed to the romatic nature of the Victorians. The novels of Sir Walter Scott had enticed their imaginations to medieval times. This jewelry made tangeable the beauty already associated with that period. The collection caused a revival in enameling techniques. Crosses, quatre-foils, and many other architectural details became popular jewelry motifs.

Jewelry designs based on nature were much in evidence at the exhibition. The Art-Journal Illustrated Catalogue made this comment about the new styles.

> The taste for floral ornament in jewelery has been very prevelent of late, and it is a good and happy taste, inasmuch as the brilliant coloring of an Enamelled leaf or floret is an excellent foil to a sparkling stone; and we have scarcely seen the design for jewelery at any period more tasteful, elegant, and appropriate, than they are at the present day.

The Crystal Palace Exhibition was a success from every point of view. The Queen and royal children enjoyed it so much that they visited many times. This was an added incentive for the public. It was estimated that over six million people visited the exhibition.

This success instigated a series of exhibitions. The United States had a Crystal Palace Exposition in 1853. It was promoted by P.T. Barnum, and yes, it was called the Crystal Palace Exposition. In 1855 an International Exhibition was staged in Paris. England scheduled another one for 1861.

# 1840-1860
## Fashions In Clothing And Jewelry

**Illustration from Godey's Lady's Book, August, 1850.**

England and America looked to Paris for fashion. These were always seasoned by the English form for 'correctness,' and 'Americanized' for the United States. In January 1850, Godey's Lady's Book found it necessary to print the following: "We have always taken care in preparing our descriptions of fashion and fashion from foreign authorities, to translate, as far as possible, the French terms and idioms, for as a correspondant justly says 'it is presumed the Ladys Book is read and intended more for American than French ladies.' Moreover, it may be noticed that our magazine is the only one that does this among all the numerous pretenders in the same path. It is true, there are, now and then, names of articles that have naturalized into our language, for which there is no translation. For instance, the Spanish, Mantilla; the French mantelet, berthé; a raché or glacé silk; tulle, etc, etc. With these exceptions, if our friends, any of them, will take the trouble to look back through the last volume, they will find no other foreign word introduced. The importance of this, in magazines destined for circulation in remote districts, where no language but our own is spoken or written, will at once be recognized. For those whom a city life had not made familiar with the proper names of articles, we annex a collection of terms most generally in use.

Berthe is a cape of lace, of almost the shape of those so fashionable a few years since, and called "low capes', in common parlance.

Tulle, or illusion—common fine silk net lace.

Ruche, a ruffle or quilling of lace or ribbon.

Corsage, waist of a dress.

Boquet de Coeffure and boquet de carrsage—bouquets for the waist and head.

Glace silk, a summer or thin silk."

In the 1840's and 1850's, as in all Victorian times, it was highly improper for "Meladies" ankle to show. Therefore, dresses were long and full with two or three flounces. Daytime (or morning) dresses usually had high necklines, pointed waists, and long sleeves even in the summer. Over this was worn a decorative apron and a Berthe. During the day bonnets shuggly covered the head and ears. For evening, dresses were low cut and the arms were exposed. The head was uncovered. Flowers and fruit were woven into the hair.

Throughout this period, women kept their ears covered. During the day, they were hidden under a bonnet; for evening they were covered with clusters of curls. As Godeys stated in 1855, "We give up the ear. Pretty or not, it cannot afford to be shown. Any face in the world looks bold with the hair put

10

away so as to show the ears. They must be covered. The curveline of the jaw needs the intersecting shade of the falling curl, or of the plait of braid drawn across it. So evident is it to us that nature intended the female ear to be covered—(by giving long hair to women, and making the ears concealment almost inevitable as well as necessary to her beauty)—that we only wonder the wearing of it covered, by hair or cap, has never been put down among the rudiments of modesty."

Very little jewelry was worn during the day. With bonnets or curls covering the ears, ear-rings were "almost wholly out of date except as worn on what may be termed state occasions."[1] Jewelry was limited to hair ornaments, brooches, and bracelets. Of these, bracelets were by far the most popular. An article in the World of Fashion states: "Bracelets are now considered indispensible; they are worn in the following manner; on one arm is placed the sentimental bracelet, composed of hair and fastened with some precious relic; the second is a silver enamaled one, having a cross, a cassolette, or anchor and heart, as sort of a talisman; the other arm is decorated with a bracelet of gold net work fastened with a simple noeud, similar to one of narrow ribbon; the other composed of medallions of blue enamel, upon which are placed small bouquets of brilliants, the fastening being composed of a single stone; lastly a broad gold chain, each link separated with a ruby and opal alternate."

Yes, you read it correctly! The women actually wore five bracelets (two on one arm; three on the other), and mixed a variety of materials—hair, silver, gold net, gold chain, enameled medallions, brilliants, rubys, and opals. The arms were available to decorate so they used them to the fullest.

By the end of 1855 the neckline was worn lower. Necklaces once again came into fashion. According to the December issue of Godey's, the most popular ones were made of hair. "Now that dresses are cut away from the throat more than for many years past, necklaces are once more in vogue. Hair necklaces are made in transparent globules or beads, and united in a continuous chain, or separated by a gold bead, either plain or chased, with a handsome gold clasp. Pendants of hair are almost necessary to this style of necklace. One of

11

Illustration from Godey's Lady's Book, February, 1855.

the most effective, and apparently most simple, is a cross
woven of hair and enframed by small diamonds; this is
suspended on a narrow black velvet ribbon, a band always

enhances the purity of a white throat and neck. A simple gold chain the light Venetian link, with no pendant but a small medallion passing once around the neck, is very suitable for a young girl. Nothing can be more in taste than a necklace on a thin, bony or discolored neck. Very few women in our country should venture upon one after thirty."

"Skirts are made very full," stated Godey's Magazine in 1855. "Fashion exacts an immense use of crinoline. Many are gathered at the waist into large round and hollow plaits. The front of the skirt is not as full or as long as the back; the first should leave the foot visible, while the second just clears the ground, or, for every dress, forms a demi-rounded train. Underskirts are arranged so as to meet the exactions of the modern hoop. Corsets are cut much shorter, no longer compressing the hip. Crinoline is worn with one or two flounces, the object being as much breath as possible to the figure."

By January 1859, skirts had become so wide Godeys' complained that "Young ladies are now presenting a very formidable appearance of amplitude. The wand of fashion has transformed that most slender girls into the appearance of haystacks." This obvious disapproval did not deter their announcement, in the next issue, of a new "self supporting tournue." On the contrary, they were quite enthusiastic about it! "That this invention should not have been made long ago, is surprising, for it is very simple and yet the best article to give beauty to the human figure. All other devices to give rotundity to the shape betray themselves, while this yields to the figure and makes no sign of its existence in the gait of a lady. The light pliant springs which proceed from the steel waistband, below or above the edge of it, as may be needed by short or long waists, perform their office admirably. These are represented by the vertical bands. The horizonal ones represent broad tapes, which sustain the general drapery. Nothing could be invented so well calculated to meet the demands of those who, in full dress, wish to present the realization of a well shaped and graceful figure. This Tournure is now generally adopted by fashionable ladies in all parts of the country, and is prized because it never loses its ability to sustain and round the skirts. Without suggesting that it is employed for such a purpose. The demand for it is very great, but the large manufactory in this city will be able to supply every dress and millinary establishment in the country, during the present season. Ladies will be delighted to throw away the cumbersome articles hitherto used to improve the figure, and adopt this admirable invention, which has been patented."

Though Godey's Lady's Magazine was known for its beautiful colored fashion plates not every department was pleased with women's styles. "While we are no Bloomerite, we must enter our protest against the very long dresses of the present day," wrote Dr. Jno. Stainback Wilson, editor of the magazine's health Department. "They are cumbersome, uncleanly, and wastefully extravagant. They prevent freedom of motion in walking; they gather the dirt from the roads and streets as they drag their beautiful lengths alone; and they cannot possibly last. In view of all these things, then, and others that might be mentioned, our verdict is; let the skirts of dresses be sufficiently Bloomerized to swing clear of the ground, at any rate. Pointed waists are nearly as bad as corsets. They compress and paralyze the muscles beneath them; while the internal organs, the stomach, liver, spleen, etc. are crowded downward, thus causing a train of most common and serious disorders to which women are subject."

Death was a very real and present part of life in Victorian times. It demanded respect not only for the 'departed,' but also for the feelings of the living. A death was always followed by a period of mourning. This usually consisted of a year spent in "full mourning" and another in "half mourning." Some widows were known to mourn the rest of their lives.

During this time women were subject to very rigid dress codes. These applied not only to widows but also to daughters, aunts, sister-in-laws, and cousins. Godey's Lady's Book helped keep the ladies up-to-date on what was appropriate. In their fashion section for March 1855, were these recommendations: "Mourning attire for a daughter— Mourning dress of parametta cloth trimmed with robings of crape; small crape collar with cuffs. *Walking-Dress*—Dress of black silk and an overskirt of crape; crape collar and sleeves, Crape and silk bonnet with fall, entirely black inside; black parasol; jet brooch and chain; black kid gloves. *Attire for an Aunt*—Black poplin dress for the street; black velvet bonnet and black cloth mantle; white collar and sleeves.

*Evening Dress*—Barege or glace silk flounces; collar and sleeves, with little but rich embroidery; white kid gloves."

Furs were very much on the fashion scene. This fact was brought out by an article in the January 1859 issue of Godey's. "Furs are at the height of favor and were never more universally worn. Ermine bands are used for trimming opera-cloaks, or sorties du bal; dark fur, and sable, and mink for velvet cloaks, etc., intended for the street. A Victorine, or cape with lappets, or round cloak, with cuffs and a small muff, are considered a full set. The Victorines are usually quite deep, coming half way to the waist behind—the cape to the waist and below it. The cloaks are as deep as ordinary talmas, and with the capes, have a collar. The muffs are still quite small. Furs are lined usually with quilted silk, and ornamented by rich cords and tassels. Sable, Hudson's Bay, and mink are the favorites among the expensive furs—Siberian squirrel, and a mixture of the gray and white fur in stripes, are among the less expensive ones."

## HAIRWORK JEWELRY

Victorian women wore jewelry not only as a decorative accessory but also as an outward expression of their innermost feelings. To them it was perfectly natural for Queen Victoria to have a bracelet made from her children's baby teeth. This may seem far-fetched to today's generation, but in those days it was a high privilege to have a part of a loved one near. To have carelessly disposed of the teeth would have been throwing away a part of her children.

This sentimental nature fostered an increasing interest in hair jewelry. For years it had been popular to own a lock of a loved one's hair. This was usually kept in a special compartment in the back of a brooch, a locket, a ring, or even in a watch fob. In the early years of the nineteenth century hair began to be used for the actual making of jewelry.

Hairwork became a drawing room pastime, just as popular as crocheting or tatting. What could be more rewarding than working with the hair of a loved one. This pastime spread throughout Europe. In December of 1850 Godey's Lady's Book introduced it to American Women:

*Of the various employments for the fingers lately introduced among our countrywomen, none is, perhaps more interesting than that we are about to describe, viz. hairwork; a recent importation from Germany, where it is very fashionable. Hitherto almost exclusively confined to professed manufactures of hair trinkets, this work has now become a drawing-room occupation, as elegant and as free from all annoyances and objections of litter, dirt, or unplesant smells, as the much practiced knitting, netting or crochet can be; while a small hankerchief will at any time cover the apparatus and materials in use. By acquiring a knowledge of this art, ladies will be themselves enabled to manufacture the hair of beloved friends, and relatives into the bracelets, chains, rings, ear-rings, and devoices, and thus insure that they do actually wear the momento they prize, and not a fabric substituted for it, as we fear has sometimes been the case.*

The work was done on a round table. It could be done while sitting or standing, depending on the height of the table. Many ladies preferred to stand because their full dresses sometimes interfered with the dangling weights on the hair.

Preparation of the hair was most important. Not only must it be boiled in soda water for fifteen (15) minutes, but it also had to be sorted into lengths and divided into strands containing from twenty to thirty hairs. All this before the actual work began! Truly, this was a labor of love.

Godey's article gave complete directions for preparing the hair and included patterns for two types of chains and bracelets. Working with these directions and subsequent patterns in Godey's Lady's Book and Peterson's Magazine, many finely executed pieces were made.

The watch chain was by far the most popular piece of hairwork jewelry. By providing her love with a chain from her hair, a young lady was assured that she would be in this thoughts may times a day. Hair bracelets combining the hair of each child was a popular keepsake for a mother (see II-17 page 84). A guard chain was always useful, and open work crosses and ear-rings were quite lovely (see I-12 page 28 and I-19 page 30).

When the hair work was completed it was sent to the jeweler for fittings. Beautiful clasps with compartments for photographs (see I-18 page 29), closures mounted with stones (see I-17 page 29), and even miniatures were used to complete bracelets. A variety of fitting were available for finishing brooches and ear-rings. To make long necklaces or guard chains, the jeweler used small gold tubes to join the sections of hair.

If the lady did not trust her own talents for doing hairwork, there were other methods for obtaining this jewelry. The monthly issues of Godey's Lady's Book included illustrations of hair jewelry that could be ordered through the editor. One had only to choose from the many designs and send in the hair along with the proper amount of money. Below are two pricelists from Godey's Lady's Book:

| | August 1855 | March 1859 |
|---|---|---|
| Breast Pins | from $4.00 to $12.00 | $4.00 to $12.00 |
| Ear Rings | from $4.50 to $10.00 | $4.50 to $10.00 |
| Bracelets | from $3.00 to $15.00 | $3.00 to $15.00 |
| Rings | from $1.00 to $ 2.00 | $1.50 to $ 3.00 |
| Necklaces | from $4.50 to $ 7.00 | $6.00 to $15.00 |
| Fob Chains | from $4.00 to $ 8.00 | $6.00 to $12.00 |
| The charms of Faith, Hope and Charity | | $4.50 |
| Hair Studs | | $5.50 to $11.00 (set) |
| Sleeve Buttons | | $6.50 to $11.00 (set) |

There were jewelers in London and New York whose primary business was to make the hairwork jewelry that was so much in demand. Linherr and Company of New York was one of the most famous. At the Crystal Palace Exposition of 1853, in addition to their full line of hair bracelets, brooches, necklaces, and chains, they displayed a full size tea set made entirely of hair. The October 8, 1853 issue of Gleasons Pictorial Drawing-room Companion spoke highly of this display. The following excerpt from this article gives an indication of how popular hairwork jewelry had become.

It is a very modern fashion to so braid and form the hair as to make not only an outside ornament of itself, but also to produce the most beautiful and delicate effect. The perfection to which this new art has been brought, has led to the general adoption of these ornaments by the ladies, and they are now almost as much worn by the "upper ten" as are golden ornaments; and that the effect—to say nothing of the pleasant idea of thus wearing the hair of those we love and cherish—is incomparably superior to metallic jewelry, no person of good taste will venture to deny.

Some hairwork pieces were made of horsehair. Because it was coarser than human hair, it was easier to work. Consequently, it became the perfect material for a beginner. After mastering the art in horsehair one was then ready to proceed to work the precious hair of a friend or a relative.

Indeed it was precious and not only because of the sentiment involved. In the 1850's hair was an expensive commodity with a vast array of commercial uses. Every spring hair merchants visited festivals, fairs, and markets throughout France and Germany. They offered young girls ribbons, combs, and trinkets in exchange for their hair. "The quantity of hair produced by the annual harvest was calculated at 200,000 pounds weight."[2] This hair was made into artificial ringlets, false plaits, beards, moustaches, perukes, and jewelry. Its value was often triple that of silver.

The comment by Leigh Hunt that appeared in the May 1855 Godeys' sums up beautifully the Victorian's love of hair:

> Hair is at once the most delicate and lasting of our materials, and survives us, like love. It is so light, so gentle, so escaping from the idea of death, that with a lock of hair belonging to a child or friend, we may almost look up to heaven and compare notes with the angelic nature—may almost say, "I have a piece of thee here, not unworthy of thy being now."

## Daguerreotypes and Gutta-Percha

In the 1840's everybody who was anybody had a photographic sitting. A sitting was an accurate description since the subject had to sit in the sun for up to thirty minutes in order to get the proper exposure.

Louis J. M. Daguerre perfected this photographic process. In 1839, he sold it to the French government. That same year Samuel F. B. Morse, inventor of the telegraph, saw these new daguerreotypes and was fascinated. On his return to the United States, he shared his new interest. Soon photography was flourishing.

Thanks to daguerreotypes, we have pictures of notable people such as John Quincy Adams, Andrew Jackson, Daniel Webster, Henry Wadsworth Longfellow, and Harriet Beecher Stowe. It is estimated that by 1849, Americans were being photographed at the rate of three million a year.

The Daguerreotype is identified by the mirror-like reflection of its background. Since the pictures were under glass, a proper container was an important consideration. Thus the daguerreotype case and locket came into existence.

Materials most often used for these cases were molded

paper, composition, and gutta-percha. The latter two materials are of the greatest interest to the jewelry and accessory minded because many decorative articles were made from them.

In 1854 Samuel Peck of Connecticut patented a composition case made of shellac, sawdust, and coloring matter. When this mixture was heated, it could be pressed in a mold to create many pleasing designs. The locket on page 32 is made of this type of composition.

Although many of today's generation have never heard of gutta-percha, it was very prevelant during the Victorian era. Made from the sap of a Malayan tree, its usefulness was discovered during the rubber making process and introduced to Paris in 1842. The Crystal Palace Catalogue of 1851 included this definition: "The Isonandra Gutta, the source of the gum-elastic, known as gutta-percha, one of the most useful substances introduced into the arts during the present century—."

Because it was very durable and highly impressionable, it lent itself well to the Victorian taste for embellishment. In its finished state it is black or brownish. This dark color made it a natural material for mourning jewelry, but it was by no means used exclusively for that purpose. Lockets, brooches, bracelets, and walking cane heads were but a few of its many uses. The October 1855 Godey's listed this unique use:

> Gutta percha for a Decayed Tooth—Procure a small piece of gutta-percha, about as much as will fill the cavity in your tooth, nearly level; drop it into boiling water, and while in the soft state press it into the tooth; then hold in the mouth cold water to harden the gutta-percha.

The Gutta Percha Company displayed many items at the Crystal Palace Exposition in 1851. Included were a sculptural-like group entitled the "Deer and Hounds," a huge, highly embellished sideboard, a chaise lounge with a back of gutta percha elastic, and even printing type. This wonderful new material was one of the first natural plastics.

Many pieces of gutta-percha are still available at reasonable prices. As more people become aware of this unique material, prices are sure to rise. Examples of Guttapercha jewelry are pictured on pages 32, 33, 41, 86, 87 and 165.

## Scottish Jewelry

Queen Victoria loved Scotland and all things Scottish. Her pride in her Stuart ancestry and the popularity of Sir Walter Scott's novels made Scottish jewelry a fashionable accessory. In 1848 the Royal couple purchased "Balmoral" to use as a summer home. Since this home closely resembled the home of Sir Walter Scott, it held a romantic fascination for the young Queen and her subjects. This led to a new country house design known as Scottish Baronial. The desire for things Scottish became even more apparent.

As early as 1851 people were wearing tartans. On their arms were flexible bracelets enameled with matching plaid designs. At a state ball in Buckingham Palace, celebrating the opening of the Crystal Palace Exposition, the Royal children wore tartans and the guests wore Stuart tartans. When the Queen visited the Emperor and Empress of France in 1855, her entire family wore kilts. The Tartans fascinated the Empress, and she introduced them to Paris.

Brooches and pins were the most popular form of Scottish jewelry. Mountings were usually silver, but some gold and even enameled ones were used. Moss agate, bloodstone, cornelian, and other stones native to Scotland were popular. The most popular stone, by far, was the Cairngorm, named for the Cairngorm Mountains of Scotland in which it is found. This smoky yellow quartz is often incorrectly called smoky topaz or Scotch topaz.

Scottish jewelry was popular throughout England until the death of Albert in 1861. After his mourning period, though the jewelry continued to be made, it was never again quite as popular. Examples of Scottish jewelry can be found on page 39 and 40.

## Chatelaines *(see page 138)*

Chatelaines were a very necessary accessory to the Victorian matron. Considered a vital part of home management, they were also ornamental and prestigious. The chantelaine consisted of a large central piece which was either hooked or pinned at the waist. From this, extended chains with swivel attachments for hanging a variety of household necessities such as scissors, a sewing case with needles and thread, a knife, a vinegerette, a coin purse, a pencil, a note case, a scent bottle, and a watch and key.

Inspiration for this type of accessory may be traced to medieval times when the keeper of the keys, which were usually worn on a chain around the waist, was the person with authority. Chatelaines were in and out of fashion for several hundred years. The Art-Journal Illustrated Catalogue of 1851 made this comment about them:

> The modern chatelaine is but a reproduction of an article of decorative ornament, worn by ladies in our own country more than a century and a half ago. The watch, the scissors, etui, pincushion, and c, were then ostentatiously appended to the dresses of the ladies, quite as much for ornament as for use.

Chatelaines were made from gold, pinchbeck, silver, silver plate, stamped metal, and cut-steel. They are quite collectible. For pictures of chatelaines turn to pages 102 and 177.

## Cameos

When Victoria ascended to the throne, cameos were already immensely popular. Excavations had awakened interest in this old art, and Napoleon I had initiated "a Prix de Rome" in 1805 to encourage stone engraving. About that same time a public school was opened in Rome for the study of cameo engraving. It was founded by Pope Leo XII and met with much success.

The early cameos were made from stone. In the early nineteenth century workmen turned to shell to meet the demand for more cameos at less expensive prices. Cameos were set in rings, brooches, ear-rings, and bracelets. The men wore them in watch fobs, rings, and pins. Stone cameos were cut from onyx, agate, sardonyx, cornelian, coral, lava, and jet. The carvers of shell cameos used the shells of the Black Helmet and the pink and white Queen's Conch which were so plentiful in the seacoast towns in Italy.

Cameos made lovely, portable souvenirs for tourists visiting the ruins of Pompeii and Hercelium. When the travelers returned home their friends were enchanted with these small works of art. Within a short time Italian cameo artists had shops in England, France, and America. These craftsmen carved cameos in the ancient styles or any other designs the purchaser might select. The January 1850 issue of Godey's Magazine included the following note:

Cameos are made by cutting away background material to make a design in relief. In stone cameos a banded agate is often used. The lighter band is used for the figure of the cameo. The remainder is carved away to expose the darker ground. In shell and stone cameos the true artist takes advantage of different layers and faults in the material to enhance the design.

Stone cameos are generally more valuable than those made of shell. But the medium is not nearly as important as the artistry. The best way to judge a cameo is to examine it with a good magnifying glass. Graceful, smooth-flowing lines with much detail are signs of a good one. The inferior ones seem to have sharper lines, fewer details, and a harsh look. Be sure to hold the cameo to the light and examine it for possible cracks.

Many antique cameos were reset in the late seventeen and early eighteen hundreds. Some craftsmen were expert at copying antique pieces. This makes accurate dating almost impossible. However, there are usually some clues to help determine age.

If a cameo is made of lava, it is almost certainly Victorian. Other clues are: the style of design (Greek, Roman, etc.), types of clothing and hair styles on the figures, and the type of mounting. If the cameo is mounted as a brooch, carefully examine the pin and hook. Safety catches are a twentieth century adaptation. If the cameo has one, then it is either not older than the early ninteen hundreds or a new catch has been added. If it is an addition, this can usually be ascertained by more careful examination. Look for signs of sautering. Often the new catch is attached to a small plate jointed to the back of the brooch. Next look closely at the pin. Notice what kind of hinge it has. If the sharp point of the pin extends past the body of the brooch, it is an "oldie."

Gold, silver, pinchbeck, goldfilled, and cut-steel were used for mounting cameos. The type metal used can often give an indication of when it was made. If the mounting is pinchbeck it was probably made between the early seventeen and the mid-eighteen hundreds. Gold electroplating was patented in 1849 so, if the piece is plated, it was made after that date. Nine carat gold was legalized in 1854. A piece in 9K would have to be made after that date. A popular metal used for mountings in the 1880's was silver, but this does not mean that all cameos mounted in silver were made at that time. All the clues have to be examined before a judgment on age can be made.

Scenic cameos are generally more expensive than bust cameos. A very popular motif around 1860 was what is known as "Rebecca at the Well." There are many variations on this theme, but they usually include a cottage, a bridge, and a girl.

Technically, a cameo is made by cutting away the background of a material to make a design in relief, but there are some items called cameos that do not fit this description. Josiah Wedgewood's factory produced jasperware plaques in blue and white and black and white. These had the look of a cameo. These massed produced "cameos" were originally very inexpensive but today they are quite collectible.

Examples of stone cameos are found on pages 33, 34, 89, 91, 98, 178 and 179. Shell cameos are pictured on pages 34, 82, 93, 103, 178, 179 and 180. Some beautiful lava cameos are shown on pages 39 and 40.

**Garter Jewelry**

Victorian jewelers took designs from a variety of sources. One popular motif stemmed from the Royal Order of the Garter. This Order, founded by King Edward III in 1348 to strengthen military leadership, is the highest honor a British monarch can bestow. Members of the Order wear a blue garter buckled on their knee. Victoria was much too modest for this tradition. Instead she chose to wear it on her arm. Thus the garter became a very fashionable jewelry motif.

Bracelets displaying this design were most plentiful (see II-107 on page 99 and II-155 on page 107). Rings were made in the form of a garter, and lockets were engraved with this motif.

**Serpent Jewelry**

When Albert gave Victoria an engagement ring in the form of a serpent, he generated a revival of this ancient decorative motif. The Queen was particularily fond of this design. She owned several serpent pieces including a bracelet which she wore at her first council meeting.

The Snake motif, believed to be a symbol of good luck, was used throughout the Victorian period. On a stroll through London, ladies could be seen wearing serpent rings, serpents entwined around their arms, and serpents coiled on their brooches.

In the book "David Copperfield" by Charles Dickens, published in 1850, a character tells of window shopping with his wife:

> We look into the glittering windows of the jeweler's shops, and I show Sophy which of the diamond-eyed serpents, coiled up on white satin rising-grounds, I would give her if I could affort it.

The style was so accepted that the 1855 Godey's Magazine gave complete instructions for making a serpent bracelent using skeins of gold twist, dark green cord, and violet and green silk. It was to be worked "in imitation of hair." Four number six steel beads were used for eyes. This enabled ladies who could not afford gold serpent bracelets to wear the latest design.

**Coral**

The Victorians had a special love for coral jewelry. Since Roman times it was believed to possess the power to ward off evil and danger. Consequently, it was a favorite christening present. A look at any family portrait of the period will show this popularity. Every baby and young child pictured will be wearing a coral necklace. These were added to as the child grew, as we do the "add a bead" and "add a pearl" necklaces today. Baby rattles with coral stems, and coral teething rings were also popular.

Coral was not limited to the young. In 1845 the Prince of the Two Sicilies gave his bride, the Duchesse d'Aumale, a beautiful parue of coral jewelry. This started a fashion among women of all ages that continued to the late 1860's. The November 1855 Godey's contained this comment on coral:

*Coral ornaments are the favorite style of jewelry. The bracelets are formed of strands of coral passing round the arm several times, and finished with a long tassel of the same beads. The bracelet sultan forms a pretty summer ornament; it is composed of strands of gold cord intermixed with green silk and coral beads, wide and worked in a Gothic pattern, from which hang five small coral balls, attached to the bracelet by gold ribbons.*

Robert Phillips, an English jeweler, did much to popularize coral. He encouraged Italian craftsmen to come to England, and he entered coral jewelry in all the important exhibitions. This did so much for the economy of Naples, where most coral is found, that the king of Naples honored him for his contribution to the industry.

Coral is the calcareous skeletons of marine animals. It is found in abundance in the Naples' area. The most prized colors are deep red and angel skin pink. Because coral is easy to work, it is used for designs which call for a profusion of flowers and leaves.

Many Victorian brooches and ear-rings were made using the natural or branch coral. This was a less expensive way to use the 'stone.' Consequently, there are more of these pieces available than the highly carved ones. Some fine examples of coral jewelry can be found on pages 38 and 96.

**Cut-Steel**

England was well known for its cut-steel industry. The most noted producer was Mathew Boulton of Birmingham. He made beautiful rings and brooches, using wedgewood cameos in cut-steel frames.

A piece of cut-steel is made by riveting rosettes fashioned from thin metal to another metal plate that has been cut in a design. Although it is called cut-steel, the metal could be silver alloy or even tin. The glitter of cut-steel comes from light reflecting off the rosettes. Imitation cut-steel is made by stamping the rosettes from a sheet of metal. The best way to determine the authenticity of a piece is by looking at the back. If there are two pieces of metal and one is a solid plate with rivets showing, chances are that the piece is genuine.

Even though cut-steel glittered it was not flashy so the Victorians considered it proper for day wear. Many lovely cloak clasps, shoe buckles, brooches, and chantelaines were made. Some examples are found on pages 36, 276 and 280.

## Amethyst

The amethyst was a very fashionable stone throughout the Victorian era. Because of its ecclesiastical associations it was acceptable for wear in the latter stages of mourning. Since amethysts were plentiful they were affordable and could be worn by all classes. In a yellow gold or pinchbeck mounting, surrounded by seed pearls, they were quite lovely.

The amethyst is a member of the quartz family of stones. It is known for its violet to red-purple hue. In fact, the name amethyst is now synonymous with that color. The finest colored and most valuable are known as Siberian amethyst. This refers to the quality of the stone and not the location from which it comes.

In olden days the amethyst was believed to possess the power to protect its wearer and bring good luck. The person born in February is fortunate to be able to claim this lovely stone as a birthstone.

## Bloodstone

Victorians wore and admired the bloodstone. This ancient stone, also known as heliotrope (Heel-ee-trope), is actually a dark green chalcedony with flecks of red. The ancients believed the red to be drops of blood; hence the name bloodstone. Many magical powers were ascribed to it including the power to stop bleeding and preserve health. Even though it is one of the birthstones for March, it is seldom used today. When a piece of jewelry contains bloodstone, it is most assuredly old.

## Gold stone

Goldstone is quite often encountered in old jewelry. It was used for the ground of some mosaics and as a stone for cuff links or stick pins. Since it is neither gold or a stone, it can be added to the list of misnomers in the jewelry field. Goldstone is an imitation aventurine made of glass to which copper crystals have been added. It has a gold spangled look that is quite attractive. Once seen it is very easy to recognize.

# I. The Jewelry—1840-1860

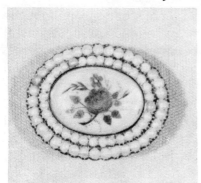

I-1. **Brooch—Early 1800's**—18K Surrounded by Pearls. Rock crystal covers flowers made of hair. 1-1/4 x 1-1/8'' $475.00 (Jeanenne Bell Collection)

I-2. **Brooch—Early 1800's**—18K with Pearls and Jet. Hair under Rock Crystal also woven hair background. 1-3/8'' diameter $350.00 (Jeanenne Bell Collection)

I-3. **Pendant—Early 1800's**—Pinchbeck with beveled glass front and back. front glass is hinged and opens. 1 5/8'' x 2-1/2'' $250.00 (Jeanenne Bell Collection)

I-4. **Locket—1840-50**—Pinchbeck— Bouquet made of hair. 3/4 x 1''. $150.00. (Jeanenne Bell Collection)

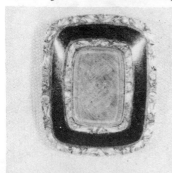

I-5. **Brooch—Early 1800's**—Pinchbeck memorial piece with black enameling. Braided hair under crystal. 1-1/4 x 1'' $125.00 (Jeanenne Bell Collection)

I-6. **Brooch—1840-50**—18K Memorial Pin with Black enameling. White and brown hair under beveled glass. 1 x 7/8'' $95.00 (Jeanenne Bell Collection)

I-7. **Brooch**—1850-70—Gold filled with Black Enameling. Hair in flat weave under beveled glass. 1-3/8 x 1-1/8'' $95.00 (Jeanenne Bell Collection)

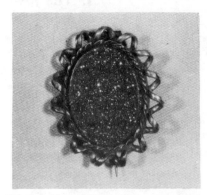

I-8. **Brooch**—1850-60—Gilt mtg. Gold Stone front. Glass covered compartment in rear. 1-1/2 x 1-1/4'' $70.00 (Jeanenne Bell Collection)

I-9. **Brooch**—1850-60—Yellow Gold mtg. with Hairwork. 1-1/2 x 7/8'' $225.00 (Jeanenne Bell Collection)

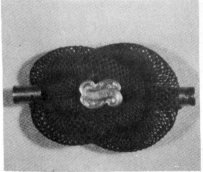

I-10. **Brooch**—1850-60—15K Yellow Gold Fittings with open weave hairwork. 1-3/4 x 1'' Engraved "Mary" $250.00 (Jeanenne Bell Collection)

I-11. **Brooch**—1850-60—15K Fittings. Open weave light brown hairwork with leaf ornamentation. 2 x 1'' $250.00 (Jeanenne Bell Collection)

I-12. **Necklace with Cross**—1850-70—Yellow Gold Fittings all hairwork cross 1-1/4 x 2'' Chain 18' L. $325.00 (Jeanenne Bell Collection)

28

I-13. **Watch chain—1840-60—**Gold Fittings with two hair patterns. Note snake and early swivel. 3/8″ Dia. x 8-1/2″ L. $125.00 (Jeanenne Bell Collection)

I-14. **Watch chain—1840-60—**Gilt Fittings-Two pieces of hairwork intertwined-Snake and early swivel. 3/4 x 8-1/2″ $95.00 (Jeanenne Bell Collection)

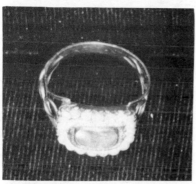

I-15. **Ring—Early 1800's—**18K with Pearls and compartment for Hair under crystal. 1/2 x 1/2″ $325.00 (Jeanenne Bell Collection)

I-16. **Ring—1850-60—**14K Fitting. Hairwork 1/8″ wide $125.00 (Jeanenne Bell Collection)

I-17. **Bracelet—1850-60—**15K Fittings. Hairwork with Amethyst in clasp. 3/4 x 6″ $250.00 (Jeanenne Bell Collection)

I-18. **Bracelet-1850-60-**Gold Fittings. Hairwork. Engraved "Sisters Hair" $260.00 (Jeanenne Bell Collection)

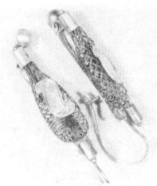

I-19. **Ear Rings**—1850-60—Gold Fittings. Open weave hairwork. Acorn look. 1-1/4″ L. $180.00 (Jeanenne Bell Collection)

I-20. **Ear Rings**—1850-60—Gold Fittings 1/4 x 1-3/4″ $180.00 (Jeanenne Bell Collection)

I-21. **Locket**—1850-60—Gold over brass rim with gold top. Cross enameled colbalt blue. Back has glass covered opening with lock of hair 5/8 x 7/8″ $65.00 (Jeanenne Bell Collection)

I-22. **Locket**—Early **1800's**—Pinchbeck-Hand engraved. 1-5/8″ Dia. $195.00 (Jeanenne Bell Collection)

I-23. **Locket**—1840-50—Pinchbeck contains daguerreotype. 1 x 1-1/2″ $250.00 (W. Baldwin Collection)

I-24. **Locket**—1850-60—Gold Filled-Glass insets 1 x 1-1/2″ $95.00 (Jeanenne Bell Collection)

I-25. **Locket—1840-60**—Gold Filled-glass inserts. Depth indicates originally contained a daguerreotype. 1-1/4 x 1-1/2" $95.00 (Jeanenne Bell Dealer)

I-26. **Locket—1850-60**—Gold Filled-Hand engraved. Button on top activates latch simular to mechanism in Hunting Case watch. 1-1/4" Dia. Has obvious repair so only $50.00 (Jeanenne Bell Collection)

I-27. **Locket—1840-60**—Gilt over brass with glass insets and tin type of baby 5/8 x 7/8" $125.00 (Jeanenne Bell Dealer)

I-28. **Locket—1840-60**—Yellow gold with 5 pearls. 5/8 x 3/8" $275.00 (Camille Grace Dealer)

I-29. **Locket—1850-70**—Gold over brass. Cross in blue enamel, leaf design in black enamel. Cross has "in memory of." Back has garter motif. Inside are pressed flowers under glass enclosure. 1 x 1-1/8" $75.00 (Jeanenne Bell Dealer)

I-30. **Locket—1850-60**—Gold Filled with 5 Turquoise stones. 1 x 2" $125.00 (Jeanenne Bell Dealer)

31

I-31. **Locket**—1855-60—Yellow Gold-filled. Variation of "Rebecca at the Well" New G.F. chain and bale. 1 x 1-1/2" $185.00 (Jeanenne Bell Dealer)

I-32. **Locket**—1860—Composition same design on inside as the one pictured below. 1-1/2 x 2" $75.00 (Jeanenne Bell Collection)

I-33. **Locket**—1850-60—Gutta Percha with Tin type and ornate interior. 1-3/4 x 2" $125.00 (Jeanenne Bell Collection)

I-34. **Locket**—Interior view of number 33.

I-35. **Locket**—1845-55—Gutta Percha with gold ornamentation. 1 x 1-1/4" $125.00 (Jeanenne Bell Collection)

I-36. **Locket**—1850-70—Gutta Percha on original black ribbon. Locket 1-1/4 x 1-1/2" $100.00 (Jeanenne Bell Collection)

I-37. **Cross—1850-60**—Gutta Percha 1-1/2 x 2-1/2'' $150.00 (Jeanenne Bell Collection)

I-38. **Brooch—1850-60**—Gutta Percha. Angel holding baby-a popular Biblical reference. 1-3/4 x 2'' $145.00 (Jeanenne Bell Collection)

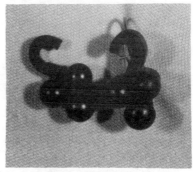

I-39. **Brooch—1850-60**—Gutta Percha. Pair of birds. 1-1/4 x 2" $85.00 (Jeanenne Bell Collection)

I-40. **Ear Rings—1850-60**—Matte finished jet balls with gutta percha back form grape motif. $95.00 (Jeanenne Bell Dealer)

I-41. **Necklace Pendant—1840-60**—Gilt brass mtg. Cornelian cameo. 3/4 x 1-1/3" $120.00 (Jeanenne Bell Dealer)

I-42. **Necklace and Earrings—1850-70**—15K Sardonyx Cameo. New wires on ear rings. Necklace drop 1 x 2''; Ear rings 3/8 x 1'' $695.00 set. (Jeanenne Bell Collection)

I-43. **Brooch—1840-60**—Pinchbeck mtg. Shell cameo 1-1/4 x 1-1/2" $150.00 (Jeanenne Bell Dealer)

I-44. **Brooch/Pendant—1850-60**—15K Beautiful sardonyx cameo with granulation. 1-1/8 x 1-7/8'' $995.00 (Jeanenne Bell Dealer)

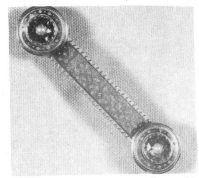

I-45. **Brooch—1850-60**—Gold over brass with some gold ornamentation. Stone cameo 3 x 1-1/4'' $195.00 (Jeanenne Bell Dealer)

I-46. **Brooch—mid 1800's**—Yellow gold with amethyst and pearls. 2-1/2 x 5/8" $350.00 (Baldwin Collection)

I-47. **Brooch and Ear Rings—1850-60**—Gold over brass. Note Etruscan influences. Granulation. Brooch 2-1/2" Ear Rings 3/4" dia. screw backs not original $175.00 (Jeanenne Bell Dealer)

I-48. **Brooch—1850-60**—Gold Filled with amethyst. 1-1/4 x 1'' $58.00 (Camille Grace Dealer)

I-49. **Brooch—1850-60**—Yellow Gold with compartment in back for hair. 1-5/8 x 1-3/8'' $250.00 (W. Baldwin Collection)

I-50. **Brooch—1840-50**—Gilt mtg. with enameled leaves and moulded cameo. $85.00 (Jeanenne Bell Dealer)

I-51. **Brooch—1850-70**—Jet-Matte and shiny finish. 1-1/4 x 1-3/4'' $125.00 (Jeanenne Bell Collection)

I-52. **Brooch—1850-70**—Gold Filled. Jet cross 1'' dia. $85.00 (Jeanenne Bell Dealer) Dealer)

I-53. **Brooch—1840-60**—Yellow Gold. Jet with seed pearls. 1 x 1-5/8'' $265.00 (Jeanenne Bell Dealer)

I-54. **Cross—1850-70**—Gilt on brass with gold ornamentation. Note tra-foils. 1-1/2 x 2-3/8'' $85.00 (Jeanenne Bell Dealer)

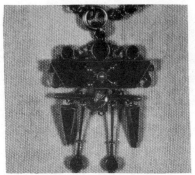

I-55. **Necklace—1850-60**—14K onyx and seed pearl chain. 14-1/2″ L. Drops 1-3/8 x 2″ $475.00 (Camille Grace Dealer)

I-56. **Brooch and Ear Rings—1850-70**—Yellow Gold with granulation and enameled flowers. Brooch 2-3/8 x 7/8″. Ear Rings 11/16 x 1-1/16″ $675.00 (W. Baldwin Collection)

I-57. **Brooch—1840-50**—15K Grapes of seed pearls. 1″ dia. $250.00 (Jeanenne Bell Dealer)

I-58. **Pendant—Early 1800's**—Cut steel. Painting on ivory. 1-5/8 x 2″ $275.00 (Jeanenne Bell Dealer)

I-59. **Ring—1850-60**—10K Flexable band made like a bracelet. Clasp in head of ring. Probably held a hankerchief. $125.00 (Jeanenne Bell Dealer)

I-60. **Bracelet—1850-60**—14K with Taille d'epergne enameling and pearls. Widest point 1-3/4″ dia. 6-1/4″ long. $675.00 (W. Baldwin Collection)

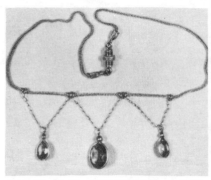

I-61. **Necklace—1840-50**—Yellow Gold-Amethyst. 16″ L. $600.00 (W. Baldwin Collection)

I-62. **Hinged Bracelet—1850-60**—Gilt on brass. Note granulation. 1/2″ wide. $135.00 (Jeanenne Bell Dealer)

I-63. **Bracelet—1850-80**—Gold Filled Note Etruscan work on drop 3/4″ wide. $55.00 (Jeanenne Bell Dealer)

I-64. **Watch Chain—Victorian**—Silver with small silver acorn and ball drop. Has 1842 four pence coin and souvenir coin. 5″ L. $55.00 (Jeanenne Bell Dealer)

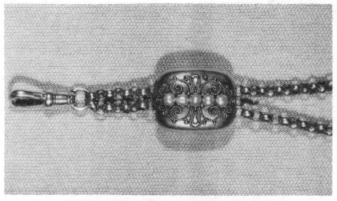

I-65. **Slide Chain—1850-60**—18K Gold. Chain 39″ L. Slide with four pearls and granulation. 1/2 x 3/4″ $1,250.00 (Jeanenne Bell Dealer)

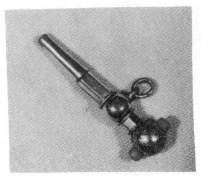

I-66. **Watch Key—1840-60**—Gold over brass with coral 1-1/2" L. Looks great worn on neck chain or watch chain $95.00 (Jeanenne Bell Collection)

I-67. **Watch Key—1850-60**—Gold Filled with bloodstone. 1-1/2'' L. $100.00 (W. Baldwin Collection)

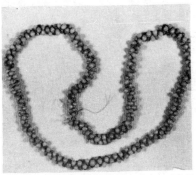

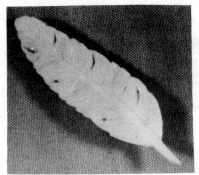

I-68. **Necklace**—Coral beads. 19" L. $200.00 (W. Baldwin Collection)

I-69. **Brooch—1850-60**—Angel skin carved coral. 2-3/4 x 3/4" $300.00 (W. Baldwin Collection)

I-70. **Brooch—1850-60**—Gold Filled. Angel skin carved coral 2-1/2 x 1-1/2" $750.00 (W. Baldwin Collection)

I-71. **Eyeglass—Early 1800's**—Glass 1-1/2" Dia. Overall length 3-1/4" $175.00 (Jeanenne Bell Collection)

I-72. **Eyeglasses—1850-60**—Can be used opened or closed. Glass portion 1-1/4" Dia. Length 3-1/8". Width opened 3-1/2" $125.00 (Jeanenne Bell Collection)

I-73. **Bracelet—1850's**—Gilt brass mtg. Lave cameos. Colors are black, putty, reddish brown, and gold brown (no two alike). 3/8 x 7/8" $750.00 (Jeanenne Bell Collection)

I-74. **Bracelet—1850's**—Silver mtg. Nine lava cameos 5/8 x 7/8" $325.00 (Jeanenne Bell Dealer)

I-75. **Scottish Brooch**—Silver-Scottish agate and cairngorm 1-1/8" Dia. $125.00 (Camille Grace Dealer)

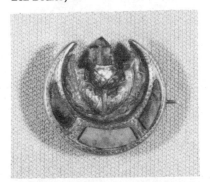

I-76. **Scottish Brooch**—English Sterling Hallmark-Scottish with agate and amethyst 7/8 x 7/8" $95.00 (Camille Grace Dealer)

I-77. **Scottish Brooch—1840-60**—Sterling mtg. Scottish agate and bloodstone. 2-5/8'' x 3/4'' $95.00 (Jeanenne Bell Dealer)

I-78. **Scottish Brooch**—Hallmarked Sterling-Cairngorm stone. 3 x 3/4″ $125.00 (W. Baldwin Collection)

I-79. **Scottish Brooch**—Silver with Cairngorm 3-1/2″ Dia. $650.00 (W. Baldwin Collection)

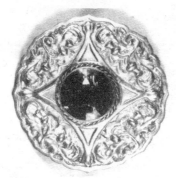

I-80. **Scottish Brooch**—Silver with Cairngorm stone 3-1/2″ Dia. $650.00 (W. Baldwin Collection)

I-81. **Scottish Bracelet**—Silver with agates and cornelian. Head 1-1/8 x 1-3/8″ Length 6-3/4″ $175.00 (W. Baldwin Collection)

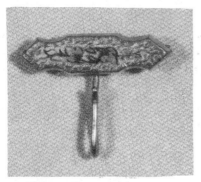

I-82. **Watch Pin**—1850-60—Gold Filled with Taille d' epergne enameling. 1 x 7/8″ $48.00 (Jeanenne Bell Dealer)

I-83. **Brooch and Ear Rings**—1850-60—Gold Filled with enameling. Ear Rings were originally collar buttons Pin 1-1/4 x 1′′. Ear Rings 1/2 x 5/8′′ $240.00 (Jeanenne Bell Dealer)

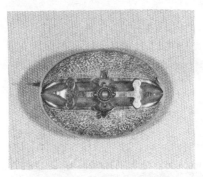

I-84. **Brooch—1850-60**—Gold Filled with gold ornamentation and seed pearl. Made to hold watch. $125.00 (Jeanenne Bell Dealer)

I-85. **Brooch—1840-60**—18K Jet with seed pearl. 1-1/2 x 5/8" $195.00 (Jeanenne Bell Dealer)

I-86. **Locket—1850-60**—10K Gold Locket on new 14K chain. 1 x 1-1/4" $195.00 (Jeanenne Bell Dealer)

I-87. **Cross—1840-60**—Gold Filled. Gutta Percha Cross 7/8 x 1-3/4" $70.00 (Jeanenne Bell Dealer)

98

I-88—**Brooch**—Early 19th century—Silver gilt frame with classical scene executed in blue and white shell cameo. Original leather case. L 650. $943.00 (A)
I-89—**Necklace**—Early 19th century—Gold panel links with central mount set with oval brown and black agate cameo ''Captor and Captives.'' Clasp has cushion shaped agate cameo. L 1,050. $1,523.00 (A) (Photos courtesy of Phillips, London 6-21-83)

I-90—**Pendant**—Early Victorian—Yellow gold with floral spray of diamonds on dark blue enamel. Embellished with pearl set bud drops. Locket on reverse side. L 1,600 $2,320.00 (A)
I-91—**Bracelet**—Early Victorian—Yellow gold hinged bangle with serpent motif with Cambridge-blue enamel. The head is set with 5 diamonds and ruby eyes. L 650. $943.00 (A)
I-92—**Brooch**—Mid 19th century—Gold oval with shell cameo of Bacchante. Signed with mark of Castellani on the cone shaped pin cap. L 900. $1,305.00. (A) (Photos courtesy of Phillips, London)

I-93—**Demi-Parure Consisting of Necklace, Brooch and Earrings**—Early 19th century—Gold cannetille set with rubies and diamonds. Original case. L 2,800. $4,060.00 (A) (Photo courtesy of Phillips, London)

I-94—**Chatelaine**—Early 19th
century— Gold with enamelling. Appendages include a
locket-base seal, locket globe
fob, a seal, a watch (a later addition) and a watch key. L 2,200.
$3,190.00 (A) (Photo courtesy of
Phillips, London)

I-95—**Croix-A-La-Jeanette**—
Circa 1835—Gold with royal
blue enamel and rose cut
diamonds. Serpent has ruby
eeys. (Some enamel damage). L
1,100 $1,573.00 (A) (Sotheby,
London 4-14-83)

I-96—**Brooch**—Circa 1840—
Cabochon sapphire with rose cut
and cushion shaped diamonds.
L7,480. $10,846.00 (A) (Photo
courtesy of Sotheby, London
4-14-83)

I-97—**Eye Pin**—Circa 1840s—Yellow
Gold with a blue enamel snake.
$900.00 (A) (Photo courtesy of
William Doyle Galleries 9-21-83)

I-98—**Brooch/Pendant and Earrings**—Circa 1840—Gold with cabachon garnets. L495. $717.75 (A) (Photo courtesy of Sotheby, London 7-28-83)

I-99—**Demi-Parure**—Circa 1835 — Necklace, earrings and brooch. Gold cannetille set with pink topaz. L 1,540. $2,233.00 (A) (Sotheby, London 4-14-83)

46

I-100—**Necklace**—Circa 1840—Gold with moonstones and garnets. $1,650.00 (A) (Photo courtesy of Sotheby, New York 10-3-83)

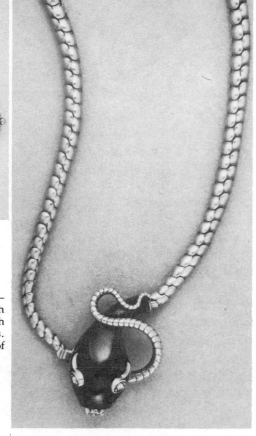

I-101—**Necklace**—Circa 1840—Gold snake necklace with cabuchon garnet head with eyes of rose cut diamonds. $2,750.00 (A) (Photo courtesy of Sotheby, New York 12-7-83)

I-102—**Necklace**—
Circa 1840—Gold
and turquoise ser-
pent. Head is Pave'
set with turquoise
and rose diamonds.
In fitted case. L 2090
$3,030.50 (A) (Photo
courtesy of Sotheby,
London 7-28-83)

I-103—**Necklace**—
Circa 1840—Gold
Snake. Head and tail
set with turquoise.
Heat set with pear
shaped diamond.
Missing two stones.
L 1,760. $2,552.00 (A)
(Photo courtesy
Sotheby, London
4-14-83)

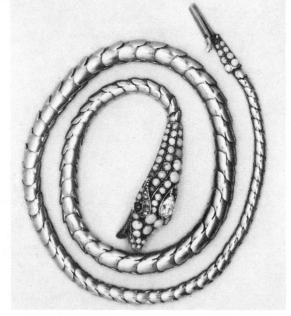

I-104—**Bracelet**—Circa 1840—
Gold with cabochon garnets.
Reverse of center garnet is a
compartment for hair. Scale
type band is flexible. $1,430.00
(A) (Photo courtesy of Sotheby,
New York 10-6-83)

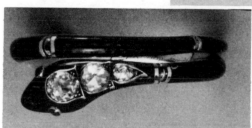

I-105—**Bracelet**—Circa 1844—
Gold snake motif. The ar-
ticulated body is decorated with
ultra-marine guilloche enamelling. Head set with 3 rose
diamonds and cabochon ruby
eyes. (Slightly imperfect) L
2,530. $3,617.90 (A) (Photo
courtesy of Sotheby, London
11-24-83)

I-106—**Pendant**—
Circa 1840—Gold
and silver with lapis
and agate stones.
Reverse has a
miniature compart-
ment. French. L 935
$1,355.75 (A) (Photo
courtesy of Sotheby,
London 4-14-83)

I-107—**Gold, Coral
and Emerald
Locket**—Mid 1800's
18K yellow gold con-
taining pink coral,
white enamel and
four square
emeralds. $950.00
(A) (Photo courtesy
of William Doyle
Galleries 12-7-83)

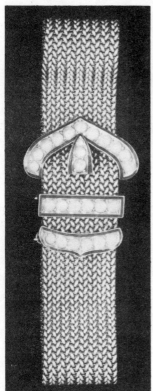

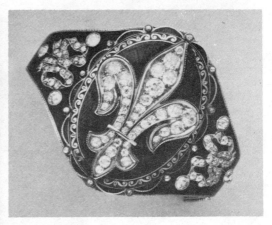

I-109—**Bracelet**—Mid 19th century—Gold hinged bangle with royal blue enamelling. Has approx. 6 cts. of old mine cut diamonds. $3,080 (A) (Photo courtesy of Sotheby, New York 10-6-83)

I-108—**Bracelet**—Mid 1800's - Gold with half pearl and royal blue enamel. L 880. $1,276.00 (A) (Photo courtesy of Sotheby, London 7-28-83)

I-110—**Brooch**—Mid 19th century—Silver and gold with carved black and white onyx ''Moonface'' cameo. Embellished with rose cut diamonds. $1,760.00 (A) (Photo courtesy of Sotheby, New York 10-6-83)

I-111—**Brooch**—Circa 1860—Gold with banded agate. L440. $638.00 (A) (Photo courtesy of Sothebys, Park Bernet and Co., London 12-15-83)

I-112—Top—**Bracelet**—Circa 2nd half of the 19th century- Gold set with pink topaz, rose diamonds and cushion shaped diamonds. The topaz and diamond cluster can be detached and worn as a brooch. L 3,740. $5,423.00 (A) I-113-bottom—**Brooch**—Circa 1840— Gold with attractive colored step cut emerald and cushion-shaped diamonds. L 27,500. $39,875.00. (A) (Photos courtesy of Sotheby, London 12-15-83)

I-114—**Victorian Coral Necklace**— $625.00 (A) (Photo courtesy of William Doyle Galleries)

I-115- Center—**Demi-Parure**—Circa 1875-80—Pendant and earrings. Gold with Roman
mosaic of bouquet of flowers. L 935. $1,355.75. (A)
I-116—**Necklace**—Mid 19th century - with matching brooch and earrings (only necklace
pictured). Gold with Roman mosaics of putti, muses and flowers. L 3,740. $5,423.00 (A)
(Photos courtesy of Sotheby, London 11-24-83)

I-117—**Brooch**—Mid 19th century Gold shaped enameled plaques with pearls and diamonds. Detachable fittings. L850. $1,232.50. (A)
I-118—**Necklace**—Mid 19th century—Gold Etruscanx style. L1,500. $2,175.00 (A) (Photos courtesy of Phillips, London 12-24-83)

I-119—**Brooch**—Circa 1840—Jet memorial piece. Some damage to reverse. 2x2½''. Jowsy & Roe, Whitby, England L35. $51.00. (D)

I-120—**Brooch**—Circa 1840-60—Jet "IN MEMORY OF MY DEAR BROTHER" Glass center for hair. 1½ x1⅛", Jowsey & Roe Whitby L40. $58.00 (D)

I-121—**Brooch & Earrings**—Circa 1870's— Gold top with gold over brass backs and taille d'epergne enamelling. Centered with black/white stone cameos (Jeanenne Bell Collection) $395.00

I-122—**Brooch**—Circa 1840-60s— 18K yellow gold with table worked hair, 3½" long. $195.00 (C)

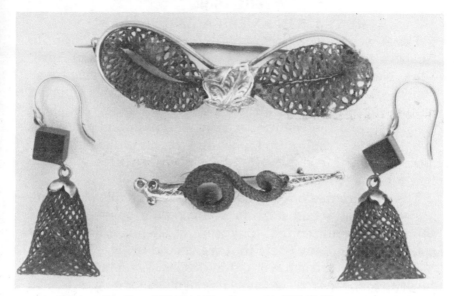

I-123—**Hairbrooch**—Circa 1850-70—18K yellow gold. $195.00 (D)
I-124—**Snake Pin**—Circa 1840-60—18K yellow gold. $265.00 (D)
I-125—**Hair Earrings**—Circa 1840-60—18K wires. Bells have gold clappers. $195.00 (C)

I-126—**Brooch**—Mid 1800s— Yellow rolled gold mounting set with beautifully done shell cameo. Center section is reversible so that the glazed compartment (reverse) can be worn in front. 2¾ x 2¼″ (Jewelry Box Antiques) $495.00 (D)

I-127—**Brooch**—Circa 1840-60— Yellow rolled gold mounting set with "three Graces" shell cameo. 2¼x2⅛″ (Jewelry Box Antiques) $389.00 (D)

## 1861-1889

## THE TIMES IN AMERICA AND ENGLAND

These years were filled with growth and change. In America the first shots of the Civil War were fired in April, 1861. Neither side expected it to last long. The mood was almost jovial as the men rushed off to fight. But this changed as the days and weeks turned into years. There was much bloodshed and the country experienced pain and suffering. People came to realize that a country at war with itself could never have a true victory. Both sides were relieved when the fighting finally came to an end.

The war created a significant change in the role of women. More than that it had actually changed their opinion of themselves. They realized that they were not delicate flowers but could withstand any trials that war could bring.

In the North women worked in offices. Washington was a favorite place to work because it was close to the troops. The Treasury Department and other government agencies hired hundreds of women to replace the men who were off fighting for the Union.

The government needed uniforms quickly so it bought a lot of new sewing machines and offered their use to any person or group who would agree to sew uniforms. Volunteers came forward quickly, and the uniforms were made. In the process the American woman grew to like the sewing machine. It became an accepted tool in the construction of clothing.

Because women were concerned about the sanitary condition of their fighting men, they decided to raise money for improvements. Sanitary Fairs, as they came to be called, became the most popular way to provide these funds. Almost every town and village sponsored at least one a year. They ranged from the church bazaar in small towns to huge fairs. Philadelphia's Fair in 1864 netted a million dollars. It included a Horticultural Department and a Picture Gallery.

Southern Belles were also becoming independent. They worked wherever needed: in the fields, overseeing large farms, or raising money for their men in uniform. "Clinging Vines" learned to shoot a rifle when it became necessary to protect their home. Many women found themselves doing things that would have been considered unlady-like in times of peace. Of course, they also had their sewing circles and provided much needed items for their soldiers.

When the war ended, many men returned home with a different perspective on life. The women they came home to were also changed. Never again would they see themselves as they were before the war. The South would rebuild, and the nation would heal its wounds, but the women had found themselves, and nothing would ever be quite the same.

Interest in women's education grew. In 1865 Vassar Female College was founded. Many other female colleges were opened, and in addition to their regular academic studies young ladies were taught independent sports such as archery, skating, tennis, and swimming.

Croquet became a popular pastime. Petersons' Magazine published an article in 1864 giving complete instructions for playing the game so women knew how to play before the men returned home. It provided a charming excuse for ladies and gentlemen to engage in an outdoor sport.

When time permitted, baseball was played between the soldiers. After the war it grew into a consuming passion. Everything that pertained to baseball or its players was a subject for comment. The January 5, 1878 issue of Frank Leslie's Illustrated Newspaper contained this interesting bit of gossip:

> Mr. Sutton, a well-known professional base-ball player was converted at a revival meeting in Philadelphia not long ago. He arose to address the meeting, and said 'I have made the first base, and, by the help of the Lord, will make a home run.'

Horseback riding became a very fashionable exercise. Fashion magazines were filled with the latest attire for riding. Leslie's Newspaper even sketched a prominent socialite taking her daily horseback ride down Fifth Avenue.

In the 1870's the Women's Property Act was passed. This allowed married women to own property. No longer did a woman's holdings automatically pass into her husbands ownership after the wedding. Not everyone viewed this as progress. Leslie's Newspaper, June 1878, complained: "Her legal rights have become so preponderant that those of her hitherto recognized lords and masters are insignificent in comparison."

The Eighties brought more marvelous new things. The light bulb Edison invented in 1879 came into use, the Brooklyn Bridge was completed, the fountain pen was perfected, the first skyscraper was built, the Statue of Liberty was unveiled, the adding machine was patented, the New York Museum was opened, and George Eastman made photography available to the masses by introducing the Kodak Camera. A period that had begun with war and violence ended with optimism and hope.

In England the year 1861 began sadly for the Queen. Her mother, the Duchess of Kent, died. For the first time Victoria experienced a personal loss. She had been so happy, so complete, that she had forgotten death could not be ruled away at her will as other things could.

Just as she was beginning to come out of her grief, another even more terrible event happened. Toward the end of November, Albert became ill. His condition became increasingly worse. On December 14th he died. Victoria was grief-strickened. The nation was stunned. Everyone went into a state of mourning.

Victoria's mourning lasted for years. It turned into an obsession to do things as Albert would have wanted them done. The remaining years of her life were dedicated to his memory. She wanted her country to know and appreciate him as she did. Writers were commissioned to record the story of his life. Monuments were built and dedicated to her dear Albert's memory.

In 1863 Edward married Princess Alexandra , the daughter of the King of Denmark. The women of Great Britain were glad to have someone to whom they could look who was not in mourning. Because Alexandra was young and attractive, she influenced fashion. She frequently wore a "dog-collar," a necklace containing several strands that fit snuggly around the neck. It was so becoming that soon all the ladies were wearing them.

From 1874 through 1880 Benjamin Disraeli was Prime Minister of England. He enjoyed a fine relationship with Queen Victoria and was responsible for getting her active again. Under his influence England expanded its imperialistic powers. Disraeli was instrumental in acquiring controlling interest in the Suez Canal for Britain. In 1877 he played a major role in having Victoria proclaimed "Empress of India."

In 1887 the English celebrated their "Jubilee Year." The good Queen had reigned for fifty years, and that was reason to rejoice! Many items added the word "Jubilee" to their product as an extra enticement to buy. There was even a "Jubilee Rug Machine" for use in the home. In May of that year the J. Theobald and Company advertized a "Grand Jubilee Prize Picture Puzzle Contest." To enter this competition one had only to purchase one of the Grand Jubilee Packets "which have been specially prepared in celebration of Her Majesty's Jubilee. This Packet contains the most marvelous value for the money, as we have determined to make it the most successful that we have ever offered. Everyone who has seen it wonders how we can possibly sell it at the price. As these articles are specially Jubilee goods every loyal patriotic person ought to possess a parcel, and treasure up the articles as momentos of this most auspicious occasion." How could any loyal subject resist that offer? The packet contained "The Queen's Jubilee Album" and "an elegant Jubilee Brooch being a beautiful heavily gold-plated Brooch in the shape of an extended Fan, with the word 'Jubilee' across it; this is no common loud cheap jewellery, but finished in the highest style of art, and could not be detected from a Brooch costing a guenia." Also included was "a Jubilee Fancy Scarf Pin, most richly finished, the center of the pin represents the Royal Arms of England in brilliant colors, surrounded by a gold-plated band bearing the motto 'Honi qui mal y pense,' surmounted with the Royal Crown in gold and crimson colours and crossed by two sceptres; besides this also a handsome Jubilee Medal bearing the Queens Head as a Medallion, and the words 'Queen Victorias' Jubilee, 1887' set in a handsome star." Surely some of these pieces are still in existence today. Many collectors would love to acquire them.

Ten years later the Queen celebrated her sixty year reign with a Diamond Jubilee. Lytton Strachey in his book "Queen Victoria" sums it up beautifully:

as the splendid procession passed along, escorting Victoria through the thronged re-echoing streets of London on her progress of thanksgiving to St. Pauls' Cathedral, the greatness of her realm and the adoration of her subjects blazed out together. The tears welled to her eyes, and while the multitude roared round her, 'how kind they are to me! how kind they are!' she repeated over and over again. That night her message flew over the Empire: 'From my heart I thank my beloved people. May God bless them!' The long journey was nearly done. But the traveller, who has come so far, and through such strange experiences, moved on with the old unfaltering step. The girl, the wife, the aged woman, were the same: vitality, conscientiousness, pride, and simplicity were hers to the latest hour.

**The Centennial Exposition**
In 1876 America celebrated its one hundredth birthday. This long awaited event was several years in the planning. "In 1872 Congress passed an act creating the Centennial Board of Finance with the authority to receive subscriptions to the capitol stock not exceeding ten million dollars, to be divided into shares of not over ten dollars each, and to use the proceeds for the erection of the buildings and all suitable fixtures and appurterands and for carrying on the exhibition to its close."[3]

Because of its historical significance, Philadelphia was chosen as the site for this great Centennial International Exposition. On July 5, 1873 Secretary Fish invited foreign nations to participate. Great Britain, France, Denmark, Germany, Switzerland, Mexico, Turkey, Brazil, Venezuela, Peru, Chile, The Sandwich Islands, Argentine Confederation, Japan, China, Australia, Bolivia, Canada, Columbia, Nicaragura, Equador, Liberia, Orange Free State, Guatemala, Honduras, and Salvador accepted.

The site of the Exposition was two hundred and thirty six beautiful acres that bordered on the Scheylkill River. Ground was broken on July 4, 1874, and the Exposition opened on May 10, 1876. Harper's New Monthly Magazine made small note of the momentous occasion: "The centennial exposition was opened at Philadelphia May 10, by an address from President Grant. The Emperor Dom Pedro assisted the President in setting the machinery in motion by starting the Corliss engine."

It was an exciting place to think about, to write about, and to visit. For months before the opening, articles were written about the country's past and future. How the early Americans lived, what they wore, and how they furnished their homes were topics for study. The country had indeed survived and prospered. The Great Exposition was tangeable proof of how far it had come.

People from far and near poured into Philadelphia. Many came by railway. The Centennial had two depots to receive them. Some utilized the steamboats that made regular runs from downtown to the Exposition. Others took the numerous horsecars and hack lines. In 1878 Leslie's Illustrated

Newspaper made this comment concerning transportation to the Centennial:

> As many as 250,000 persons were conveyed in one day from Philadelphia to the Centennial Exposition grounds and the facilities were even then not sufficient to meet the demand made of the transportation.

As early as 6:00 A.M. the lines would start forming at the ticket booths. Admission was a half dollar (50¢) and the people were more than eager to pay it. There were so many things to see that one hardly knew where to begin. There was the Main Exposition Building with exhibits from all over the world, the Machinery Hall where machinery could be seen in operation, Memorial Hall with all its wonderous works of art, the Shoe and Leather Building where one could view the actual making of shoes, the Brewers building, the Photographic Building, and many, many more. There was a Japanese Bazaar for buying gifts and a Photographic Studio. If all the walking worked up an appetite there were restaurants where foods from all over the world could be sampled.

The Exposition had its own railroad that circled the exhibitions. It provided a way to get a general feeling of the layout of the buildings and gave the feet a much needed rest. The cost of the four mile trip was five cents. People were allowed to ride as long as they liked.

One of the most visited buildings was the Department of Public Comfort. Reception rooms, washrooms, toilets, barber shops, and dressing rooms were located here. It provided a good meeting place. Lunch baskets could be checked until needed. There were umbrellas and wheelchairs available for rental.

The Women's Building was of special interest. Women had played a large part in raising money for the Centennial. Without their support it might never have taken place. The Women's Centennial Committee decided to go a step further and have their own building. They wanted "a place to exhibit work of women in such a manner as would display to advantage the individual taste and manufacture, and artistic skill of the sex."[4]

One of the more costly buildings, the Women's Pavillion, had 30,000 square feet of display area. "The walls were painted a light color, neatly panelled with blue upon the ceilings. The panels on the side walls were decorated with groups allegorical of Faith, Hope, and Charity, Art, Labor, Instruction, and the Family." It was a perfect setting for displaying their many talents. The building was lovely and the displays were well done. But not everyone shared this opinion. William Dean Howell made his views quite clear in his book "A Sennight of the Centennial:"

> It seems not yet the moment for the better half of our species to take their stand apart from the worst upon any distinct performance in art and industry; even when they have a building of their own, some organizing force to get their best work into it is lacking; many of those pictures and pincushions were no better than if men had made them.

The governments of England, France, Germany, Brazil, Spain, Sweden, and Japan built buildings to represent their countries. Japan also built a Japanese dwelling. During its erection it "created more curiousity and attracted infinitely more visitors than any other building on the grounds. It was erected by native Japanese workmen, with materials brought from home, and built in their own manner with curious tools and yet more curious manual processes."[5]

There were many jewelry displays at the Centennial, but none as striking as the Tiffany Exhibit. Their display was filled with watches, silver, jewelry, and stationary. They not only received special recognition but were presented with a gold metal.

The Centennial celebration had many positive results. The nation could take pride in its achievements and was favorably recognized by the rest of the world for its famous Yankee ingenuity. Even more important was the opportunity that the Exposition afforded the average person to become more familiar with other countries and their cultures.

## Fashions in Clothing and Jewelry

Thanks to the movie "Gone With the Wind" most people are familiar with the clothing and hair styles of the 1860's and 70's. It made real the beautiful dresses and manicured coiffurs worn by the ladies of that time. Who could ever forget the elegant dress that Scarlett made from her green velvet draperies? The scene in which Scarlett, dressed in mourning clothes, danced with Rhett Butler is still imprinted in many minds.

The jewelry of the 60's and 70's is best described as heavy, massive, and solid. Massiveness was equated with well-made and sturdy. The bigger a piece of furniture or jewelry the better it must surely be.

Colors were also visually heavy. Rich red velvets covered not only furniture and windows but also "meladies" as well. The feeling of opulence was everywhere. It was used to give an impression of wealth and importance.

The most outstanding feature of fashion was the hoop skirt which was introduced by the Princess Eugunie in Paris. It was not unusual to use as many as thirty yards of material for one skirt. Still they did tend to make the waist appear smaller, and small waists were definitely in fashion. Laced corsets were also used to minimize the waist. Some ladies wore their lacing so tight they were subject to fainting spells. To further emphasize the waist, buckles came into favor. "Buckles for waist bands have now attained colossal proportions, but these are generally imitation, and not genuine gold and silver," states Peterson's Magazine for November 1864. "The chased buckles are more distinguished than the plain dead ones, as the workmanship adds to their beauty. The mother-of-pearl buckles are worn with white dresses; and it is fashionable to wear a buckle both at the front and back of the waist."

Necklaces adorned every neck. "Necklaces or very thick chains have become indispensable with a low dress, and are also worn with high chemisettes and swiss bodices," said Petersons in January 1864. "The large round jet or coral beads are preferred for demi-toliet and married ladies often wear the thick gold chains."

Peterson's January 1864.
Fig. I—Ball dress of white silk, trimmed with black and white lace.
Fig. II—Evening dress of Blue Silk, trimmed, around the bottom, with a
deep flounce, headed by a thick chenille cord. Above the flounce is a
deep white chenille fringe, headed by a cord of the same. Backs of
white chenille.

These gold chains combined with other pieces were the height of fashion. In November of 1864 Petersons noted: "Jewels are of a very massive description, and set flat in the Cameo style; pearls and precious stones are often laid upon enamel, which has a very good effect. Necklaces are almost indispensable now with low dresses. Bold chains are six and eight times doubled and fastened here and there with thick round balls of gold, inlaid with jewels; the same style with pendant ornaments, is pretty for bracelets. Brooches are mostly round in the shape of small shields and very massive; they are made of different shades, some inclining to green, some to red and some of a deep burnish color. Pearls or smaller stones are arranged in a pattern over them."

A new way to wear chains became popular during the 1865-70 period. Instead of being worn around the neck in the traditional way they were suspended from over the top of the bonnet and draped over the bust. They were known as Benoiton Chains because a character in the play "La Famille Benoiton" wore her necklace in this manner. These long chains were made of gold, pearls, beads, or most any kind of material.

Jewelry was being worn at all times and in all places. The pieces were enormous, and many were in the costume jewelry category. "Jewelry is now being worn in out-of-door dress," comments the Lady's Book of January 1864. "The style in vogue is the Oriental-crescents, large round sequins, and long drooping ornaments being preferred. Very large ear-rings, brooches, clasps and studs are worn to match, in dimensions hitherto unheard of, and either in plain gold, or in gold and coral, or enameled. These jewels, being but a passing whim of fashion, need not be of the purest gold or precious gems. Even French ladies who have always been very particular on this point, now wear imitation jewels without the least scruple."

With loved ones off to war everyone wanted a keepsake close at hand. The locket came to be considered an important part of the total fashion picture. The May 1864 Peterson's Magazine confirmes this:

Lockets, medallions, etc. are still being worn around the neck attached to narrow velvet ribbons. Black ribbon velvet is generally used for
this purpose, as well as to tie the lace tucker which may be worn with
a low-necked dress. But frequently the velvet is selected to match the
trimming of the dress-a white dress trimmed with a scarlet ribbon
velvet, both for the locket and tucker, would be used, and with a blue
dress blue velvet etc. Two yards of ribbon velvet will be sufficient to
suspend the locket, as long ends are worn. Many ladies especially in
Paris, have latterly adopted the plan of mounting precious stones upon
black velvet for the throat, a style will be found advantageous around
throats which are neither round nor fair. Necklaces of all descriptions
are greatly in vogue but many ladies still retain the simple locket and
velvet, in preference to more costly necklets. Rosettes for the shoes
made to correspond with the trimmings of the dress, like-wise ribbon
velvet for the locket are now usually sent home with the dress by the
generality of our best dress-makers.

Because the women were involved in working for the war
efforts, hair styles became less complicated. The hair was
often worn pulled back, and nets came into fashion. In
February 1864, Petersons gave complete instructions for
making a hair-net. The article was introduced by these
words: "The Hair-net is a very pretty article of dress, and
useful also where the hair is redundant—. It is one of those
classical fashions, revived, with advantage, in the present
day, when the stiff modes are entirely out of favor. The
materials are as simple as possible, being nothing more than
a good netting silk. Brown is the prettiest color for the
general wear; but if a more dressy style be desired, the color
should be selected to suit the costume with which it is to be
worn."

Nets were so widely accepted that soon they were being used with evening attire. This was noted in the April edition of
the same magazine. "For small evening parties, dinners, or
the opera, nets, when made of fine gold braid, are very
becoming and give additional smartness to the toilet. Many
young ladies are satisfied with gold braid, fastened to the
center of the net and the hair-dress is finished; others add
flowers."

The ears were no longer considered unattractive. With the
hair worn back, earrings became fashionable again. The
November issue of Petersons stated: "Ear-rings are worn extremely large and weighty in the Grecian style; bonnets now
being so small, the ear-rings are allowed to show outside

them, and have in consequence acquired more importance than ever."

Combs became a very popular adornment for the hair. Not only were they utilitarian, but also they could be an asset to the overall fashion picture. "Combs for the hair now come within the sphere of jewels;" stated Petersons. "They are made with a wide, flat piece turned back from the teeth, and composing a very rich ornament, set with gold and precious stones; these combs are worn in the back hair; smaller ones are also sometimes used to keep back the hair in front."

The war helped prove to women just how impractical their clothes were. When one had to get up each morning and ride the omnibus to work it was painfully apparent that hugh hoops had no place on public transportation. The skirts were also much too long. They were a nuisance when walking on muddy streets, which every working woman had to do on occasion.

As early as 1874 women were holding Dress Reform Meetings. Something had to be done. By the 80's the hoops were gone, but they were replaced by the bustle. The skirts were much narrower, but the bustle did protrude. "How well the bustle performed may be judged by the story of the Washington lady who walked to church and home again with a toy rooster perched on her bustle."[6] Many women wanted to do away with this contraption. In April of 1887 the fashion editor of the Young Ladies' Journal wrote; "We are told by competent authorities that steel tournures, and all the metallic appliances which are so uncomfortable, are going out of fashion."

Things improved very quickly. Two months later the same writer made this comment:

Fashion is really becomming quite rational, after all the extravagences and eccentricities with which has too justly been charged, it has now become quite quiet and reasonable.

The ridiculous tournures, enormously protruding, which vexed seriously inclined spirits for the last few years are now almost forgotten; they have been transformed into a modest cushion, scarcely apparant, which offers a timid support to the skirt, marking the bend of the waist. Our shoes and boots, with stilt-like heels, have long been exchanged for rational chaussures with low square heels; and the absurd peak by which they terminated hurt so many feet, that it has *been found quite necessary to change it for a rational shape, neither square nor pointed, but something between the two, which looks graceful without being uncomfortable.*

*What else were we blamed for? Extravagant chapeaux, which towered high above the head-inconvenient hats, which at the theatre played the troublesome part of screens for these spectators who were unfortunate enough to sit behind them. Well here reason is triumphant, and our capotes are perfectly charming; small and well posed upon the head, they form a most beccoming frame to the face.*

*What, therefore, can modern Fashion be accused of now? It is quite rational and as practical and logical as most things are in the "Age of realism."*

Hair styles evolved from being "pulled back" in the 60's and 70's, to being "put up" in the 80's. Everyone was hair conscious. Switches of extra hair were worn by most women to supplement what mother nature had given them. The new hair styles were identified by name. The Young Ladies' Journal described three of the most popular styles in 1887.

*"The Diana Coiffure" is much in vogue. For this coiffure the hair is turned straight up from the roots, and arranged on the top of the head into a sort of rouleau, which is fastioned with a small tortoise-shell comb. Two tortoiseshell pins to match are used to fasten the ends of the front hair into loops at the sides quite high on the head.*

*"The Marie-Antoinette Coiffure" is also much in vogue. For this coiffure the hair is arranged in a rouleau; it is not brushed straight off from the face and fastened straight down, but merely rolled off and attached with pins, but so as to remain loose. This style does not suit all faces but is very beccoming to ladies who have a low broad forehead, and straight eyebrows.*

*"The Psyche Coiffure" is also very fashionable. The hair is also combed up from the roots, but it is then twisted and arranged into two loops, fastened with a small comb and pins of light-coloured tortoiseshell.*

With the new up-sweep hair styles, the comb gained new importance. "These tortoiseshell combs and pins are of quite a new style." commented The Young Ladies' Journal in January 1887, "and are among the prettiest novelties introduced this year for New Year's gifts. They are in pretty open-worked patterns, some square, some rounded, and some triangular; the pins are but reductions of the comb; they are sold in pairs."

In 1885 Charles Dana Gibson drew his first Gibson Girl. She became the epitome of what was most desirable. Women all over the country emulated her dress, hair style, manner,

Illustration from The Young Ladies' Journal, July, 1887.

and even her drooped eye-lid, head titled back pose. Alice
Roosevelt, the President's daughter, gave the American
public an opportunity to vicariously experience the thrill of a

real live Gibson type. They were shocked by her flaunting rules such as smoking in public. But since she did things they did not have the courage or the money to do, it made her even more endearing. T.R. loved her and was proud of her independent spirit even though he once stated, "I can be President or I can handle Alice. I can't possibly do both."

The mood of the world was reflected in these new "up sweep" hair fashions. In England people were ready to shed the heavy mood that Victoria's mourning had spread across the country. They were ready for some gaiety in their lives.

Americans were beginning to feel carefree and optimistic. Women were experiencing an unprecidented freedom in fashion. This lightness began to be reflected in jewelry. By December of 1887 a new style of jewelry was emerging. These changes were noted in the Young Ladies' Journal: "There are a few changes to note in fashionable jewellery, the solid, massive portebonheur is quite out of fashion; bracelets are all made in the the chain style, or else composed of a fine circle with diamonds and precious stones; gold chains and lockets for the neck are things of the past; brooches are of the most fanciful and dainty type, and are fastened here, there, and everywhere, among lace folds, close to the shoulder or near the neck; eardrops are as small as possible; diamonds are fixed in close to the ear. Combs and hair-styles are ornamented with pearls and precious stones. Jewels are now required to have at least as much artistic as intrinsic value."

So be it. Out went the old—in came the new.

## Archaeological Inspirations

Archaelogical findings exerted an important influence on jewelry designs of the 1861-89 period. The digs began in Egypt after Napoleon's conquest in 1798. The findings spurred interest in archaeological artifacts, and from 1806 to 1814 the French excavated Pompeii.

Pompeii had been completely covered by a volcanic eruption in 79 A.D. The excavations uncovered a city that had been caught unaware. It provided a glimpse of an ancient civilization almost beyond belief to the nineteenth century. Beautiful houses with frescoed walls, atriums complete with fountains and mosaic floors, jewelry made with ancient unknown goldwork methods, and everyday items made with beautiful skill and craftsmanship—all captured the imagaination of the people.

Greek artifacts were discovered on the island of Crete and Rhodes. These were sorted and made public by Author Evans. In 1848 Sir Austin Henery Layard wrote "Minevia and Its Remains," a book about the fascinating archaeological finds in the ancient capital of Assyria.

The archaeological motifs of the Egyptians, Etruscans, Greeks, and Romans were popular first in Europe, and then they spread to England. By the 1850's the theatre was using the discoveries to authenticate scenery for plays. In 1853 Charles Dean based his scenery for the play "Sardanapalus" on pieces in the British Museum. This made the public even more aware of the archaeological finds.

The ancient motifs were further stimulated in 1862 by the display of Castellani jewelry at The Great Exposition in London. It attracted much attention. The public went home convinced that the ancient styles were the most suitable for jewelry designs.

By 1864 jewelry designs, inspired by the finds, had spread to the United States. The June Issue of Petersons' Magazine noted, "the new models are all copied from the antique and give one a very good idea of the beautiful gold and jewel ornaments of Old Grecian Art."

The same publication made this comment in the November issue:

*Ear rings are now made in the antique style. They represent a large circle, in the center of which either a large ball of dead gold, or five crescents of pearls is fastened; the crescents diminish in size as they ascend. Sometimes the ear-ring is composed of a large crescent of dead gold studded with coral and fringed with gold.*

Interest in archaeological findings continued to increase. The "Treasure of Priam" was discovered by Heinrich Schlieman in 1869. In 1872 the British Museum bought some fine examples of ancient jewelry from the Castellani collection. This enabled the British to study and admire the archaeological styles. The French could satisfy their curosity by viewing the Cavalier Compana Collection at the Louvre, and the Italians could study pieces by Augusto Castelliani in the Capitoline Museum.

It was not until 1877 that the people of the United States could boast of a collection of archeological finds. In the early 1870's Luigi P. do Cesnola, a United States Consul at Larmoce, discovered the treasure vaults of the Temple of Kurium. An account of the discovery was published July 1872 in the Harper's New Monthly Magazine. Within the next five years more discoveries were made on this island of Cyprus. In July 1877 Harpers published another article in which they rejoiced at these findings being displayed in the United States.

*The Metropolitan Museum of Art had the wisdom to commence its collection of illustrations of ancient art at the very beginning of all art, and to offer to its visitors and the American public facilities for studying what no European collection illustrates-the birth of art among civilized men, and its growth in the early years.*

The treasure vaults of the Kuruin were vast. "Gold, silver, alabastor, and bronze, the work of artists and artisins dead more than twenty-five centuries ago, are here gathered; not a few specimens, a ring or two and a gem or two, but literally hundreds of ear and finger rings, bracelets, necklaces, amulets and ornaments in vast variety."

Harpers described many of the pieces. It had this comment on the ear-rings:

*It can not fail to strike the observer that the present form was a favorite, and many in this form are evidently Phoenician of an early date. Simple crescents of plain gold are numerous. After these come*

73

plain crescents with raised edges and wire ornamentations. Then
enamels beautify the crecsent. Precious stones are placed on them, or
form pendants. Then the crescent swells into a solid gold form. Then
the hollow gold is shaped in lobes with charming surface ornaments.
Then we see agates cut in new-moon form, and set in gold with
delicious granulated patterns. There is no end to the varieties of earrings. There are bunches of fruit, rosettes, plaques with impressed im-
ages ear-rings with pendants in every form, and ear-rings with pendants, in the modern form, where a small ornament fits close on the
lobe of the ear.

The article also gave an excellent description of granula-
tions:

This style of work, known in Etruscan jewelry, characterizes much of
this ancient Greek work, and is a puzzle to modern goldsmiths. We il-
lustrate a gold ornament—a round brooch or amulet—for the sake of
describing this remarkable style of work. The surface of this object
present to the eye the appearance of a gold disk stamped in a die, or
crossed by numerous fine wires at right angles with each other. On
examining it with the magnifying-glass, however it is found that the effect is produced by minute globes of gold, each one perfectly round
and smooth, soldered on the surface in exact lines, each globe
touching the next. There are on the surface of this small object, a little
over an inch in diameter, upward of nine hundred of these globes.
How were they made, and how were they soldered on in such absolutely true lines? The ablest gold-workers in America (and that is to
say the albest in the world) tell us that they can not explain it.

Revival jewelry was already in fashion by the time the
Metropolitan Museum acquired Cesnola's finds. The Harpers
article stated:

There are some things here in silver which, were they perfect, would
ravish the eyes of our lady readers, and over which some of them who
love old art will bend in delighted rapture. These are silver belts worn
by the ladies of Cyprus in the ancient years. Within the past year or
two a fashion has prevailed among ladies in America of wearing
broad metallic belts of silver or other metal. Could an American lady
possess one of these belts of Cyproit made in its original freshness, or
its facsimile, she would be very happy.

Ten years later (1887) the ancient style jewelry was still
being worn. But instead of being made of gold, the designs
were now executed in silver. This is confirmed by an article
in the Young Ladies' Journal of January 1887:

Jewels of old silver, finely wrought in the imitation of Ancient jewelry,
are also among the favorite trinkets of fashion just now. There are

*beautiful bracelets composed of detached ovals fastened together by very fine chains. Brooches to match, and exquisite chantelaines of the most beautiful workmanship.*

Many famous jewelers made jewelry based on archaeological findings. The most famous were Robert Phillips, Carlos Giuliano, and Castellani.

## Castellani

One of the most familiar names in nineteenth century design is Castellani. Actually there were several Castellanis who played an important role in jewelry styles.

Fortunato Pio Castellani was born in 1793, the son of a goldsmith. In 1814 he went to work for his father and excelled at the craft. He became fascinated with Etruscan jewelry while working in an advisory capacity to the Papal government in 1836. They needed his expertise on goldwork to advise them on purchases of artifacts from a tomb discovered at Cervetri.

He was intrigued with the Etruscan art of granulation and wanted to learn this ancient technique. After many unsuccessful attempts to capture the art of the tiny granules he went in search of someone who might have knowledge of this ancient art. In a remote mountain village he found some men and women to whom this art of working gold had been passed from generation to generation. He persuaded them to come to Rome to live and work with him. It was not long before his workshop was known throughout Italy.

Castellani's sons, Alessandro (1824-1883) and Augusto (1829-1914), were both active in their father's business. When the revolutionary upheavels stated in 1848, the shop was closed. In 1851 Fortunato retired and turned the business over to his sons. They became involved in the revolution. Eventually Alessandro fled to Paris and Augusto went to London. They took their enthusiasm for Etruscan work with them and shared its technique with other artists in those cities. Thus the design spread to new areas.

Alessandro became an expert in archaeological artifacts. He was a collector and a dealer. Some of his customers were the museums of England, Europe, and America. In 1868 he published a catalogue entitled "Italian Jewelry as Worn by the Peasants of Italy, Collected by Signor Castellani."

Augusto was very involved in the business and strove to carry on his fathers traditions. Later his knowledge and interest led him to become the Director of the Capitoline Musuem in Rome. He was the author of "Antique Jewelry and Its Revival," published in 1862.

When the Castellani jewelry was displayed at the 1862 International Exposition in London, it drew much attention. The name Castellani and their crossed capitol "C" trademark became known throughout the world.

Jewelry showing the Etruscan granulation influence is pictured on pages 34, 36, 37, 100 and 102.

## Jet

At the death of her beloved husband, Queen Victoria went into a period of mourning which was to last the rest of her life. This unexpected death left the English subjects shocked and grieved. All the nation went into mourning.

It was customary to be "in mourning" for a period of two years. The first year only black was allowed to be worn. This was a time of full mourning and elaborate regulations as to appropriate dress for each relative of the departed was followed. The second year was spent in "half-mourning". The bereaved could wear a few things that were not black such as amethyst because of its ecclesiastical associations, but for the most part all jewelry and clothes were dark.

Jet was an obvious solution to the problem of jewelry suitable during this period. Victoria had first worn jet during the mourning period for William IV, her predecessor, and it was natural for her to wear it while in mourning for his husband.

Jet is a hard, coal-like material. A type of fossilized wood. The finest jet was mined in the town of Whitby, England. The industry started there in the early nineteenth century and by 1850 there were fifty jet workshops. Because it lent itself well to carving and kept a sharp edge, it was used extensively. By 1873 there were more than two hundred jet shops in this one small town.

Because jet is extremely light weight, it was the perfect material for making the enormous lockets, necklaces, brooches and bracelets that were so popular in the 1860's and 70's. The success enjoyed by the jet factories led to many imitations. French jet, which is neither French nor jet (it is black glass, was cheaper to manufacture. It gave the jet industry some competition, but because it is much heavier, it was used mostly in the making of beads and smaller items.

Today, it is illegal to mine jet in Whitby. The jet is in seams in the walls of the cliffs on which parts of the town were built. Consequently, the very existance of the town was threatened by those who extracted the velvety substance. The two jet cutters in the town today have to rely on the pieces that wash up on the shore of this sea coast town.

This makes the jet of the Victorian era more precious than ever. Good, well-made examples of Whitby jet are sure to appreciate in value.

For ways to differentiate between jet and other visually similar materials such as Gutta-Purcha, bog oak, glass and onyx, read Section III. Examples of jet jewelry are pictured on pages 27, 33, 35, 41, 82 and 83.

## Diamonds

Diamonds were discovered in South Africa in 1867. A peasant boy, playing near a river, found a pretty stone and took it home. A traveler passing through the village saw the boy's prize and suspected what it might be. He was right; it was a diamond valued at $2,500. Word of the "find" spread, and the diamond rush began. Within a few years this new source was supplying the Paris demand. Diamonds were very much in fashion.

Diamonds have always been in demand. The Greeks appreciated the stone's hardness and called it 'Adamas,' meaning unconquerable. Consequently, it was often worn into battle. The stones were not cut or faceted as they are today but worn in their natural pointed shape.

These early diamonds were found in streams of India. These 'alluvial' diamonds required no mining because the natural erosion of the earth uncovered them. Until 1871 alluvial diamonds were the only ones available to man.

By chance it was discovered that diamonds were buried deep inside the earth in what is now known as 'pipes.' These pipes are thought to be part of extinct volcanoes. The rock surrounding the diamond is called 'blue ground.' It is estimated that an average of two tons of blue ground must be mined to find a single carat of diamonds.

Diamonds are judged by weight, cut, clarity, and color. Consequently, three stones each weighing one carat could vary thousands of dollars in price. A carat weighs two hundred (200) milligrams which is equal to one hundred (100) points. Hence a half carat is fifty (50) points, and twenty five (25) points equals a fourth of a carat.

The cut of a diamond is very important. It takes an expert to decide the proper cut for each stone. The proper proportions will enhance the stone's brilliance and increase its value. Most diamonds today are cut brilliant and have fifty eight (58) facets.

The clarity of a diamond is determined by the purity of the stone. Flaws such as dark inclusions and feathers can greatly decrease the value. A diamond is considered to be flawless if there are no visable flaws when the stone is examined using a ten power loupe.

Diamonds come in a variety of colors. Some are colorless, many have a yellowish tinge, and a few have a blueish tinge. When fancy colors such as green, violet, brown, blue, red, and yellow are found in quality stones, they are very expensive and highly collectible. Since diamonds tend to pick up color from surrounding objects, a white background is best when determining a stone's true color.

From the 1880's through the 1920's the Tiffany mounting was the most popular setting used for a diamond. Someone at Tiffanys came up with a six prong setting that became known as a "Tiffany" mounting. It became so fashionable that the average person would ask for it by name. This infuriated the other jewelers. They did not like the fact that a customer had to use a competitor's name to describe the type of setting they wanted.

Because the diamond has always been highly prized, there have been many imitations. These include rock crystal, zircon, spinel, Strass glass, and diamond doublets. Today's popular imitations are cubic zirconia, YAG, and strontium titanate. Because these synthetic stones look very much like diamonds to the untrained eye, it is wise to buy from a reputable source.

## Opals

In 1870 a hugh opal field was discovered in Australia. This prompted Queen Victoria to try again to lift the veil of superstition that had befallen the stone. The novel, "Anne of Geurstein," written by Scott and published in 1829, was responsible for the opal being considered 'bad luck.' Lady Heromine, a character in the book, always wore an opal in her hair. Its irridescent glow seemed to reflect her every mood. When she came to a tragic end, the opal's mysterious powers were blamed.

The opal was one of Queen Victoria's favorite stones. She gave them as wedding gifts to her daughters and wore them herself. Still the superstition remained. When Napoleon presented the Empress Eugenie with a parure of opals, she refused them. Even today some people think it is unlucky to wear an opal unless it is a birthstone. Others believe as the ancients did that the stone brings good fortune to its wearer.

There are three types of opals; precious, fire, and common. The precious is the kind most people associate with the word 'opal.' It has a beautiful multicolored irridescence that changes when exposed to different angles of light. The most common color of precious opal is white. There are also black opals, but they are very rare. Opals may also be found in colors of gray, blue, or green.

The fire opal is named for its orange color. It is not opalescent, and it does not have the rainbow-like colors. The best of this type are clear and transparent. Another variety of the fire opal is the Mexican Water Opal. It is usually light brown or colorless.

The so-called common opals are varied. There are agate opals, wood opals, honey opals, milk opals, and moss opals. Most of these the average person would never identify as an opal.

Because opals contain as much as thirty percent (30%) water, they require very special treatment. If a stone gets too dry, it tends to crack or lose its irridescent quality. In the book "Gemstones of the World," Walter Schumann suggests the best treatment is to "saturate the stone with oil or water and to avoid the aging process by storing the piece in moist absorbent cotton."

## Garnets

Throughout the ages garnets have been worn and admired. Although the word garnet usually conjurs up pictures of a wine red stone, they can be found in every color except blue.

Actually garnets are a group of stones that have the same structure but differ chemically. The garnets most associated with the name are almadine and pyrope. They are also the most common.

The pyrope (PIE-rope) garnets were popular during the 1860-1889 period. Their deep rich color was a favorite accessory for the massive clothing of the 1860's and 70's. These Bohemian garnets, fashioned in lighter scale mountings, continued to be popular in the 1880's and 90's. They are red or reddish brown in color and tend to be more transparent than the almadine garnet. Most pyrope garnets are mined in Czechoslovakia, Australia, and South Africa.

The almadine (AL-man-dine) garnet tends to have a slightly purplish tint. The most common variety of garnet, it is found in Brazil, India, Australia, Czechoslovakia, and Sri Lanka.

A lesser known variety of garnet is the dementoid (deh-MAN-toid). Its rich emerald green color and diamond-like luster make it the most valuable of garnets.

The garnet is the accepted January birthstone. Some believe that it empowers it wearer with truth, constancy, and faith. Ancient man wore it for protection against being struck by lightning. No matter what reason is chosen for wearing garnets, they always seem to be admired and enjoyed.

## Mosaics

Mosaics were popular souveniers for the Victorian traveler. Not only did they picture scenes that had been visited, but they were made using ancient methods made popular by the excavations. Most of these tiny works of art were made in Florence and Rome.

The mosaics from Florence are commonly known as "petra dura." These works of art are made by cutting designs out of stones such as malachite and cornelian, and fitting them together in a black background stone. This was done so expertly that a magnifying glass is needed to verify that the design is indeed made from pieces and not painted. Flowers and birds were the favorite motifs.

The mosaics from Rome have an entirely different look. They are made of tiny rectangular bricks of glass. As early as the eighteenth century, the Vatican was making pieces to sell to visitors. The motifs are typical Roman ruins and other familiar scenes of Rome. Many designs were taken from mosaics found in the ruins of Pompeii. Again a magnifying glass is needed to fully appreciate the craftsmanship that went into creating these souvenir pieces.

Mosaics are highly collectible. The price depends on the material used for the mounting and the workmanship of the artist. A beautiful example of petra dura is pictured on page 84. A Roman mosaic pin is shown on page 160.

## Pique and Tortoise Shell

The popular French definition of the word Pique is "dotted" or "cracked." This is an apt description of the beautiful work done in tortoise shell or ivory.

The most frequently encountered pique is done in tortoise shell, which comes from the hawksbill turtle. Even though this is the smallest of marine turtles, it usually weighs between one hundred and two hundred pounds. Both the mottled upper shell and the lower "yellow belly" are used for ornamental purposes.

Tortoise shell is one of nature's natural plastics. It can be heated and moulded or cut into many forms. For pique the shell is heated and a design is formed (star, cross, etc.). Into this design "dots" or "cracks" are drilled. These minute spaces are inlaid with silver or gold rods. The hot tortoise shell emits a glue-like film which, along with the natural contraction caused by the cooling shell, snuggly seals the metal.

Many lovely pieces were made using this process. Pique has been in and out of fashion since the sixteenth century. In the nineteenth century it was popular in the 1820's and the 1870's. Today it is highly collectible. When a piece comes on the market it is purchased quickly by a collector. Since pique is not being reproduced it most assuredly will continue to appreciate in value.

# II. The Jewelry—1861-1889

**II-1. Brooch**—Jet marked "Whitby" 2 x 1-1/2'' $120.00 (Jeanenne Bell Collection)

**II-2. Bracelet—1860-70**—Jet strung on elastic with petra dura. 1-1/4" wide. $495.00 (Camille Grace Dealer)

**II-3. Bracelet—1860-70**—Jet strung on elastic with shell cameos 3/4 x 1-1/2" wide $495.00 (Camille Grace Dealer)

**II-4. Jet Cameo—1860-70**—Surrounded by rose cut jet. 1-1/4 x 1-1/2'' $150.00 (Jeanenne Bell Dealer)

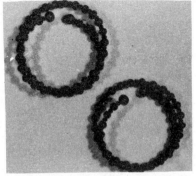

**II-5. Beads—1860-80**—8 MM Matte finished jet on chain. $95.00 (Jeanenne Bell Dealer)

**II-6. Bracelets—1870-90**—Matte jet balls with shinging jet bead spacers. End matte ball 8 MM $85.00 pair (Jeanenne Bell Dealer)

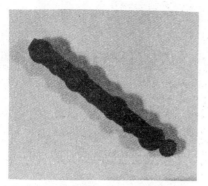

II-7. **Brooch—1870-89**—Matte jet balls 5 MM and crepe stone on Gutta Percha 2-1/8 x 1/4" $55.00 (Jeanenne Bell Dealer)

II-8. **Bracelet—1860-70**—18K Gold-8" long. Each lava cameo 1-1/4 x 1-1/2-7/8" high relief. $1495.00 (Lucile and Sam Mundorff Dealers)

II-9. **Bracelet—1860-70**—22K gold Lava cameo 7/8 x 1". Band 1 x 1/2" $975.00 (Lucile and Sam Mundorff Dealers)

II-10. **Brooch—1860's**—18K mtg. Lava Cameo 1-3/4 x 2-1/8" $850.00 (Jeanenne Bell Collection)

II-11. **Brooch—1860-70**—18K Mosaic has black onyx background with multi colored flowers beautifully worked cluster of grapes. Compartment for hair in rear. Piece swivels so that hair can be in front. 2 x 2-1/4" $750.00 (Jeanenne Bell Collection)

II-12. **Pendants—1860-80**—1-1/21 x 2-1/4". Petra Dura 1-1/2 x 1-7/8" $500.00 pair (Camille Grace Dealer)

83

II-13. **Pendant**—Same as No. 12 with different design. One of pair.

II-14. **Bracelet**—1860-70—15K gold mtgs. Petra Dura Center Plaques 1-7/8 x 2-1/4" 2 side pieces 1-1/8 x 1-1/4" Length 6-1/2" $2,200 (Jeanenne Bell Dealer)

II-15. **Bracelet**—1860-70—10K Locket Clasp. Three strands of hair. 1-1/4" dia. x 6" L. $295.00 (Jeanenne Bell Collection)

II-16. **Bracelet**—1860-70—10 K Fittings. Hairwork 3/4 x 6-1/2" $325.00 (Jeanenne Bell Collection)

II-17. **Bracelet**—1860-70—10K Locket clasp with 4 weaves of hairwork in 3 colors. 1x7" $325.00 (Jeanenne Bell Collection)

II-18. **Bracelet**—1860-70—9K Locket clasp-4 weaves of hairwork. 1" wide x 7-1/8" L. $295.00 (Jeanenne Bell Collection)

84

II-19. **Brooch and Earrings—1850-70—** 14K Hairwork pin 1-3/4 x 5/8". Earrings 5/8" dia. $475.00 (Jeanenne Bell Collection)

II-20. **Brooch—1850-70—**Gold Filled Fittings and gold ornamentation. Hairwork 2-1/4 x 1-1/2" $165.00 (Jeanenne Bell Collection)

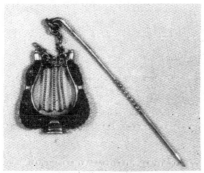

II-21. **Scarf Pin—1860-80—**Gold Filled Fittings. Hairwork is finished all around. Harp motif was popular for many years. $65.00 (Jeanenne Bell Collection)

II-22. **Scarf Pin—1880's—**Gold over brass fitting. Hairwork, popular Horse shoe motif. 1/2 x 5/8" Pin 2 1/2" L. $65.00 (Jeanenne Bell Collection)

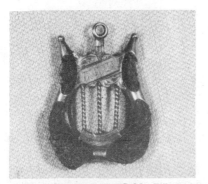

II-23. **Fob—1850-80—**Gold Filled Fittings. Open weave Hairwork. Finished on one side only. 5/8 x 7/8" $55.00 (Jeanenne Bell Collection)

II-24. **Watch Chain—1860-80—**Gilt brass fittings. Light brown hairwork. Masonic fob, hand engraved and enameled 13" L $125.00 (Jeanenne Bell Collection)

II-25. **Watch Chain**—1860-80—Gilt brass fittings. Hairwork in 3 patterns. 3/8″ dia. 15″ L. $85.00 (Jeanenne Bell Dealer)

II-26. **Watch Chain**—Gold over brass fittings. Double length of hairwork in 3 patterns. Note fob with hand holding Amethyst. 3/8″ x 18″ $145.00 (Jeanenne Bell Collection)

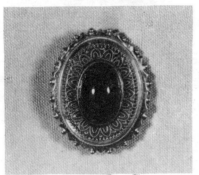

II-27. **Brooch**—1860-80—Yellow Gold Cabochon Garnet and granulation work. Glassed compartment in back for hair. 1-1/2 x 1-1/4″ $395.00 (W. Baldwin Collection)

II-28. **Locket**—1850-70—Gutta Percha with Anchor motif. 1 x 1-1/4″ $120.00 (Jeanenne Bell Collection)

II-29. **Cross**—1860-70—Gutta Percha with anchor of hope. 2-1/16 x 3-3/4″ $145.00 (Jeanenne Bell Collection)

II-30. **Bracelet**—1860-70—Gutta Percha 1-1/4-2″ wide. $155.00 (Jeanenne Bell Collection)

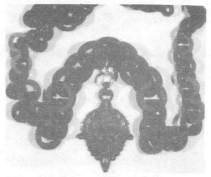

II-31. **Necklace—1860-70**—Gutta Percha. Chain lengths graduate from 1″ to
5/8″ Drop 1-3/4 x 3″. A fine example of
the massive style. $140.00 (Jeanenne Bell
Collection)

II-32. **Brooch**—Inscribed Mary 1879.
Painted carved wood with gold ornamen-
tation 1-3/8 x 1″ $65.00 (Jeanenne Bell
Collection)

II-33. **Ring—1870-80**—9K Gold with hair
band. Engraved "Hugh." Blocks spell
"Brother." Memorial piece 3/8″ wide.
$195.00 (Jeanenne Bell Collection)

II-34. **Locket—1860-80**—Gold Filled 7/8 x
1-1/4″ Mint Condition. $95.00 (Jeanenne
Bell Dealer)

II-35. **Locket—1860's**—Gold Filled. Contains two tin types. Note the button on top
that opens like hunting case watch. 1-1/2″
dia. $165.00 (Jeanenne Bell Dealer)

II-36. **Locket**—Inside view of 35.

II-37. **Locket**—**1850-70**—Pinchbeck 1-1/2 x 2-1/2" $185.00 (Jeanenne Bell Collection)

II-38. **Locket**—**1850-70**—Gilt over brass with some gold ornamentation. Two blue stones and two red stones. 1-1/8 x 1-3/8" $125.00 (Jeanenne Bell Dealer)

II-39. **Locket**—**1850-70**—Gold Filled with Gold top and bottom. Taille d' epergne enameling. 1-1/4 x 1-3/4" $225.00 (Camille Grace Dealer)

II-40. **Locket and chain**—**1870-80**—Gold over brass with banded agate and Seed Pearls. 1-3/8 x 2" $95.00 (Jeanenne Bell Dealer)

II-41. **Locket**—**1870-80**—Gold over brass with some gold ornamentation. Moonstone in center. Contains a lock of hair. 1-1/4 x 2-1/8" $145.00 (Jeanenne Bell Collection)

II-42. **Locket**—**Hallmarked 1879**—Sterling 1-1/4 x 1-3/4" $95.00 (Jeanenne Bell Dealer)

II-43. **Cross-1860-80**—Gold top. Back is gold over brass. 1-5/8 x 2-3/8" $85.00 (Jeanenne Bell Dealer)

II-44. **Locket Fob—1860-80**—Gold Filled with gold stone. 1 x 1-5/8" Attached to book chain 1/2 x 16" L. $130.00 (Camille Grace Dealer)

II-45. **Vinigrette and Slid Chain—1880's** —Gold Filled Chain 27" L. 3/4 x 1" $175.00 (Camille Grace Dealer)

II-46. **Locket and Bookchain—1880- 90**—Gold Filled Locket 1-1/8 x 1-1/2" Chain 1/2 x 18" L. $195.00 (Camille Grace Dealer)

II-47. **Bookchain Necklace—1860-80**— Gold filled with stone cameo drop 1 x 1-1/4". Chain 19" $195.00 (Jeanenne Bell Collection)

II-48. **Bookchain Necklace—1860-80**— Gold over brass bookchain with small stone cameo. 7/8 x 1-1/2" drop $195.00 (Jeanenne Bell Collection)

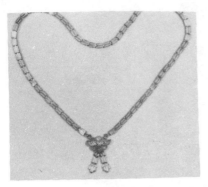

II-49. **Bookchain Necklace—1860-80—** Gold over brass. Flat Links 1/8″ Drop 3/4 x 1-1/4″ $155.00 (Jeanenne Bell Collection)

II-50. **Bookchain Necklace—**Same as 49 unclasped.

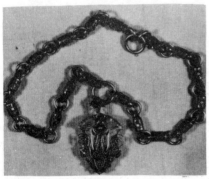

II-51. **Bookchain and Locket—1860-70—** Yellow gold 1-1/4 x 2-1/8″ Chain length 20″ $1,500.00 (W. Baldwin Collection)

II-52. **Locket—1860-80—**Gold Filled with original mesh chain 1/4 x 19″ L. Locket 1 x 1-1/2″ $225.00 (Jeanenne Bell Collection)

II-53. **Necklace—1860-70—**Gold Filled with 19″ original chain. Drop is 1-5/8 x 2″ Note chain is at top left side of drop. $185.00 (Jeanenne Bell Collection)

II-54. **Necklace—**same necklace shown unclasped.

II-55. **Bracelet—1850-70**—Gold over brass with gold ornamentation. Quatre Foils are pink gold. Leaves are green gold. Bookchain style 1/4 x 7" L $70.00 (Jeanenne Bell Collection)

II-56. **Bookchain and Locket—1860-70**—Gold Filled. Locket has mosaic bird 1-1/8 x 2". Chain 3/8 x 18" $450.00 (Camille Grace Collection)

II-57. **Brooch—1850-70**—14K Gold. Stone cameo with enameling 1-1/4 x 1-1/2" $725.00 (Jeanenne Bell Collection)

II-58. **Slide and Chain—1860's**—Gold top slide with enameling and stone cameo. Chain is new Gold Filled 52" $250.00 (Jeanenne Bell Collection)

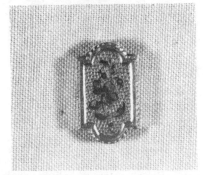

II-59. **Slide—1860-70**—Gold Filled with Taille d' epergne enameling 5/8 x 1-1/4" $125.00 (Jeanenne Bell Dealer)

II-60. **Slide—1860-70**—Gold with enameling 9/16 x 7/8" $225.00 (W. Baldwin Collection)

II-61. **Victorian Chain—1860-80**—Silver over brass. Some gold ornamentation. Note anchor 5″ L. $36.00 (Jeanenne Bell Dealer)

II-62. **Watchchain—1860-70**—Gold over brass with some gold. Drop has ambrotype 1/4″ wide. Drop 1″ Dia. $80.00 (Jeanenne Bell Collection)

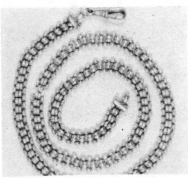

II-63. **Watchchain—1870-90**—Gold Filled. 1/4 x 20-1/2″ Makes nice neckchain for today. $90.00 (Jeanenne Bell Dealer)

II-64. Slidechain—1860-70—18K heavy. Chain 64″ L. Slide with enameling and pearls 3/4 x 1″ $1950.00 (Jeanenne Bell Collection)

II-65. **Bookchain—1870-1880's**—Silver 1/2 x 17-1/2″ L. $250.00 (W. Baldwin Collection)

II-66. **Bookchain—1870-80's**—Silver. Originally had a locket attached 5/8 x 16-1/2″ L. $295.00 (W. Baldwin Collection)

II-67. **Watchchain—1870-90**—Silver with Tassell 8-1/2" L. $58.00 (Jeanenne Bell Dealer)

II-68. **Brooch—1860-70**—Gold Filled Mounting. Shell cameo 1-3/4 x 2" $285.00 (Camille Grace Dealer)

II-69. **Brooch—1860-80**—Gold Filled Mtg. Shell Cameo 2-1/4 x 2-5/8" $225.00 (W. Baldwin Collection)

II-70. **Brooch—1860-80**—Silver Mtg. Shell Cameo 1-3/4 x 2-1/4" $195.00 (Camille Grace Collection)

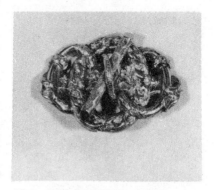

II-71. **Brooch—1860-70**—14K 2-1/8 x 1-1/2" $325.00 (Jeanenne Bell Dealer)

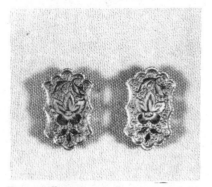

II-72. **Collar Buttons—1860-80**—Gold with black enameling 5/8 x 1" $185.00 (W. Baldwin Collection)

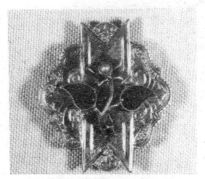

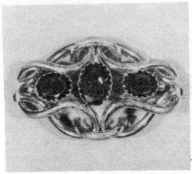

II-73. **Brooch—1860-80**—Gold with onyx and 1 pearl. 1-3/4 x 1-1/8" $175.00 (W. Baldwin Collection)

II-74. **Brooch—1860-70**—Gold Filled with garnet colored stones. Typical massive style 2-3/4 x 1-3/4" $98.00 (Jeanenne Bell Dealer)

II-75. **Brooch—1860-70**—Gold over brass with garnets 2 x 1-1/2" $65.00 (Jeanenne Bell Dealer)

II-76. **Brooch/Pendant—1870-80**—Gold with tassels 1-1/4 x 3-1/8" $650.00 (W. Baldwin Collection)

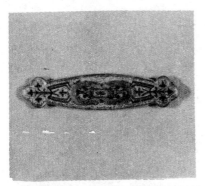

II-77. **Brooch—1860-70**—Gold top with black Taille d' epergne enameling 2-3/8 x 5/8" $78.00 (Jeanenne Bell Dealer)

II-78. **Memorial Brooch—1860-70**—Gold with black enameling. Nice tin type $125.00 (Lucille and Sam Mindorff Dealers)

II-79. **Brooch—1870-80's**—Gold Filled. Crepe stone. 2-1/4 x 3/4" $85.00 (Jeanenne Bell Dealer)

II-80. **Brooch—1870-80'**—Crepe stone 2-1/2 x 1/2" Chipped corner so only $45.00 (Jeanenne Bell Dealer)

II-81. **Brooch and Ear Rings—1870-80's**—Gold Filled mtg. Crepe stone Pin 1-3/4 x 1/4". Ear Rings 3/8 x 3/4" $150.00 (Jeanenne Bell Dealer)

II-82. **Brooch—1870-80's**—Gold Filled with onyx and pearl 2-1/4 x 3/8" $78.00 (W. Baldwin Collection)

II-83. **Brooch and Ear Rings-1860-80**—Gold Filled with "Robin's Egg Blue" enameling. Ear Rings were originally color buttons and have been converted with 14K wire. All pins are 1 x 5/8" $195.00 set (Jeanenne Bell Collection)

II-84. **Brooch and Ear Rings—1860-80**—Gold with garnets and pearls. Brooch 1-1/2 x 2". Ear Rings 3/4 x 2-1/4" $695.00 (W. Baldwin Collection)

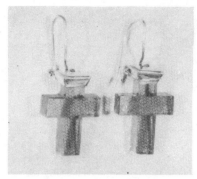

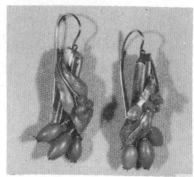

II-85. **Ear Rings**—1850-70—Gold Filled. Topaz colored glass crosses 5/8 x 1-3/8" $68.00 (Jeanenne Bell Dealer)

II-86. **Ear Rings**—1860-70—Gold with coral 3/4 x 1-3/4" L. $245.00 (Camille Grace Dealer)

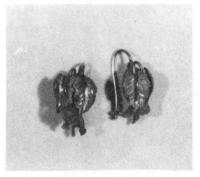

II-87. **Ear Rings**—1850-70—Gold Filled. Pink and green gold leaves. Imitation coral stones 1/2 x 7/8" $85.00 (Jeanenne Bell Dealer)

II-88. **Ear Rings**—1860-70—Gold Filled with gold ornamentated. Taille d' epergne enameling 1/2 x 1-1/2" $165.00 (Jeanenne Bell Collection)

II-89. **Ear Rings**—1860-70—Gold Filled with garnets 3/4 x 2-1/8" L. $195.00 (Camille Grace Dealer)

II-90. **Ear Rings**—1860-70—Gold Filled-often called hollow gold. 1-3/4" L. $145.00 (Jeanenne Bell Dealer)

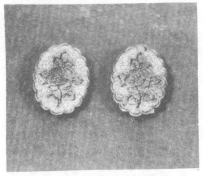

II-91. **Ear Rings—1860-80**—Gold Tops-Gold over brass backs. Black enameling. Originally collar buttons now have 14K posts $125.00 (Jeanenne Bell Dealer)

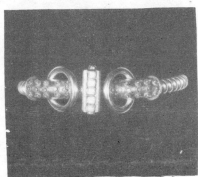

II-92. **Bracelet—1860-s**—Gold over brass with torquoise stones and granulation. $185.00 (Jeanenne Bell Dealer)

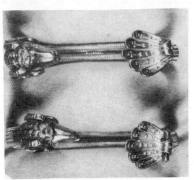

II-93. **Pair of Bracelets—1860's**—Gold over silver. Rams head and mesh. 1/4 x 3/4" $285.00 pair (Jeanenne Bell Dealer)

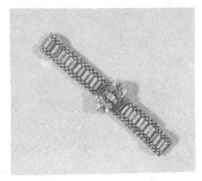

II-94. **Bracelet—1850-70**—Gold Filled. Bracelet 1/2" wide. Slide 7/8" $145.00 (Jeanenne Bell Dealer)

II-95. **Bracelet—Patent date Nov. 7, 1871 and June 26, '72**—Gold Filled. Slide clasp has 5 Persian torquoises 1 x 1/4" Mesh bracelet 1/2" wide $185.00 (Jeanenne Bell Dealer)

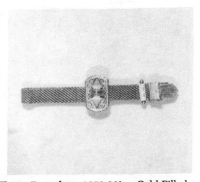

II-96. **Bracelet—1870-80's**—Gold Filled. Taillo d' epergne enameling marked W.E.W. & Co. 3/8" wide band glide 5/8 x 1" $145.00 (Jeanenne Bell Dealer)

II-97. **Bracelet—1870-80's**—Gold Filled mesh 1/2" wide. Top is 1/2 x 1" Black enameled $140.00 (Jeanenne Bell Dealer)

II-98. **Bracelet—1870-80**—Gold Filled with stone cameo mesh 1/4" wide; Cameo 5/8 x 7/8" $185.00 (Jeanenne Bell Dealer)

II-99. **Pair of Bracelets—1870-80**—Gold over brass. This type bracelet was usually worn in pairs. $185.00 (Jeanenne Bell Dealer)

II-100. **Bracelet—Dated May 13, 1884**—Gold over brass 3/8" wide. Visible repairs so only $120.00(Jeanenne Bell Dealer)

II-101. **Bracelet—1860-80**—14K Gold Clasp has Taille d' epergne and seed pearls 1/2" wide. $650.00 (Jeanenne Bell Dealer)

II-102. **Bracelet—1860-70**—Gold Filled with stone onyx cameo. Bracelet 7/8" $225.00 (Jeanenne Bell Dealer)

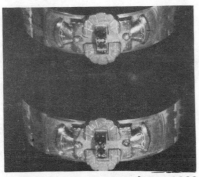

II-103. **Pair of Bracelets—1860-80**—Gold over brass. Mkd. W.E.W. & Co. Adjustable band. Each bracelet has 3 garnets and two pearls. 3/8" wide. $195.00 (Camille Grace Dealer)

II-104. **Hinged Bracelet—1860-70**—Gold Filled with Taille d' epergne enameling. $275.00 (Camille Grace Dealer)

II-105. **Hinged Bracelet with safety—Pat'd July 21, 1874 H&B Co.**—Gold Filled with some gold. Beautiful Taille d' epergne enameling 3/4 to 7/8" wide $250.00 (Jeanenne Bell Dealer)

II-106. **Bracelet—Pat. June 19, 1883**—Flexible Gold over brass with embossed design. $68.00 (Jeanenne Bell Dealer)

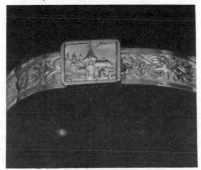

II-107. **Bracelet—Pat. dates Jan. 1, 1879 and Feb. 26, 1884**—Gold Filled 1/2" wide $95.00 (Jeanenne Bell Dealer)

II-108. **Bracelet—1870-80**—Gold over brass Mesh 1/2" wide with metal core $80.00 (Jeanenne Bell Dealer)

II-109. **Hinged Bracelet—1880-90**—Yellow Gold Filled with pink and green gold designs $225.00 (Jeanenne Bell Dealer)

II-110. **Baby Bracelet—1880-90**—Gold Filled. Engraved "Baby" Black enamel 1/4" wide adjustable closure $68.00 (Jeanenne Bell Dealer)

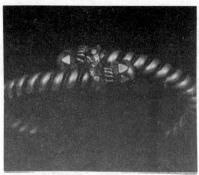

II-111. **Bracelet—1870-80**—Silver. Flexible. Note Etruscan influence $75.00 (Jeanenne Bell Dealer)

II-112. **Bracelet—1880-90's**—Gold over brass 1/8" Twisted wire. Ends approximately 3/8" $85.00 (Jeanenne Bell Dealer)

II-113. **Bracelet—1860-80**—Silver chain with gold designed links 7-1/2" L. Note Acorn drop. $85.00 (Jeanenne Bell Dealer)

II-114. **Bracelet—1860-80's**—Silver. Acorn drop. $68.00 (Jeanenne Bell Dealer)

II-115. **Necklace—1860-80**—14K Gold. Onyx, pearls and enameling. Chain 18″ long drop 1-3/8 x 1-1/2″ $650.00 (W. Baldwin Collection)

II-116. **Necklace—1860-80**—Gold with cabachon garnet. Drop 1-1/8″ Dia. Chain 61″ Long $975.00 (W. Baldwin Collection)

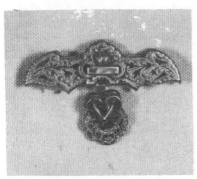

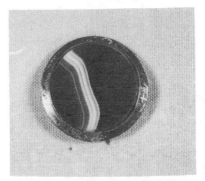

II-117. **Brooch—1860-70**—Gold Filled with Taille d' epergne enameling 1-1/4 x 1″ $95.00 (Camille Grace Dealer)

II-118. **Brooch—1860-80**—Gold. Agate 1-1/4″ Dia. $165.00 (W. Baldwin Collection)

II-119. **Brooch—1870-80's**—Gold Filled. Key Motif 2-3/4 x 3/4″ $58.00 (Jeanenne Bell Dealer)

II-120. **Brooch—Pat. June 5, 1887**—Gold Top. Back gold over brass 2 x 5/8″ Note same motif as bracelet 109. $58.00 (Jeanenne Bell Dealer)

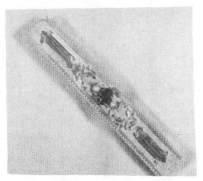

II-121. **Brooch**—1870-80—Gold Mtg. Garnet with 2 seed pearls 1-3/8 x 3/8" $285.00 (Wayne Collection)

II-122. **Brooch**—1860-80—Gold over brass. Mosaic in black onyx with flowers of white, red, and green. 1 x 3/4" $65.00 (Jeanenne Bell Dealer)

II-123. **Necklace Drop**—1860-80—Gold over brass with Venetian glass inset. Note granulation 1 x 1/2" $65.00 (Jeanenne Bell Dealer)

II-124. **Necklace**—1860-80—Gold Filled on black ribbon 32" L. $75.00 (Jeanenne Bell Collection)

II-125. **Chantelaine**—1870-90—Gold Filled with note pad. 7-1/2" Long. Pin 2-1/2 x 4" $325.00 (Jeanenne Bell Dealer)

II-126. **Pencil**—1870-80—Gold Filled with black enameling 2-1/4" L. $58.00 (Jeanenne Bell Dealer)

**II-127. Brooch/Pendant—1880-90's—** Gold Filled. Shell Cameo 1-1/2 x 2" $250.00 (Camille Grace Dealer)

**II-128. Baby Ring—1860-80—**10K Gold $60.00 (Jeanenne Bell Dealer)

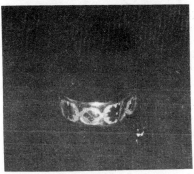

**II-129. Childs Ring—1860-70—**14K Gold. "Hettie" engraved inside. $70.00 (Jeanenne Bell Dealer)

**II-130. Ring—1860-70—**18K Shell cameo. Massive mounting. Cameo 1 x 1-1/4". $395.00 (Camille Grace Dealer)

**II-131. Ring—1870-80's—**10K Cornelian intaglio 1-1/4" Dia. $350.00 (Camille Grace Dealer)

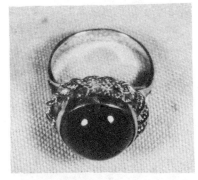

**II-132. Ring—1860-80—**Gold Cabachon garnet. Head 5/8" $280.00 (W. Baldwin Collection)

103

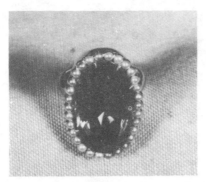

II-133. **Ring—1860-80**—Gold Amethyst and pearl. Head 3/4 x 1-1/8″ $795.00 (W. Baldwin Collection)

II-134. **Ring—1860-80**—9K Amethyst and pearl $450.00 (W. Baldwin Collection)

II-135. **Ring—1860-80**—Gold Cornelian intaglio $325.00 (Lucille and Sam Mundorff Dealers)

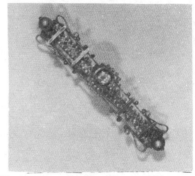

II-136. **Brooch—1860-80**—Gold over brass with some gold ornamentation. Clear stone and 2 pearls 2-1/4 L. $58.00 (Jeanenne Bell Dealer)

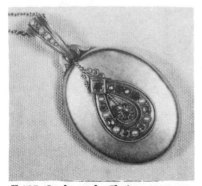

II-137. **Lock and Chain—1870-90's**—18K Gold with 2 rubies, 9 dematoid garnets, 12 pearls, and 4 diamonds with granulation. 1-1/4 x 2-1/4″ Chain 24″ $950.00 (Camille Grace Collection)

II-138. **Brooch—1880-90**—18K Gold with 6 diamonds 1-7/8 x 7/8″ $850.00 (Camille Grace Collection)

II-139. **Ear Rings—1880-90**—Gold with onyx and pearls 5/8 x 1-1/2″ L. $225.00 (Camille Grace Dealer)

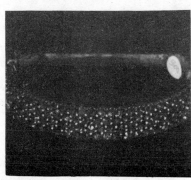

II-140. **Bracelet—1870-90**—Gilted Silver with 4 rows of rose cut garnets 1/2″ wide $575.00 (Camille Grace Dealer)

II-141. **Brooch—1880-90's**—Gold over brass. Bohemian Garnets 1-3/8″ Dia. $165.00 (Camille Grace Dealer)

II-142. **Brooch—1880-90's**—Gold over brass. Crescent and star. Bohemian garnets 1-3/8″ x 1-1/2″ $185.00 (Camille Grace Dealer)

II-143. **Brooch—1880-90's**—Gold over brass Crown of bohemian garnets 1-7/8 x 1″ $195.00 (Camille Grace Dealer)

II-144. **Brooch—1880-90's**—Gold over brass. Bohemian garnets 1-1/8 x 1-1/8″ $185.00 (Camille Grace Dealer)

105

II-145. **Pencil—1871 Pat. date**—Gold Filled Mother of Pearl 1/4" Dia. 2-1/2" L. $58.00 (Lucille and Sam Mundorff Dealers)

II-146. **Brooch—Hallmarked 1889-90—** Sterling 1-3/4 x 1-1/8" $95.00 (Camille Grace Dealer)

II-147. **Watch Pin—1880-90**—Gold Filled 1-7/8 x 1-1/2" $65.00 (Jeanenne Bell Dealer)

II-148. **Brooch—1880-90's**—Gold Filled Mtg. Painting on Porcelain 3 x 2-3/4" $145.00 (Jeanenne Bell Dealer)

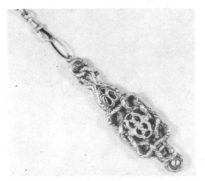

II-149. **Lorgnette and Chain—1880-90** —French hallmark sterling. Chain length 61" closed 7/8 x 2-7/8" $450.00 (W. Baldwin Collection)

II-150. **Lorgnette opened.**

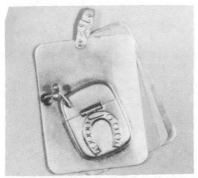

**II-151. Notecase—1885-1910—**Silver plated. Front and back slide apart to reveal horn page. Note coin holder on top with horseshoe motif 2 x 2-1/2" $95.00 (Jeanenne Bell Collection)

**II-152. Bracelet—1887 English Hall-mark—**Sterling. Hinged bangle 5/8" wide $165.00 (Jeanenne Bell Dealer)

**II-153. Watch Pin—1880-1900—**Gold Filled. 7/8 x 1" $58.00 (Jeanenne Bell Dealer)

**II-154. Cigar Cutter Fob—1880-90—**Sterling 1/2 x 1-3/8" $55.00 (Jeanenne Bell Dealer)

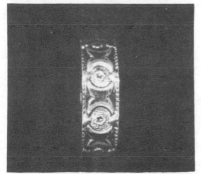

**II-155. Ring—1870-85—**Gold Filled 1/4" wide $38.00 (Jeanenne Bell Dealer)

**II-156. Brooch—1880-1910—**Silver with amethyst and 3 baroque pearls. Enameled trim 1-3/8 x 1" $125.00 (Camille Grace Dealer)

107

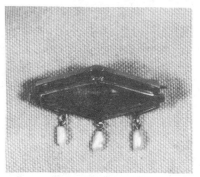

II-157. **Brooch**—1880-1910—Silver with amethyst and 1 baroque pearl 1-3/8 x 1-7/8″ $100.00 (W. Baldwin Collection)

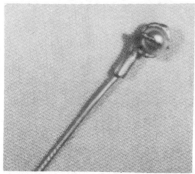

II-158. **Scarf Pin**—1880-90—Gold over brass. Claw set 6 MM pearl $32.00 (Jeanenne Bell Dealer)

II-159. **Scarf Pin**—1870-80—Gold Filled with blue enameled ground 5/8″ Dia. $35.00 (Jeanenne Bell Dealer)

II-160. **Scarf Pin**—1880-1900—14K Yellow Gold with Torquoise and diamond $95.00 (Jeanenne Bell Dealer)

II-161. **Scarf Pin**—1880-90—Gold over brass. 3/4″ Dia. $28.00 (Jeanenne Bell Dealer)

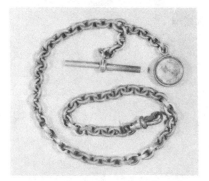

II-162. **Watch Chain and Fob**—Silver over brass with compass fob. 12-1/2″ L. Compass 1/2″ Dia. $65.00 (Jeanenne Bell Dealer)

II-163. **Watch Chain—1880-90**—Gold over brass fittings. Hairwork chain with Locket fob. Probably American Locket 7/8 x 1-1/8". Chain 109-1/2" $125.00 (Jeanenne Bell Dealer)

II-164. **Locket—1880-90**—Gold Tops. Tripple picture holder 7/8 x 1-1/4" $125.00 (Camille Grace Dealer)

II-165. **Locket—1880-90**—9K Heart 3/4 x 1" $185.00 (Camille Grace Dealer)

II-166. **Brooch and Bracelet—1870-90** —Sterling: French Hallmark. Black enameled with pearls. Jointed bracelet 3/8" wide $250.00 Bracelet 1-5/8 x 1-1/2" $175.00 (Camille Grace Dealer)

II-167. **Brooch—1870-90**—10K Gold 2 x 1-1/4" $225.00 (Jeanenne Bell Collection)

II-168. **Brooch—1880-90**—Gold over brass mtg. Pyrite 2-1/8 x 1/4" Drop 1/2" Dia. $65.00 (Jeanenne Bell Dealer)

II-169. **Brooch—1870-90**—Yellow Gold fitted with rose cut imitation garnets and sapphires. 1-3/4 x 1-1/8 $38.00 (Jeanenne Bell Dealer)

II-170. **Bracelet—1880-1900**—Silver over brass. Mosaic flower insets 1/2 wide x 7″ L. $48.00 (Jeanenne Bell Dealer)

II-171. **Brooch—1880-1900**—Gold over brass mtg. with celluloid Cameo. 1-1/2 x 2″ $22.00 (Jeanenne Bell Dealer)

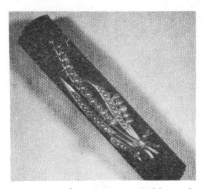

II-172. **Brooch—1870-90**—Gold with onyx and seed pearls 2-5/8 x 1/2″ $295.00 (W. Baldwin Collection)

II-173. **Watch—1870-80**—Sterling case. A.W. Watch Co. Waltham Mass. Key Wind, key set. Movement marked AM. Watch Co. $165.00 (Jeanenne Bell Dealer)

II-174. **Watch—1879**—14K Gold hunting case. Engraved "Josei from John" Dec. 25, 1880. Mint Condition. $800.00 (Anne Noblitt Collection)

II-175. **Watch—1880**—Gold Filled hunting case with movement by Tavannes Watch Co. 16 size. $249.00 (Jeanenne Bell Dealer)

II-176. **Watch—1880's**—Sterling Case. Key wind-key set movememt. Beautifully engraved case. $165.00 (Jeanenne Bell Dealer)

II-177. **Watch—1880**—.935 silver. 1-1/2″ Dia. Enameled flowers on face. Key wind-key set. $175.00 (Jeanenne Bell Dealer)

II-178—**Locket**— 1870-90. Gold navette shaped with applied floral spray of diamonds on dark blue translucent enamel. L 800. $1,160.00 (A) (Photo courtesy of Phillips, London 6-21-83)

II-179—**Brooch**— 19th century - Gold with enameled ivory miniature portrait. Circular frame surrounded by rose-cut diamonds. $660.00 (Photo courtesy of Sotheby's New York 4-10-84)

II-180—**Pendant**— Mid Victorian - Gold with pave set cushion shaped rubies and diamonds in pear design. Enameled leaves and diamond set branch are detachable. L 7,000 $10,150.00 (A) (Photo courtesy of Phillips London 6-21-83)

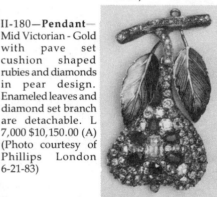

II-181—**Brooch**—Circa 1850-70 - Gold with oval sardonyx cameo. Embellished with 4 seed pearls and 8 single cut diamonds. $990.00 (A) (Photo courtesy of Sotheby's New York 10-6-83)

II-182—**Pendant/Brooch**—Circa 1850-70. Gold with sardonyx cameo of Hagar and Ishmael. (some damage) Spaulding & Co. $990.00 (A) (Photo courtesy of Sotheby's New York 10-6-83)

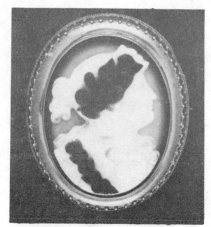

II-183—**Brooch**—Mid 19th century. Gold with oval sardonyx cameo. $660.00 (A) (Photo courtesy of Sotheby's New York 10-6-83)

II-184—**Pendant**—Mid 19th century. Gold with a black and white onyx cameo. Frame enameled in pale blue and white. With earrings (not shown). Fitted case. L1,200 $1,740.00 (A) (Photo courtesy Phillips, London 9-20-83)

II-185—**Brooch**—Circa 1860-70. Yellow gold with cameo and 6 assorted diamonds. $32.500 (A) (Photo courtesy of Wm. Doyle Galleries New York 9-21-83)

II-186—**Bracelet**—Circa 1860. Gold snake motif with woven body and eyes set with old mine diamonds. $2,200.00 (A) (Photo courtesy of Sotheby's New York 10-6-83)

113

II-187—**Bracelet**—Circa 1860. Gold with Italian mosaics of allegorical figures representing the four seasons. Reverse has glazed compartments. Fitted case. $4,950.00 (A) (Photo courtesy Sotheby's New York 10-6-83)

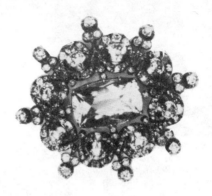

II-188—**Brooch**—Victorian. Gold with cushion shaped aquamarine set in a pierced silver collet. Surrounded with diamonds. L1,500. $2,175.00 (A) (Photo courtesy of Phillips, London 10-18-83)

II-189—**Pendant**—Gold centered with old cut diamond. Oval cambridge blue enamel surrounded by rose diamonds and half pearls. Fitted case. L1,600. $2,320.00 (A) (Photo courtesy Phillips, London 9-20-83)

114

II-190—**Necklace** —Circa 1875. Gold micro-mosaic beetle. Gold chain. Italian $1,210.00. (Photo courtesy of Sotheby's New York 4-10-84)

II-191—**Brooch**—Second half of nineteenth century. Gold with enameled repousse plaque representing St. George and the dragon. Cerulean enamel frame. L495.00 $718.00 (A) (Photo courtesy of Sotheby's, London 12-15-83)

II-192—**Pendant/Brooch**—Circa 1860-70. Gold with sardonyx cameo "The Triumph of Love". $1,540.00 (A) (Photo courtesy of Sotheby's New York 12-7-83)

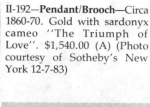

II-193—**Pendant**—Circa 1850-70. Gold with oval sardonyx cameo of Roman maiden. $935.00 (A) (Photo courtesy of Sotheby's New York 12-7-83)

II-194—**Bracelet**—Circa 1860. Gold embellished with black button pearls, and cushion shaped rubies and diamonds. L15,400 $22,330.00 (A) (Photo courtesy of Sotheby's London 4-14-83)

II-195—**Brooch**—Circa 1870. Girandale style set with rubies and diamonds. L3,520 $5,104.00 (A) (Photo courtesy of Sotheby's, London 4-14-83)

II-196—**Earrings**—Circa 1875-80s. Gold with diamonds and royal blue enameled star within borders of white enamel. L770 $1,116.50 (A) (Photo courtesy of Sotheby's, London 11-24-83)

116

II-198—**Demi Parure - Pendant & Earrings.** Circa 1870. Pierced with a six pointed star within a diamond crescent motif. (2 stones missing) L3,080 $4,466.00 (A)
II-197 (center) **Brooch**—Circa 1860. By "Castellani". Gold centered with a carved ruby cameo of the head of cupid with a border of cushion shaped diamonds. L11,000 $15,950.00 (A) (Photos courtesy of Sotheby's, London 11-24-83)

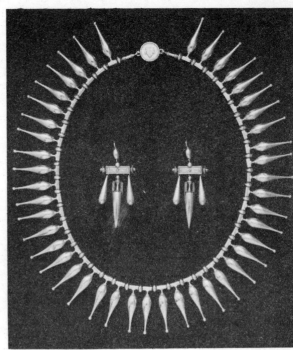

II-199—**Necklace and Earrings**—Circa 1875-90. Gold Hellenistic style with fringe of pod motif. L2,090 $3,030.50 (A) (Photo courtesy of Sotheby's, London 7-28-83)

II-200—**Pendant**—Circa 1860's. Gold with enameled plaque. Encircled with diamonds. Reverse has hinged compartment. L950 $1,377.50 (A) (Photo courtesy of Phillips, London 9-20-83)

II-201—**Earrings**—1875-95. Gold classical Greek style with filligree and granulation. L2,090 $3,030.00 (A) (Photo courtesy of Sotheby Park Bernet & Co. London 12-15-83)

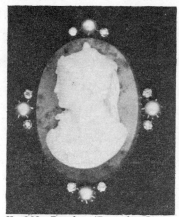

II—202—**Pendant/Brooch**—Circa last quarter of 19th century. Gold with hard stone cameo of Elizabethan lady. Embellished with 4 pearls and 8 old mine diamonds. Reverse has glazed compartment and hinged pendant loup. ''Tiffany & Co.'' $2,530.00 (A) (Photo courtesy of Sotheby's, New York 12-7-83)

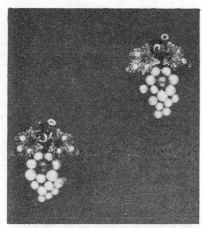

II—204—**Earrings**—Late 19th century. Gold mountings with grapes of multi-colored pearls. Leaves are studdied with 12 small old European cut and old mine diamonds. Screw backs added later. $770.00 (A) (Photo courtesy of Sotheby's, New York 10-5-83)

II-205—**Bracelet**—Gold hinged bangle with owl and Latin motto. By Carlo Giuliano. L1,800 $2,610.00 (A) (Photo courtesy of Phillips, London 1-28-84)

II-203—**Chatelaine Watch**—Circa 1880. Gold with enameled scenes depicting themes of love and music in pearl set bezels. Gilt oval cylinder movement. 5 inches long. $3,300.00 (A) (Photo courtesy of Sotheby's, New York 2-14-84)

119

II-206—**Pendant**—
Victorian. Gold with
diamonds. Reverse has
compartment for picture
of hair. L600 $870.00 (A)
(Photo courtesy of
Phillips, London 4-26-83)

II-207—**Pendant/Brooch**-
—Circa 1875-90. Gold
with tinted crystal intaglio
of a stag on a cliff. (slightly damaged) Reverse has
glazed compartment.
$495.00 (A) (Photo
courtesy of Sotheby's,
New York 10-5-83)

II-208—**Brooch**—Circa 1880. Gold
with sardonyx cameo and pale blue
and white enameling. L770.
$1,116.50 (A) (Photo courtesy of
Sotheby's, London 4-14-83)

II-209—**Brooch/Pendant**—Last quarter of
nineteenth century. Gold with sardonyx
cameo. Mounting embellished with rose
cut diamonds. L1,650 $2,392.50 (A) (Photo
courtesy of Sotheby's, London 4-14-83)

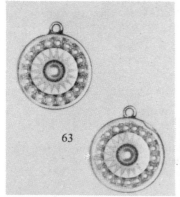

63

II-210—**Earrings**—Gold dish shaped with
half pearl set in blue enamel star centers.
Surrounded by a half pearl hoop. Signed
C.G. in oval cartouches. Carlo Guilliano.
L400 $580.00 (A) (Photo courtesy of
Phillips, London 6-21-83)

120

II-211—**Pendant**—Gold and enameled box panels set with sapphires, emeralds, garnets, and rubies with pearl and diamond solitaire center and pearl drops. Earrings en suite (later fittings). Each piece signed 'G. G.' in oval cartouches. Carlo Guilliano. L5,200 $7,540.00 (A) (Photo courtesy of Phillips, London 6-21-83)

II-212—**Pendant**—Circa 1865. Gold centered with a blue sapphire and pearls. Signed "E R" by Ernesto Rinzi. This has a long slide chain (not shown). L2,200 $3,190.00 (A) (Photo courtesy of Sotheby's, London 4-14-83)

II-214–Right—**Clips** —Gold (converted from a buckle). Black and white enameling. Signed "C.G." on both sections. Carlo Giuliano. L442 $609.00 (A) (Photo courtesy of Phillips, London 6-21-83)

II-213—**Earrings**—Last quarter of the nineteenth century. Gold with powder blue, crimson and black enamel. L1,320 $1,914.00 (A) (Photo courtesy of Sotheby's, London 4-14-83)

II-215- **Demi-Parure.** Consisting of pendant and earrings. Circa last quarter of the nineteenth century. Gold with enameling, seed pearls and rose diamonds. (slightly imperfect) L1,210 $1,754.50 (A) (Photo courtesy of Sotheby Park Bernet, London 12-15-83)

II-216—**Bracelet**—Circa 1870-90. Gold hinged bangle set with foiled backed rectangular mixed cut 3.8 cts. emerald surrounded by rose cut diamonds and flanked by pearls. L2,600 $3770.00 (A) (Photo courtesy of Phillips, London 4-26-83)

II-217—**Earrings**—Circa 1860s-Pique. (Nancy Bechtold Collection) $450.00

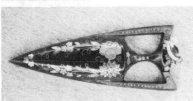

II-218—**Pendant**—Circa 1840s-Pique. (Norma Benjamin) $225.00

II-219—**Bracelet**—circa 1860-70. Yellow gold filled with black taille d'epergne enameling. No hinge. Strung on wide elastic. (Marilyn Feaster Collection) $225.00

II-220—**Cross Pendant**—circa 1860-80— Jet 4¼ x ¾'' (Jowsey & Roe Whitby, England) L68 $99.00 (D)

II-221—**Cross**—Jet 2½ x 4''. (Jowsey & Roe, Whitby, England) L68 $99.00 (D)

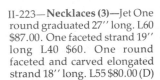

II-222—**Necklaces (2)**—Circa 1860s — Jet (1) 18'' long 12 dia., (1) 23'' long. (Jowsey & Roe, Whitby) L95 each $140.00 ea. (D)

II-223—**Necklaces (3)**—Jet One round graduated 27'' long. L60 $87.00. One faceted strand 19'' long L40 $60. One round faceted and carved elongated strand 18'' long. L55 $80.00 (D)

II-224—Left — **Brooch** — Circa 1860-70— Jet with painting on porcelain of Vagabond Boy. 2''x1½''. (Jowsey & Roe, Whitby, Eng.) L75 $109.00 (D)
II-225-Right —**Brooch**— Circa 1860-80— Jet mounting with a painting on porcelain. 1⅝''x2'' (Jowsey & Roe, Whitby, Eng.) L79 $109.00 (D)

124

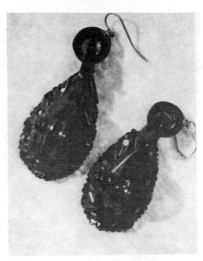

II-226- **Earrings**—circa 1860s—Jet with paintings on porcelain. 2'' x ¾'' (Jowsey & Roe) L95 $138.00 (D)

II-227— **Earrings**—Circa 1860-70s—Jet 2'' x ¾'' (Jowsey & Roe, Whitby, England) L75 $109.00 (D)

II-228— **Necklace**—circa $860s— Jet segments 1½ x 1¼'' each. 18'' long. (Jowsey & Roe, Whitby, England) L110 $160.00 (D)

II-229–**Earrings**—Circa 1860s—Jet with pink shell cameos 2¼ x 1''. (Jowsey & Roe, Whitby, England) L75 $109.00

II-230— **Bracelet**—Circa 1860-80 -Jet chain and lock. 8'' long. Lock ½ x ¾''. (Jowsey & Roe Whitby, Eng.) L50 $73.00 (D)

II-231–**Locket/Pendant**— Circa 1870s — Jet (does not open) Photo in back compartment. 2'' x 1¾'' (Jowsey & Roe, Whitby) L65 $95.00 (D)

II-232—**Pendant Drop**— Circa 1860-80. Jet frame 2⅛'' x 2''. (Jowsey & Roe, Whitby) L65 $95.00 (D)

II-233–**Cross/Pendant**—Circa 1860-80. Jet 3½'' x 2¼'' (Jowsey & Roe Whitby) L80 $116.00 (D)

II-234– **Cross Pendant**—Jet faceted beads. 3¾'' x 2½''. (Jowsey & Roe, Whitby) L50 $73.00 (D)

# 1890-1917

## THE TIMES IN AMERICA

In the United States the years from 1890 to 1917 were filled with extremes and contraditions. The nineties were both gay and naughty. The country was taking on airs of worldliness, but it still had the innocence of youth. America had become the leading industrial nation in the world. Its wealth was incomparable. In New York, Societies "400" could boast of more diamonds than most of Europe's Royalty. At the same time others were living in slum tenements. A single room housed as many as nine people.

In April of 1898 Congress declared war on Spain. It was described by some as "a great little war." Many people began to feel it was the country's "Christian duty" to be imperialistic.

It was also a time of social unrest. Union and management waged bloody battles. Cox's army marched to Washington. Women demonstrated for the right to vote.

More than ever women were involved in the world of business. By 1910 there were 386,765 women employed in offices, an increase of 385,835 since 1870. They were also playing the stock market. The first brokerage firm owned by a woman opened on Wall Street in 1869 and was an immediate success. They could become rich by investing in the market, but they still could not vote.

Women were also making headlines. Nellie Bly, a reporter for the New York World, captured the country's attention as she set out to beat Jules Verne's fictional record of traveling around the world in eighty (80) days. All American followed her travels via her newspaper accounts. She traveled 24,899 miles in seventy three (73) days, thus beating the record. This stunt, staged by Joseph Pulitzer to increase newspaper sales, also succeeded in proving the world was growing smaller, and women's abilities were getting larger.

The bicycle was the plaything of the nineties. Men, women, and children of all ages spent every possible minute riding the many varieties available. The demand was so great that companies in totally unrelated businesses began to manufacture bicycles. The Chester Frost & Company, wholesale jewelry manufacturers, included bicycles in their 1896 catalogue. "The bicycle is no longer simply a luxury or a toy for children and idle men but an article of everyday necessity for thousands," it stated. The "biggest seller" weighed twenty five pounds and sold for $100.00. Other bicycles were priced from $94.00 to $120.00

Godeys estimated in 1896 that there were 10,000,000 bicycles in the world, and cyclists traveled over 100,000,000 miles. In Paris there was a riding school on the Champs Elysees. For four dollars one could attend until "throughly proficient." According to Godeys there was even a bicycle ambulance. "The bicycle ambulance is a humanitarian invention for removing sick people; it runs more easily and makes less noise than the regulation vehicle. It has met with instantaneous success in Chicago."

The most revolutionary form of transportation in this time period was the automobile. It began as a novelty for the rich and succeeded in changing the entire country. In 1903 the automobile made its first "cross country" trip. The journey took fifty two (52) days, but it proved to the world that it could be done. By 1917 a car could be bought for as little as $345.00. There were an estimated 4,700,500 on the roads of America. Car salesmen bragged that their product "would out last a horse by many years, and none had ever died of hoof and mouth disease."

In 1903 the Wright Brothers helped loosen the strings that had bound man to the ground. This first heavier than air flight caused a surge of hope in the hearts of men who had always wanted to ascend into the heavens. Little did they realize that in less than fifteen years this marvelous new machine would be used in a World War. Man was indeed reaching new heights, but hate and greed were still alive and well.

Entertainment was a booming business during these years. In 1893 Thomas Edison invented the Kintoscope. It required a nickel for operation, and by 1905 hundreds of these "nickelodeons" were is use. Records were selling at a brisk pace. The nation was singing, and sheet music sales soared. With the quickening pace of life, it was only natural for music and dance to become more lively. The dance team of Vernon and Irene Castles introduced new steps to the American public. Dancing became very fashionable.

In 1900 there were over 2,000 theatres in the country. Vaudeville acts were on tour. America was entertained by everything from comedy routines to dog acts. There were also top attractions such as Ethel Barrymore, Enrico Caruso, and Harry Houdini. George M. Cohen's talent filled theatres with music and the hearts of people with song.

By 1910 there were ten thousand movie houses in the country. People were entranced by "the bigger than life" stars on the screen. They became emotionally involved with these film stars, and Mary Pickford became "America's Sweetheart."

When the rumblings in Europe erupted into war in 1914, most Americans did not want to get involved. In fact many believed that the country would not become a part of the struggle. But on April 6, 1917 a Declaration of War was passed by Congress and signed by President Wilson. Willing or not America was in it.

## THE TIMES IN ENGLAND

On January 22, 1901 at 6:30 P.M. Queen Victoria died. Great Britain was stunned. Most people could not remember a time in which she had not been their Queen. Even though they had already turned away from Victorian standards, her physical loss was still incomprehensible.

As late as December 1896 Godeys Magazine noted: "Queen Victoria has just had her picture taken; it is that of a hale and hearty old lady in the perennial white cap; in spite of rumors as to her abdication, the Queen holds the reins of state with a firm grip, and seems in no haste to hand them over to the still jolly and giddy Prince of Wales."

This attitude toward Edward was very prevalent. Throughout his childhood he had shown little ability for his lessons. His parents regarded him as a slow and incapable student. Conscious of the position that would someday be his, they pushed him in his studies and structured his ever waking hour.

When he came of age it is little wonder that he rebelled. He filled his life with things he wanted and sought pleasure at every opportunity. This lifestyle caused Victoria much distress and displeasure. She was more than embarrassed when he was required to appear in court as part of a divorce proceeding.

In 1863 Edward married Princess Alexandra the lovely daughter of the King of Denmark. Victoria hoped that marriage might settle him down, but it did not. Edward continued his womanizing, and Alexandra learned to live with it.

When Edward finally became king at age fifty nine (59), he surprised everyone with his abilities. He spoke several languages fluently and was interested in International Affairs. On his visits to India, Ireland, and Russia he displayed an innate ability to grasp existing situations. Still it was hard to overcome the image which had been his label since childhood.

King Edward loved wealth. Money was the standard by which he judged people. The nouveau riche were quickly accepted into British society much to the dismay of the gentility. His short reign was filled with the pursuit of pleasure. Some people went to the extreme in this pursuit. It is indicative of this time period that the phrase "if you can't be good—be careful," from the 1912 production of "The Girl in the Taxi" became popular.

The rich middle class was satisfied and complacent while a feeling of unrest and dissatisfaction was prevalent among the poor and working people. Britain had its share of labor disputes and women suffragettes, but for the most part the upper class lived a self-centered existence. They felt Britain's place in the world was established and invincible.

In 1910 Edward's short reign ended. It was also the end of an era of supremacy for Great Britain. Never again would she be the great world power and ruler of the seas. By 1914 she was drawn into the war. The world and Britain would never be the same.

# THE COLUMBIAN EXPOSITION
## 1893

Throughout the nineteenth century expositions and exhibitions played a unique role in the development of art and industry. In 1893 Chicago was the host city for the World's Columbia Exposition. The event was planned to celebrate the 400th anniversary of the discovery of America. Countries from all over the world were represented. The visitor was given a mini-tour of the world past and present. The architecture of the "Magic City" had an old world look. A source of "wonderment and admiration," it was described as a "composite of the most exquisite architecture of the Moors and the symmetrical and utilitarian construction of the present."[8] This sentiment was shared by many and resulted in scores of public buildings being built in this style in the succeeding years.

With a 50 cent admission ticket, the visitor could tour the buildings, view the exhibitions, and marvel at the canals complete with gondolas from Venice. The Midway was an exciting place where everyday people could mingle with visitors from all over the world. Belly dancers from Egypt, Dahoney cannibals from Africa, East India jugglers, and natives from Java were just a few of the "people attractions." The Egyptian dancers received an unusual amount of attention. The writer of the *Magic City* described the dance as "a suggestively lascivious contorting of the abdominal muscles, which is extremely ungraceful and almost shockingly disgusting."

The real star of the show was the new and exciting "electricity." "A more wonderful, magical sight was never seen than that revealed by the marvelous displays of electrical apparatus, machinery and devices made in the Electric Building."[9] The Columbian Exposition Album included this description.

*The interior of the Electricty Building, either by day or night, but especially at the latter time was a place to conjure by. Crackling sparks—lightning in the miniature—flew from buzzing dynamos, luminous balls of everchanging colors chased one another along cornices, up pillars, and round corners; mysterious automatic wands traced irridescent words and eraces them again with magic touch; and the voice of far-off singers were heard as if near by, echoed from the Atlantic Coast along conducting wires.—It was a wonderland, the enchanted throneroom of Electra.*

132

This great new power was also bringing new wonders for everyday use. The Popular Science Monthly was very enthusiastic about these new possibilities: "The greatest novelty in cooking appliances at the fair is unquestionably the apparatus for cooking by electricity.—The electric current is conducted into plates of enamel, where it meets with resistence and is converted into heat. These plates were attached to specially constructed ovens, boilers, griddles, flatirons, etc. An ordinary stewpan, coffee or tea pot, or steam cooker may be heated on the 'disk heater.' An outfit of articles necessary for a private house costs $60.00 or $77.50 if a heater for a kitchen boiler is included." In less than twenty years the electric range was a popular household appliance. The marvelous power of electricity was benefiting the average working man.

Although the Centennial Exposition included a Women's Building, the Columbian Exposition had "the first full, complete representation ever accorded to women."[10] Miss Sophia Hayden of Boston designed the building and supervised its construction. Statuary ornaments were by Miss Alice Rideout of California. The interior decorations and art works were also the work of women. The library was filled with books written by the fairer sex. A model nursery provided a play room and attendants to care for children. Thousands of women made use of this "infant check-room" while they visited the sights of the fair.

A good over-all view of the grounds could be seen from the Intermural Railway. Its elevated tracks followed the boundary lines of the Fairgrounds. Of course it was operated by electricty. Another means of transportation was the moving sidewalk. "The charge was only five cents, and this permitted the patron to ride thereon as long as he desired, but notwithstanding the cheapness and comfort, the enterprise was not very liberally patronized."[11] That was probably because the moving sidewalk went only 2,500 feet down a long pier and back. Who wanted to look at a lake when there were so many more interesting sights to see?

Visitors to the fair were exposed to brilliant displays of jewelry. American jewelers were well represented. Tiffanys and Gorham had their own pavillions. There were displays by twenty nine jewelry manufactures from New England. They were jointed by other companies from all over the world who were showing their finest pieces. Tray after tray of rings, chains, bracelets, ear-rings, and watches provided a spectacle of delight. The Venetian Glass Works had their own building. Thirty Venetian artists could be seen at work making mosaics, etchings, and blown glass items. The jewelry was not only an attractive addition to the wardrobe, but it also provided a nice souvenir of the fair.

Another interesting attraction was the World's Congress of Beauties. This building had forty ladies from forty nations on display. The men came to gaze upon the beautiful women. The ladies came to see the marvelous costumes made by the famous Worth.

One of the most visited attractions of the Fair was the Byzantine Chapel designed by L.C. Tiffany. It provided a beautiful setting in which to highlite his talents for working with stain glass, mosaics, and metal. The public was curious to see his designs which were considered very new.

The Expositions was a hugh success. More than twenty seven million people paid the price of admission to see the wondrous sights. It was a memorable experience that not only affected the architecture of the country but also announced to the world that the United States had come of age.

## THE FASHIONS IN CLOTHING AND JEWELRY

The "fin de siecle" (end of the century) mood that enveloped the country created a desire for the dramatic in dress and jewelry. Designers endeavored to make the most of this by designing fashions that were exciting and risque. Dress that accentuated the figure came into fashion. The Princess style dress was revived even though the dressmakers hated the time involved to fit it properly.

The figure was definitely gaining a new importance in fashion. As early as 1909 an under-endowed lady could improve her bust by wearing "Nature's Rival Air Form—a corset waist, bouyant and light, that gives instantly the natural, well rounded bust of a beautiful women." The Sahlin Company offered the slender woman "a perfect form and corset combinded." It was advertised to be "the only garment that, without padding or inter-lining, produces the stylish high bust, straight waist and long hip." For the woman with a figure problem another advertiser cited the new styles "demand the Princess Chic Figure Shaper." They claimed it would give "better results in figure shaping than other new corsets, at a trifle of their cost."

The apparatus used for shapely figures did not always mix well with the new inventions. Godey's July 1896 issue reported this conflict:

> Electricity and corsets are apparently inimical. One of the professors in the Girls High School in Oakland, California discovered that the steels in the young women's corsets seriously affected the electrical apparatus and rendered experiements uncertain; health waists, which did not contain steels, made no disturbance. A galvanometer is placed at the door which immediately indicated the wearers of the obnoxious stays.

Accessories were becoming more daring. "Gloves with tiny purses in the palm for containing car-fare are not strikingly new," commented Godeys Magazine in July, 1886. "The stocking, however, with a small pocket inserted on the outer portion of the knee is quite fin de siecle. This receptacle is supposed to hold the watch or such jewelry as one is not wearing. On silk stockings these pockets are elaborated with embroidery." This was quite daring since the skirt had to be lifted in order to deposit the treaure.

Midsummer Calling Gowns, August, 1902.

The wicked look of the snake was very much in fashion. "A wiggling gold serpent having overlapping scales of various hues, forms one of the latest queen chains," reported the Ladies' Home Journal in October 1891. "The tail terminates the swivel for the watch, while the head holds suspended in its wicked looking jaws a struggling bird of pearls and rubies."

Even with this sinister element, clothing and accessories had a light, delicate look. Bodices were soft and designers wasted no time in creating a profusion of lace pins. The Ladies' Home Journal described several in an 1891 article "Novelties in Jewelry."

> Some enterprising jeweler has invented a lace pin that, owing to its uniqueness and ingenuity, will fill the hearts of the novelty-seeking class with ecstacy. It represents an enamel rose bud at the end of a twig on which a single green leaf is suspended. When this leaf is compressed the petals of the rose fall open and disclose a photograph circled with rubies, diamonds and sapphires.
>
> An oddity, that cannot fail to inspire comment, is a lace pin representing a vulture about to seize a fluttering bird from its nest. The vulture is of rich gold with an oblong opal inserted in its back, while its victim is of diamonds and emeralds.
>
> Two variegated love birds circled by a laurel wreath in which small diamonds nestle, constitutes a lace pin that will be seen this autumn.

Hats were an intricate part of any wardrobe. They were designed in a variety of styles. Russian turbans and English box turbans "with crowns matching the suits and bordered with fur or feather ranching" were popular. The October 1896 issue of Godey's stated that "Oceans of plumes will be greatly worn. Creme felt hats with trimmings of the same color are stylish for evening wear. Dainty capotes of bright-hued velvet studded with gems or embroidered in gold are the proper thing for the theatre."

Royalty still exerted an influence on fashion. As late as 1891 Queen Victoria's approval affected a fashion's acceptance. The Ladies' Home Journal confirmed this in its fashion suggestions for October. "Long sleeves will continue in fashion during the winter, and the women who like delicate lace ruffles falling down over their hands and making them look so small, may indulge in this fancy, and not only have the knowledge that they are in good taste, but also that it is a fashion approved by the Queen of England."

Because Alexandra was attractive, she influenced fashion even before she became Queen. High necklines and collars complemented her long, graceful neck. Realizing this she wore them frequently. This started a fashion that prompted an 1896 Godeys Magazine to note: "High neck-dressing is in the rage just now. A neck band of velvet or ribbon about two and a half inches being the regulation depth. In order to increase the height, a pleating of silk or ribbon, growing narrower in front and extremely high and flairing at the back, is sewn on the inside of the band." For evening Alexandra favored choker type necklaces or "dog collars." Soon women all over England, Europe, and America were wearing them. Pearls were another of her favorites. This made them even more desirable to the general public.

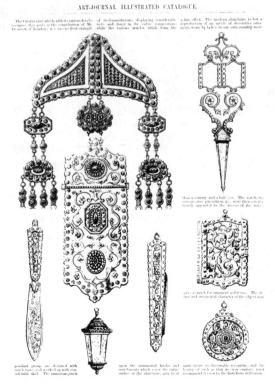

Chantelains had gone out of style in the 1860's, but Alexander revived the fashion by wearing one. In 1887 the Young Ladies' Journal felt it necessary to explain to the younger generation what a chantelain was: "The chantelaine consists of an ornamental hook to fasten to the waistband, from which depend five chains, each upholding some article necessary to the work-table for instance, a thimble-holder, a pair of scissors made so as to fasten in their points when not wanted, a pincushion and a yard measure. In some models the latter are exchanged for a silver pencil-case, and a scent-bottle, or a tiny note-book, while some ladies perfer a silver whistle or a circle for suspending a bunch of keys." By 1891 chantelaines were beginning to show signs of the Art Nouveau influence. The October issue of the Ladies' Home Journal described one; "For a chantelaine holder, a silver albatross with outstretched wings, from the feathers of which many fancy chains depend, will undoubtedly meet with approval among those of artistic taste."

King Edward was an avid sportsman. His horses won the English Derby on three occasions, and this was a constant source of pride. His passion for racing caused the horseshoe to become a decorative motif. Cuff links, fobs, pins, and brooches were just a few of the items that were either made in this shape or carried its motif.

Even with all these influences the American woman felt that Royalty was losing its glamour. In 1902 the Delinator complained, "Queen Alexandra follows fashion at a distance and seeks rather the appropriate and the beautiful than the georgeous."

Stars of the theatre played an increasingly important role in the evolution of fashion. An article in the Young Ladies' Journal explained how new styles came into existence:

The theatre is where new models are introduced. When a play is being rehearsed, the principal actress has long consultations as to the dress and coiffure she is to wear with her modiste and couturiere. Together they invent models suited to the role and person of the actress, and generally get up something very striking and infinitely becoming. Ladies who see an actress look extremely pretty with a certain bonnet on stage, of course wish to have a simular coiffure. They run to the modiste who is the happy inventor of the new model and ask for a similar one, and thus it is that bonnet gets to be the great

139

The increase in women's activities led to changes in the wardrobe. Bicycling was a favorite pastime, and clothing materials were chosen with this fact in mind. "For Cycling," stated Godey's in 1896, "the stitched alphines (a hat) of English cloth or of felt are greatly used; they stand any amount of wear and tear and are very comfortable. Young girls are wearing cycling costumes of white pique or mohair. The former possess the advantage of laundering easily; the latter are only suitable for certain occasions, such as a tea, or for wear at fashionable summer resorts."

Magazines were filled with articles on cycling. Everything from the proper way of mounting a cycle to their care and maintenance was discussed. Some people even tried to improve on it. These new ideas were not always appreaciated as a note in the 1896 Godey's illustrated. "A woman has applied for a patent curtain screen for women bicyclists who desire to conceal their identity from public gaze. Verily the way of feminine cyclist is hard enough without interposing further difficulties. Fancy a woman with such an awkward arrangement flapping about her having the courage to wheel at all."

With the hands busily engaged in keeping the cycle on the road, coin purses were attached to a chain and worn around the neck. A good example of this type coin holder is pictured on page 161. Watches and lorgnettes were also worn in this manner. It is interesting to note that the chains were rather long, so long that when sitting the attached articles usually rested in the lap.

The whistle bracelet was another popular bicycling accessory. It was a "protective ornament" for women who took long rides by themselves. The shrill whistle could be heard for a distance of two miles. It was used to summon help in case of an emergency.

Golf became a popular sport among women in the 1890's. Godey's Magazine was quite adament about the proper costume for this sport. "The fancy suits sold in the shops are quite unsuitable for resisting the wear and tear which the inveterate golfer must inevitably encounter. She must not be afraid of a little rain or a modicum of mud and should wear thick laced boots either black or tan, with broad low heels, or shoes with leather or cloth legging reaching to her knees. A suit of stout Scotch tweed or English homespun in small checks or mixed colorings is the best choice; it is made with a rather short and well-fitted skirt, a Norfolk or Eaton Jacket, or an openfronted coat; a stiff shirt or a shirt waist is worn beneath, and an alpine or tam of the same material as the gloves, covers the head. A covent coat or a silk-lined golf cape is necessary to put on after finishing the game, as one is always heated." One wonders how they could have played at all.

By 1910 there were 386, 765 women working in offices. As this number increased, it became apparent that working women had a unique set of clothing problems. In June of 1909 McCalls' Magazine published an article by Miss Pearl Merwin titled "Practical Dress for the Business Woman." She recognized that women who work really did not have time to shop for clothes. She sympathized with the many problems but took a firm stand on the importance of proper business attire. "Clothes for business wear should be simple and modest, almost to the point of severity. Therefore the tailored gown should be the business woman's standby. The question of trimmings, in the way of laces, ribbons or handwork of any kind is almost eliminated. Suits of a manish type, with straight skirts of walking length, semi-fitting with notched collars, lapels and pockets are the safeguard for business women. The perfectly plain tailored shirt waist is the proper thing in the way of a third garment, and should be worn with a linen collar and a bow of lace, or of the beautiful and fancy designs now so much in vogue." Miss Merwin also gave pointers on the proper head gear, shoes, and gloves. On the subject of jewelry she was very firm. "Much jewelry is in bad taste for office and business wear. One, two or three pieces inconspiciously worn are about enough; but when it comes to having the fingers loaded and numbers of showey 'beauty pins' and beads and cheap brooches and loud and fancy hair combs, etc., it denotes not only poor taste and judgement, but rather a weak character as well."

**McCall's Magazine, June, 1909.**

The business women or isolated farm wife could keep abreast of the latest fashions by looking through mail order catalogues. The Montgomery Ward Company and Sears Roebuck Company had catalogues that could fulfill any woman's dreams. In 1909 Macys published a 450 page Spring and Summer Catalogue that was mailed to thousands of homes. Everything from suits to bathtubs were ordered through the mail.

In 1913 Carmen Lowery, the Author's grandmother, aged fourteen (14), orderd a ring from a mail order catalogue. Although it cost only 32¢, she can still remember the thrill of wearing it to town. Samuel Noblitt, the Author's grandfather, remembered that "a pretty little ring could be ordered from the Gay Lyn Company for only 20 cents." He was known to have ordered several before his courting days were over.

Women who did not work outside the home were bombarded by advertisements to sell products to their friends and neighbors. Most of these companies offered jewelry as an incentive. A choice of a "heavily plated chain bracelet with lock and key (similar to the one pictured on page 186), or a solid gold shell belcher birthday ring" was given for selling twelve (12) cent packages of "Imperishable Perfume". Another perfume company offered "a gold shell ring and a silver chain bracelet with lock and key warranted for five years" for selling ten packs of "Rosebud Perfume" at ten cents each. If a lady wanted a "beautifully engraved gold filled watch", she had only to sell 100 gold filled "ladies beauty pins" at five cents each. McCalls' Magazine encouraged women to "raise clubs" by selling subscriptions. Each subscription was given a premium. Watches, opera glasses, and rings were given according to the number sold. For example, a Walthan gold filled hunting case watch was free with 48 subscriptions, but even one subscription entitled the seller to a gold filled ring set with a genuine opal. These offers enabled many women to wear jewelry who did not have the money to buy it.

In June 1909 McCalls' Magazine had an article entitled "Jewelry for the Prospective Bride." This article is especially important because it introduced ear rings with screw backs. "Earrings are very fashionable once more, and the sort most used are the long drop varieties, although the pearl hoop earrings shown in one of our illustrations are also new and very becoming. All the latest varieties of earrings are made with a little screw to fasten on each side of the lobe of the ear, so that it is not necessary to have the ears pierced. Very beautiful are the amethyst drop earrings made in this style and also earrings of black or white pearls. —Bracelets this year are worn over the transparent lace sleeves as well as the bare arm." The article pictures two bracelets that were reported to be "revivals from the days of our grandmothers." To a trained eye these would never be confused with any other period than the early 1900's. One was a "wide bracelet with knobs of turquoise matrix set in a filligree gold setting," and the other was "a lovely cameo design. A most charming amethyst and baroque pearl pendant necklace" was pictured, and it was noted that "amethyst jewelry of all sorts is extremely fashionable at present."

Opals had lost their unearned reputation for being unlucky. They were being used in the newest designs. "During the last few years a reaction has taken place and American women are accepting the magic gem," an article in the August 1886 edition of Godey's Magazine commented. "Many superb designs are seen at the jewellers, one of the latest being a golden eagle with outstretched wings, thickly studded with opals, the edges being incrusted with tiny scintillant diamonds. The shimmering changeful fire of the opal renders it suitable for articles of jewelry to be worn in the evenings, the light glinting upon the evanescent hues of the lovely gem in a most fascinating manner,—. There are striking designs of butterflies, dragon flies and beetles, in opals associated with emeralds and diamonds. These stones admirably express the brilliant beauty of the insects."

New stones were being used. "Like canines, every stone has its day," noted the Ladies' Home Journal in 1891. "At present the Alexandrite appears to be in the ascendency. This jewel comes from Siberia, and is of a beautiful dark-green transparent color, which under any artificial light changes to that of pidgeonblood ruby. The Alexandrite is cut like a diamond and is being used by the leading jewelers for lace pins, bracelets and other ornaments."

It was not long before the automobile began to influence fashion. A dustcoat with a belted or buttoned waist was a necessity. As early as 1902 the Marvin Smith Company of Chicago, Illinois listed several "automobile style ladies' rain coasts," and "ladies and misses automobile Machintoshes," in their catalogue. Scarfs that covered the hat and tied under the chin were essential for women, and goggles were a "must."

The hobble skirt became popular between 1910 and 1915. It was a straight skirt that became narrow at the hemline. Walking was difficult because only small steps were possible. Women felt very sleek and sophisticated in them so they endured the inconvenience in order to be fashionable.

The sleek look was also becoming fashionable in jewelry. The effects of the Cubist art movement and the geometric machine designs were seen in the straight lines and rectangular shapes being used in jewelry motifs. Safety match holders and knives like the one on page 189 were displayed in catalogues along with those embellished with curlicules and flowers of the late eighteen hundreds. A 1916 catalogue lists such innovative items as a sterling cigarette making case with separate parts for tobacco papers and matches ($12.50); a sterling cigarette case with an engine turned front bordered in blue enamel ($12.50); and a sterling combination pocket knife and screw pencil ($3.75).

The same catalogue included sterling silver articles for women. A vanity case (a compact with space for powder puff, coin holder, mirror, and cards) with an engine turned front and a plain back, was $16.50. A hand engraved one was only $10.00. This tends to prove that the engine turned design was more desirable.

Throughout this time period brooches continued to have a very delicate, light look. They were frequently decorated with enameling and pearls. Bar pins and circle brooches were also very fashionable. The jewelry from this time has a charm all its own.

# ART NOUVEAU

The Art Nouveau style was a rare, exotic flower that bloomed for a tantalizingly brief time in the garden of art and design. Seeds for this new style had been gathered from many times and places. The roots can be traced back to the mid-eighteen hundreds when the "naturalistic school" was producing designs based on nature. In his book "The Analysis of Ornament," Ralph Wornum wrote "one particular feature of the school is, that it often substitutes the ornament itself for the thing to be ornamented." This is exactly what the Art Nouveau designers did (i.e., the Metro Lamp Post in Paris).

More seeds were planted at the International Exhibition of 1862 in London. The Japanese exhibited their wares here for the first time and attracted much attention. After the Exhibition the goods were sold. Many of the items were purchased by a store in which Arthur Lazenby Liberty was employed. Liberty was to play an important part in the style that would come to be known as Art Nouveau.

The Centennial Exposition in Philadelphia in 1876 contributed to the style when it invited the Japanese to build a house on the grounds and to hold a Japanese bazaar. This provided the American public an opportunity to view, at first hand, the ancient arts of the Orient. They were fascinated by the superb skill and craftsmanship that went into these works of art. The designs were so different that the Americans were intrigued.

William Morris further nourished the style with his Arts and Crafts movement. His emphasis on handcrafting and the importance of designers and craftsmen working together played an important part in the new movement.

But it took the social climate and mood of the late 1880's for the style to emerge. The fin de siecle (end of the century) had put the world on a psychological edge. There was an almost unreal feeling, perhaps from being suspended from the end of one century to the beginning of another—a one foot in the boat and the other on the shore sort of thing. This feeling was expressed by the impressionist artist of the day. If the mood of the country could have been painted, it would have definitely been pastel—soft and hazy. At the same time people were more daring. Maybe it was because of all the progress that had been made in the nineteenth century and the promise of what the new century might bring. People were confident and ready for anything. The time was ripe for Art Nouveau.

The French took the best from the past—the naturalistic designs of the 1850's, the free flowing lines and enameling techniques from the Orient, the pride in craftsmanship of the Arts and Craft's movement, the sensuousness of the fin de siecle—combined it in their own inimitable way and Viola!—Art Nouveau.

Since Art Nouveau was a decorative period style, its influence was felt in all phases of design. Henri de Toulouse-Lautrec painted posters in this style. Antonio Gaudi (Spain) and Victor Horta (Belgium) designed buildings in the new style; furniture and accessory designers were also using the new motifs.

Art Nouveau had an important influence on the jewelry designers of the period. It provided a form of expression for them which seemed to be unlimited. All the forces of nature could be captured in the free flowing asymetrical lines.

One of the foremost Art Nouveau designers was Rene Jules Lalique (1860-1945). He was one of the few designers who was also a trained jeweler. In 1885 he acquired a fully equipped workshop. Business was good. By 1900 he was able to move to a larger location. That same year his works were exhibited at the Exposition Universalle in Paris. It was a lucky year for him. All his work on display at the Exposition was bought by Colouste Gulbenkian, a millionaire from Germany. More attention was drawn to his work when Sarah Bernhardt became his patron. She commissioned him to make two pieces of jewelry for her, and his reputation was made! Since she was considered the greatest actress of the time, her clothing and jewelry were highly publicized. This kept his name in the limelight and assured his place in posterity.

Because this new style was art—an expression of the designer—materials were of much less importance than the skill involved in its design and execution. Consequently, jewelry was made using materials such as horn, ivory, tortoise shell, and carved glass. Lalique used the dramatic and exotic as motifs. Orchids, irises, snakes, dragonflies, and sensuous women's heads are some of the motifs he made popular. The stones he used reflect the mood of the work.

They consisted of opals, moonstones, and a variety of semi-precious stones. His pieces were highlited by beautiful enameling techinques.

In England William Morris (1834-1896) had long been an exponent of craftsmanship. He studied at Oxford and was an artist and poet. In 1851 he visited the Crystal Palace Exhibition in London and was appalled by the machine made goods that everyone else thought so marvelous. He felt that industry was ugly and that it dehumanized men by taking away their creativeness. Fascinated by the Middle Ages, he wanted to return to the hand made methods of producing jewelry, furniture, and accessories. In 1861 he founded "Morris and Company." Here he made the famous Morris chair and sold many handmade items. He helped found the Arts and Craft's Exhibition Society in 1886, which provided a "showcase" for the work of its members. Morris believed that there should be no distinction between the designer and the craftsman, and that the best art was achieved when artists worked in partnership. Morris died in 1896, but his ideas lived on in the minds of his fellow artists.

C.R. Ashbee (1836-1942) was a famous name in English Art Nouveau jewelry. Greatly influenced by the philosophy of William Morris, he did much to foster craftsmanship in his country. In 1887 he founded the School and Guild of Handicrafts. Though most of his work was done in gold and silver, he kept to the Art Nouveau tradition of using moonstones and blister pearls. Many fine examples of Ashbee's work can be seen at the Victoria and Albert Museum, including his famous Peacock necklace.

Liberty and Company in London, England had a most important influence on the Art Nouveau style. Before anyone had ever used the term Art Nouveau, the style was being offered by this company. In fact, the Art Nouveau style was known as "stile Liberty" in Italy for quite some time. A. L. Liberty had always been intrigued by the designs of the Orient. He had been employed by Farmer and Rogers when they purchased part of the Japanese exhibit from the International Exhibition of 1862. When he opened his own shop in 1876, it was devoted exclusively to goods from India, Japan, and other parts of the Orient. The aesthetics patronized his shop, and it became a dominant force on the fashion scene. During the Art Nouveau period, Liberty and Company had its own group of jewelry designers. Their work helped further the popularity of jewelry in this design.

In the United States Louis Comfort Tiffany was the proponent of the Art Nouveau style. At an early age he decided to be an artist. He studied with George Inness and in 1867 was allowed to enter a painting in the National Academy of Design Exhibition. Elated by this accomplishment, he decided to go to Paris to study. During his two years of study and the years of travel that followed, his philosophy of art changed. He decided to delve into all forms of art. In 1878 he formed his own company. Louis C. Tiffany and Company specialized in interior design and did both commercial and residential work. Their most prestigeous commission was to redecorate parts of the White House.

In 1880 L.C.T. joined his father's business as Director of Design. His job was to design jewelry, and he had a separate floor in which to display his creations. Because of his father's wealth, he never had to worry about the cost of his items. He would spend any amount of money to achieve the effect he desired. Although he wanted his work to be used and enjoyed by all people, the costs involved in manufacturing made this impossible. When he died in 1932 he had spent $11,881,000 of the $13,125,000 that had been left to him by his father.

Samuel Bing was the man responsible for the application of the name Art Nouveau to the style. He was a dealer in Japanese art and became interested in the new style of work. In 1895 he opened a shop "L'Art Nouveau" at 22 Rue de Provence in Paris. He gathered work from all the designers in the new style—jewelry by Lalique and glass by Tiffany—and offered them for sale. So successful was his business that its name became synomymous with the style.

Characteristic motifs of Art Nouveau designs are flowing lines, exotic flowers, asymetry, plant shapes, sinister looking reptiles, and women with mystical faces and long flowing hair.

Materials used were varied. Many of them had little intrinsic value. Horn, copper, tortoise-shell, ivory, carved glass, and shells were some of the most popular.

Near colorless stones such as opals and moonstones were popular. All types of pearls were used. Semiprecious stones were more favored by the designers than diamonds.

Art Nouveau jewelry is extremely popular at the present time. Because of this many pieces are being reproduced. Be sure to buy from a reputable dealer who will guarantee the authencity of the piece. Fine examples of Art Nouveau may be found on pages 170-175.

## Enameling

It is not surprising that the Art Nouveau jewelry designers made use of ancient enameling techniques. The scope and range of enameling could produce an endless variety of effects. One enamel could be applied on top of another to create the varied, flowing colors so indicative of the period. Colors could be opaque or transparent. The possibilities were unlimited and enamel's durability made it suitable for everyday use.

Enamel is a glass-like mixture of silica, quartz, borax, feldspar, and lead. Metalic oxides are added to produce the desired color. These materials are ground into a fine powder and applied to the article being embellished.

Firing at a temperature of about 1700 degrees fahrenheit is required to melt the mixture and bond it to the article. Care must be taken since the melting point of the article should be higher than that of the enameling mixture. Each color is fired separately. The color with the highest melting point is fired first. Those requiring progressively less heat are fired in succession. The methods of enameling are named according to the method used to prepare the article being decorated. The most popular of these are cloisonne, clampleve, basse-taille, and plique-a-jour.

For cloisonne (Kloy-zoe-NAY) (partition), a design is drawn on the article and traced with fine gold wire. This wire forms "Partitions" into which the enamel mixture is poured. Since powdered enamel tends to shrink when fired, several firings are sometimes necessary for each color. After all colors are fired, the enameling is polished-off even with the top of the wire.

Champleve (Shomp-leh-VAY) (to cut out) is an enameling technique in which the designs are "cut out" from the background of the metal. The metal between these cut out areas becomes an intricate part of the design. The hollowed areas are filled with enamel and fired in succession of hardness. After firing is completed, polishing is required to finish the piece. Good examples of champleve are pictured on page 185.

In Basse-taille (Bahs-TAH-ye) (shallow-cut) the designs are cut or engraved in the metal. But instead of just filling these depressions, the entire piece is covered with a transparent enamel. Many beautiful designs can be achieved using this method because the color varies with the depth of the design. An example of basse-taille can be seen in picture III-155. Quite often a piece will use both basse-taille and cloisonne. See pictures III-152 and III-153.

Plique-a-jour (Pleek-ah-ZHOOR) is an enameling method that was used to full advantage by the Art Nouveau designers. It is an especially delicate method in that the enameling has no backing—only sides. To achieve this feat the enameling mixture is used in a molasses type form. Sometimes a thin metal or mica backing is used and removed after firing. Cellini used a layer of clay to back his pieces while firing. Whatever material is used, the results are quite lovely. The enameling has the effect of stained glass or gem stones. These translucent enamels are seen at fullest advantage when held to the light.

Taille d'epergne (TAH-ye de A-purn), an ancient form of enameling, was popular in the mid-nineteenth century. After a design was deeply engraved or cut into a metal, it was filled with powdered enamel. The piece was then fired and polished. Although any color could be used in taille d'epergne, the Victorians favored black or blue. See pages 91 and 99 for fine examples of this technique.

Niello (nye-EL-oh) is considered a form of enameling even though it is not a "true enamel." A mixture of sulphur, lead, copper, or silver is used instead of the powdered glass enamel. After the design is engraved into the metal, the niello mixture is applied. The piece is fired and then polished to remove the niello from all but the incised portion of the design. All niello is black. It is easy to distinguish from black enameling because it lacks sheen. Instead it has a metallic-like luster. Good examples of niello are found in the Siamise jewelry of the 1950's.

The metals used in enameling were as varied as the methods. For champleve and cloisonne, copper and bronze were often used. Gold and silver provided an excellent base for all enameling techniques. Although the metal used is of prime consideration when determining value, the execution of design and the clarity of colors are of the utmost importance. A piece well done in copper using several enameling techniques can sometimes be more valuable than one in gold using one color and technique.

Enameled jewelry is highly collectible. People who are aware of the time, effort, and talent that combine to create these tiny works of art appreciate and treasure them. Although little enameling is being done today in the United States, many lovely pins made in the early 1900's are still available at moderate prices. If you are interested in collecting enamels of this period, now is the time to buy.

### Amber

Amber beads were popular during the 1890-1917 period and continued to be through the 1920's. According to Marilyn Roos, an amber dealer, it was a different form from what we see today. The inclusions and air bubbles were considered unattractive so the amber was melted to remove them before forming the beads. Sometimes the beads even had a celluloid core.

Amber is fossilized tree resin. Over fifty million years ago trees taller than the redwoods of today grew along the shore of the Baltic Sea. The Glacier Age caused them to be swept into the sea. There they solidified under ice and pressure. Scientists believe that the trees probably had a fungus of some type because the resin was so loose it even surrounded dew drops. Amber often has insects, petals of flowers, seeds, and bark locked inside. These add to the value of the gem.

One of the oldest gems known to man, amber has been revered through the ages. The Greeks called it "lectron", which is the root word for electricity. Ancient man wore it for protection against disease. As recently as the nineteen hundreds doctors melted amber and mixed it with honey to make a remedy for throat ailments. People even believed that wearing an amber necklace would cure a goiter.

Although light yellow (honey colored) is the color most associated with the name, it can also be brown or red (cherry amber). Color varies according to the depth of water into which the tree fell. Amber can be translucent, opaque, or a mixture of both.

The "feel" of amber is very distinct. The best way to become acquainted with it is to actually handle a piece. It is so light weight that long beautiful strands can be worn with ease.

Amber is not only a lovely accessory, but it can be a good investment. It can be worn with a feeling of safety no longer associated with diamonds. When buying amber, as with any fine gem, always deal with a reputable source.

To insure the beautiful luster of amber take care to protect it from hair-spray and perfume. A bath in warm water and gentle detergent will keep it sparkling clean.

Celluloid, glass, and plastic have all been used to imitate amber. Tests to determine the authenticity of a piece can be found in the "Is it Real?" section of this book.

## Celluloid

A marvelous new material made it possible for people of modest means to have combs, bracelets, necklaces, and brooches that looked much more expensive than they actually were. Celluloid, the trade name given this material by its inventor John Wesley Hyatt in 1869, was widely used in the 1890-1917 period. Celluloid is an artificial plastic made from pyroxylin and camphor. Combs that looked like tortoise, bracelets and necklaces that could pass for ivory, and pins of every description were made from it.

In December 1896 Godey's Magazine included an article on gifts for Christmas. It recognized the affordability of celluloid items:

> Much less expensive are the neat celluloid goods, either silver mounted or adorned with a small miniature or cameo head; here again twenty-five cents to a dollar will purchase much that is attractive in the way of trinket sets, little fancy boxes, trays, pocket combs, brushes, and mirrors.

Because celluloid was highly flammable, its use in jewelry manufacturing was discontinued when safer plastics became available. Since celluloid jewelry was made for a limited time, it stands to reason that these pieces will become more collectible and increase in value. At the present time, however, good bargains can still be found.

## Pearls

Pearls were a favorite of Queen Alexandria, and women throughout the ages have prized them. A visit to most any art museum will evidence this fact with portrait after portrait of women wearing pearls with pride. They were used for necklaces, bracelets, earrings, and rings and were sometimes even sewn on to dresses for decoration.

Pearls are formed in mullusks. They begin when a tiny irritant enters the oyster. It reacts by secreting a substance called narce (NAY-kur) to surround the intruder. The gradual building up of this substance creates the pearl.

The oriental pearl is the most desirable of pearls. It does not necessarily come from the Orient but derives its name from the luster associated with pearls from that region. They are always formed by nature in sea water. The ones of best quality are found in the Persian Gulf.

Fresh water pearls are found in rivers all over the world. Between 1896 and 1899 pearls valued at over a half million dollars were found in the White River in Arkansas. Pearls are also found in edible clams and oysters, but these usually lack the lustre of the more valuable ones.

Pearls come in many shapes and sizes. When a pearl becomes attached to the wall of a shell and forms a flat back, it is called a button pearl. Blister pearls are another misformation, and the name provides an apt description. Blister pearls and button pearls are quite lovely when set in earrings, brooches, and rings. Another malformed pearl is known as the Baroque pearl. It was perfect for the Art Nouveau jewelry designs and made the ideal appendage for the lavaliers that were so popular during this same time period.

The round pearl is the most desirable and hence the most valuable. It is ideally suited for the popular "string of pearls." Small round pearls that weigh less than a grain are called seed pearls.

156

Pearls come in a variety of colors: pink, cream, white gold, orange, and black. The color depends on the type of mullusks and the water in which it is found. Black pearls, which are really grey, are the most valuable.

Shape, color, and weight are all factors in determining the value of a pearl. Blemishes or any irregularities dimish the value. A perfect pearl is always allowed one blemish because it can be drilled in that spot. It takes many years to collect a perfectly matched string of pearls. Consequently, they can be most expensive. Prior to the perfecting of cultured pearls, they were more costly than diamonds. Mrs. George Gould, one of the Society 400, owned a necklace assembled for her by Tiffanys. It was valued at more than a million dollars.

Cultured pearls are real pearls that man has helped nature develop. As early as 1883 Mr. K. Mikimoto was able to produce semi-spherical ones. It took many more years of experiments and the help of several men to perfect the round cultured pearl.

To produce a cultured pearl an irritant is placed inside the oyster. The natural reaction occurs, and the pearl is formed, but this takes many years. To hasten the process a round Mother of Pearl bead is now used as an irritant. Even with this headstart, it takes from three to seven years to produce a cultured pearl.

They are many types of imitation perals. The most common is a glass ball covered with essence d'orient, a liquid made from fish scales. Plastic is also used to imitate pearls, but it does such a poor job that it usually fools no one.

There are international laws and agreements concerning various aspects of the pearl industry. It is against the law to sell an imitation pearl as a natural pearl. Even cultured pearls must be so designated.

There is no other gem quite like a pearl. To keep this rare beauty special attention is required. Because elements in the air cause deterioration, the average life span is only 100 to 150 years. That is not to say that in that length of time they will turn to dust; only that they will no longer have their inner sheen. To lengthen the life span, always take care not to expose them to perfume or hair spray. Never clean them with a commercial jewelry cleanser unless it specifies "safe for pearls." A gentle wiping with a soft cloth after wearing will prolong the luster and insure another generation the joy of wearing them. By all means do wear and enjoy them.

## Moonstones

The moonstone was a popular stone in the 1890-1917 period. It filled the designer's need for a stone with little color, and its moonish glow added a mystical touch to any piece it adorned.

The moonstone is a type of translucent feldspar. It was so named because of the blue white sheen that seems to glow from within. Some moonstones are colorless; others have a pearly look. They are even found as moonstone cat's eye.

Since the stone is a symbol of the moon, it had romantic associations. Like the moon it symbolized love, romance, and passion. Many felt that it had powers of persuasion in these areas. Consequently, it was a favorite stone to give a sweetheart. The moonstone is one of the June birthstones, but it is seldom used today.

## Peridot

King Edward VII considered the peridot his goodluck stone. His perference made it popular throughout his reign. Because of its olive green color, the mineralogical name for peridot is olivine, although it is not uncommon to find yellow-green, or even brownish peridots.

Peridots have been mined for over 3,500 years on the small island of St. John in the Red Sea. Other mines are located in Burma, Bohemia, Norway, Australia, Brazil, and South Africa. In the United States peridots are found in Arizona, New Mexico, and Hawaii.

Because peridots are fairly soft and tend to be brittle, they are not too popular with today's jewelry designers. But a table or emerald cut stone mounted in yellow gold is quite beautiful, especially to someone born in August. The magical properties ascribed to the peridot include the power to overcome timidness. It must work because most Leo's never seem to have this problem.

# III. The Jewelry—1890-1917

III-1. **Brooch—1880-1900**—Gold Filled 2-3/4 x 2" $48.00 (Jeanenne Bell Dealer)

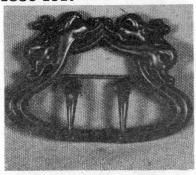

III-2. **Brooch—1880-1900**—Silver 2-1/8 x 1-1/2" $95.00 (W. Baldwin Collection)

III-3. **Necklace—1880-1910**—Silver with amethyst stones 16" chain Drop 1-1/2 x 3" $300.00 (W. Baldwin Collection)

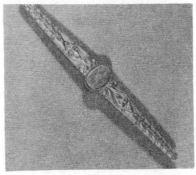

III-4. **Brooch—1890-1910**—Gold Filled 3-1/2 x 1/2" $38.00 (Jeanenne Bell Dealer)

III-5. **Initial Pin—1890-1910**—Gold over brass 1-3/8 x 1-1/8" Initial "N" $24.00 (Jeanenne Bell Dealer)

III-6. **Initial Pin—1890-1910**—Initial "B" $24.00 (Jeanenne Bell Dealer)

III-7. **Childs Pin—1880-90**—Gold top. Engraved "PET" 1 x 1-1/4" $38.00 (Jeanenne Bell Dealer)

III-8. **Brooch—1890's**—Gold Filled with rose cut garnets 1-3/8 x 1" $32.00 (Jeanenne Bell Dealer)

III-9. **Pin**—1890-1910—$135.00 (Jeanenne Bell Dealer)

III-10. **Mosaic Pin—1890-1910**—9K Roman mosaic 2 x 3/4" $195.00 (Camille Grace Dealer)

III-11. **Pin—1890-1910**—9K with seed pearls 1-1/4" L. $125.00 (W. Baldwin Collection)

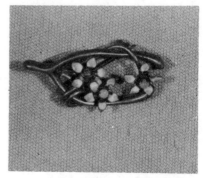

III-12. **Pin—1890-1915**—Yellow Gold Filled with enameled petals and moonstones. Wishbone motif 1-3/8 x 1" $28.00 (Jeanenne Bell Dealer)

160

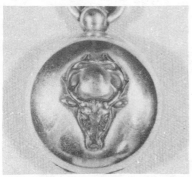

**III-13. Money Holder and Original Chain—Pat. 1903**—Silver over brass. Popular for lady bicyclist rider 1-1/4" Dia. Original sterling chain $180.00 (Jeanenne Bell Dealer)

**III-14. Coin Holder**—1890-1910—Gold over brass 1-1/4" Dia. $65.00 (Jeanenne Bell Dealer)

**III-15. Locket**—1890-1910—Gold 1" Dia. $185.00 (W. Baldwin Collection)

**III-16. Locket**—1890-1910—18K 1-1/2" Dia. These initial lockets were very popular $350.00 (Jeanenne Bell Dealer)

**III-17. Locket**—1890-1910—1/4 Gold Shell Marked W & H Co. 1" Dia. $70.00 (Jeanenne Bell Dealer)

**III-18. Locket**—1890-1910—Yellow Gold Filled 3/4" Dia. $38.00 (Jeanenne Bell Dealer)

III-19. **Locket—1890-1910**—Gold Filled 1″ Dia. $38.00 (Jeanenne Bell Dealer)

III-20. **Locket—1890-1910**—Gold over brass with engraved flowers 1-3/8″ Dia. $48.00 (Jeanenne Bell Dealer)

III-21. **Locket—1890-1910**—Gold FIlled Mkd. E. IRA. R. Initials both sides 1-3/8″ Dia. $32.00 (Jeanenne Bell Dealer)

III-22. **Locket—1890-1910**—Gold Filled Initial "B" 1″ Dia. $38.00 (Jeanenne Bell Dealer)

III-23. **Locket—1890-1910**—Gold Filled. Obviously some never had their initials inscribed 5/8 x 1-3/8″ $35.00 (Jeanenne Bell Dealer)

III-24. **Locket—1890-1910**—Gold Filled Mkd. S. B. & Co. 1/2 x 1″ $36.00 (Jeanenne Bell Dealer)

III-25. **Locket—1890-1900**—Gold Filled with rose cut clear stone 1-2/1″ Dia. Mkd. Hayden Mfg. Co. 11499 $58.00 (Jeanenne Bell Dealer)

III-26. **Locket—1890-1910**—Gold Filled with 2-1/2 MM opal 1 x 1-3/8″ Often worn as a watch fob $58.00 (Jeanenne Bell Dealer)

III-27. **Locket and Fob—1090's**—Gold Gilt over brass 2-1/2 MM opal 1 x 1-3/8″ $60.00 (Jeanenne Bell Dealer)

III-28. **Locket—1890-1900**—Yellow gold filled with brilliant stone 5/8 x 1-1/8″ heart $38.00 (Jeanenne Bell Dealer)

III-29. **Locket—1890's**—14K with 4 small diamonds 1-1/8″ Dia. $375.00 (Jeanenne Bell Collection)

III-30. **Locket—1890-1910**—Gold Filled with seed pearls set in cross. 1-1/2″ Dia. Mkd. HAC Co. $68.00 (Jeanenne Bell Dealer)

163

III-31. **Locket and Fob—1880-1910—** Gold Filled 1 x 1-1/8" $55.00 (Jeanenne Bell Dealer)

III-32. **Locket—1890-1910—**Gold Filled Mkd. "austen & stone" with red stones and seed pearls 1-1/4" Dia. $75.00 (Camille Grace Dealer)

III-33. **Locket—1890-1915—**Gold Filled with alternating white and green stones 1" Dia. Original chain 18" $48.00 (Jeanenne Bell Dealer)

III-34. **Locket and Fob—1890-1910—** Gold over brass. Mkd. W & H Co. 1 x 1-1/4" $38.00 (Jeanenne Bell Dealer)

III-35. **Locket—1890-1910—**Gold Filled 3/4" sq. $38.00 (Jeanenne Bell Dealer)

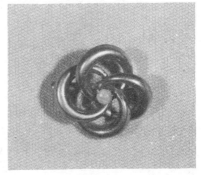

III-36. **Locket—1890-1910—**Gold Filled 3-1/2 MM opal 3/4" Dia. $55.00 (Jeanenne Bell Dealer)

164

III-37. **Lavalier—1890-1910**—18K Gold with paste stones 3/8 x 1-1/2" on new 14K chain. $120.00 (Jeanenne Bell Dealer)

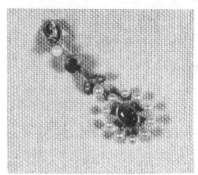

III-38. **Lavalier—1890-1910**—15K Yellow gold with amethyst and pearls. 7/16 x 1-3/8" $325.00 (W. Baldwin Collection)

III-39. **Lavalier—1890—1910**—14K Yellow gold with amethyst on original chain 3/8 x 5/8" $195.00 (Jeanenne Bell Dealer)

III-40. **Necklace and Ear Rings—1890's** —14K with brilliant. Pendant 5/8 x 1-1/4" Ear Rings 3/4" L. $295.00 (Jeanenne Bell Collection)

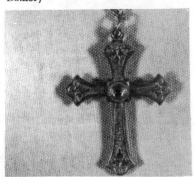

III-41. **Cross—1880-1910**—Gold over brass. Has Apostles Creed inside 1-1/4 x 2" $75.00 (Lucile and Sam Mandorff Dealers)

III-42. **Cross—1890-1910**—Gutta Percha on new gold filled chain 1-3/8 x 2-5/8" $75.00 (Jeanenne Bell Dealer)

III-43. **Cross—1890-1910**—Gold over copper with seed pearls 5/8 x 1" On new gold filled chain $55.00 (Jeanenne Bell Dealer)

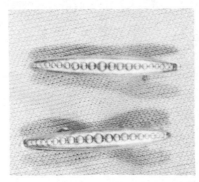

III-44. **Pins—1890-1915**—Gold Filled 1/16 x 1" $22.00 pair (Jeanenne Bell Dealer)

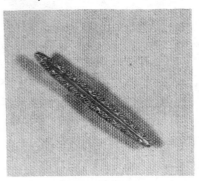

III-45. **Lace Pin—1890-1915**—10K Yellow Gold 1-3/4" L. $75.00 (W. Baldwin Collection)

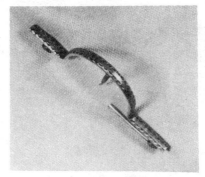

III-46. **Boquet Pin—1880-1915**—Sterling 2-1/4" Wide projects 1" $85.00 (W. Baldwin Collection)

III-47. **Brooch—1880-1910**—Gold over brass with brilliant. Note Horseshoe 2 x 1" $32.00 (Jeanenne Bell Dealer)

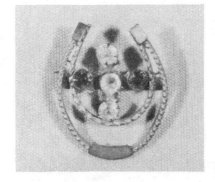

III-48. **Brooch—1890-1910**—Gold over brass with brilliant and green glass "stones" Horseshoe design 1 x 1-1/4" $24.00 (Jeanenne Bell Dealer)

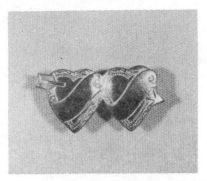

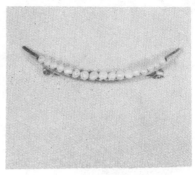

III-49. **Heart Pin**—1890-1910—Gold over brass with popular double heart motif 1-1/2 x 3/4″ $22.00 (Jeanenne Bell Dealer)

III-50. **Brooch**—1890-1910—10K Yellow Gold with 17 pearls in crescent shape. 1-3/4″ $145.00 (Jeanenne Bell Dealer)

III-51. **Brooch**—1890's—Gold with onyx and pearl. 1″ Dia. $165.00 (W. Baldwin Collection)

III-52. **Brooch**—1880-90's—Black enamel over silver mtg. Jet flower with seed pearls. 1-1/2 x 2-1/8″ $95.00 (Jeanenne Bell Collection)

III-53. **Brooch**—1890-1910—Gold Filled with some gold and rose cut stones in the cross. 2 x 3/4″ $55.00 (Jeanenne Bell Dealer)

III-54. **Brooch/Pendant**—1890-1910—14K with center diamond and seed pearls. 1-3/4″ Dia. $425.00 (Mignon Stufflebam Collection)

III-55. **Pendant Necklace—1890**—Dust rose glass pendant on dusty rose silk cord. Note crescent and stars pendant 1-1/4 x 3" Cord 42" L. $48.00 (Jeanenne Bell Dealer)

III-56. **Brooch—1880-1910**—Gold over brass. Star design with imitation pearls and topaz colored stone. $38.00 (Camille Grace Dealer)

III-57. **Brooch—1890-1910**—Gold Filled with 4 moonstones 1-1/2 x 1-1/4" $50.00 (Camille Grace Dealer)

III-58. **Locket—Inscribed Dec. 23, 1903**—Gold shell 1-1/8" Dia. Mkd. S O B & Co. $55.00 (Jeanenne Bell Dealer)

III-59. **Neckchain—1890-1910**—Gun metal 59-1/2" Long. $125.00 (W. Baldwin Collection)

III-60. **Brooch—Early 1900's**—Gold over brass with glass peridots 2-3/4 x 2" $38.00 (Jeanenne Bell Dealer)

III-61. **Brooch—1890-1910**—Silver over brass with faceted purple stone 3 x 2-1/8″ $22.00 (Jeanenne Bell Dealer)

III-62. **Brooch—1890-1915**—Gold over brass with coral colored "stone" 2 x 2″ $35.00 (Jeanenne Bell Dealer)

III-63. **Clip Pin—turn of the century**—Silver over copper. Used to clip on dress and money was pinned inside dress for safe keeping 1-1/2 x 2-1/2″ $48.00 (Jeanenne Bell Dealer)

III-64. **Necklace—1880-1910**—Silver over copper. Ladies head on original chain. Grey imitation pearls. Head 1-1/4″ x 1-5/8″ Chain 25″ L. $65.00 (Jeanenne Bell Dealer)

III-65. **Locket—1890-1910**—Gold Filled. Note bats and moon, 3 brilliants 1-1/8″ Dia. $120.00 (Camille Grace Dealer)

III-66. **Locket—1885-1914**—Gold Filled Mkd. "Lady Fair" 1-1/4″ Dia. $125.00 (Camille Grace Dealer)

III-67. **Locket—1890-1910**—Gold Filled. Mkd. J.G.F. Co. Bust of lady. 1-3/8″ Dia. $125.00 (Camille Grace Dealer)

III-68. **Locket—engraved 9-19-1908**— Gold Filled. Two girls: one has turquoise around neck; the other has clear stone around her neck. 1-1/2″ Dia. $125.00 (Camille Grace Dealer)

III-69. **Locket—1885-1910**—Gold Filled. Mkd. W & H Co. Girl blowing bubbles 1-1/4 Dia. $145.00 (Camille Grace Dealer)

III-70. **Watchpin—1885-1910**—Gold Filled 1″ Dia. $120.00 (W. Baldwin Collection)

III-71. **Brooch—1885-1910**—14K Yellow Gold with 2 diamonds 1-1/8 x 1″ $650.00 (W. Baldwin Collection)

III-72. **Locket—1890-1910**—Yellow Gold Filled. Girls head and clover. 1″ Dia. $125.00 (Camille Grace Dealer)

III-73. **Locket—1890-1910**—Gold Filled Mkd. B&B Sunbonnet girl. 1-1/8″ Dia. $95.00 (Camille Grace Dealer)

III-74. **Locket—1890-1910**—Gold Filled with 9 brilliant. 1-1/4″ Dia. $195.00 (Camille Grace Dealer)

III-75. **Locket—1890-1910**—Yellow Gold Filled. Girl with stars 1-1/4″ Dia. $135.00 (Camille Grace Dealer)

III-76. **Locket—1890-1910**—Gold Filled 1-1/4″ Dia. $85.00 (Camille Grace Dealer)

III-77. **Locket and chain—1885-1910**— Gold Filled with 4 diamonds, 2 opals, and 2 garnets. 1-1/4″ Dia. 16″ L. chain. $300.00 (Camille Grace Dealer)

III-78. **Locket—1885-1910**—Gold Filled $120.00 (Lucile and Sam Mundorff Dealers)

III-79. **Match safe**—1890-1910—
Sterling. Nouveau 1-5/8 x 2-1/2" $175.00
(W. Baldwin Collection)

III-80. **Belt Buckle**—Art Nouveau—
Silver over brass 3 x 2" $145.00 (Mary
Holloway Collection)

III-81. **Locket**—1890-1914—Mkd. Gold
shell. Elgin American Mfg. Co. body of
yellow gold; flowers of pink, green and
yellow gold 1-3/8" Dia. $95.00 (Camille
Grace Dealer)

III-82. **Brooch**—1890-1910—Gold on
copper with typical Nouveau head and
brilliant 1-3/ × " L. $58.00 (Jeanenne Bell
Dealer)

III-83. **Brooch**—1885-1910—2-1/4" Dia.
$650.00 Art Nouveau (Camille Grace
Dealer)

III-84. **Brooch**—Art Nouveau—Silver
over copper 1-3/8 x 2" $125.00 (Jeanenne
Bell Dealer)

III-85. **Brooch—Art Nouveau**—Copper, probably has silver plate originally. 2-1/4 x 2" $100.00 (Jeanenne Bell Collection)

III-86. **Brooch—Art Nouveau**—Mkd. "Sterling on top. German silver on back" 1-1/8" Dia. $150.00 (W. Baldwin Collection)

III-87. **Belt Buckle—Dated June 25, 1901**—Silver 1-3/4 x 1-1/2" $75.00 (Camille Grace Dealer)

III-88. **Pin—Art Nouveau**—Gold over brass. Head 1 x 1" $95.00 (Camille Grace Dealer)

III-89. **Brooch—Art Nouveau**—Yellow Gold 7/8 x 7/8" $195.00 (W. Baldwin Collection)

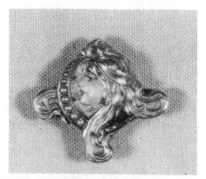

III-90. **Watch Pin—Art Nouveau**—14K Yellow Gold with emerald face and pearls 1-5/16 x 1-3/15" $800.00 (W. Baldwin Collection)

III-91. **Buckle Pendant—Art Nouveau** —Mkd. Sterling. Originally part of a belt buckle. Makes a handsome pendant. 2-3/8 x 3" $95.00 (Camille Grace Dealer)

III-92. **Cross—Art Nouveau**—Gold Filled 1-3/8 x 2-1/4" $65.00 (Jeanenne Bell Dealer)

III-93. **Chantelaine—Note Pad-Art Nouveau**—Silver over brass. Pad 1-3/4 x 2 3/4". Clip 1-5/8 x 1-3/4" $175.00 (Jeanenne Bell Dealer)

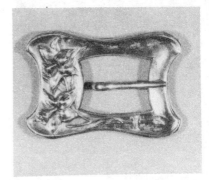

III-94. **Brooch—Art Nouveau**—Mkd. "Sterling top. W.B. Co." Star punch 3 x 2" $85.00 (Jeanenne Bell Dealer)

III-95. **Brooch—Art Nouveau**—Mkd. "Sterling top. W.B. Co." Two punched stars in back 3 x 2" $95.00 (Jeanenne Bell Dealer)

III-96. **Brooch—1890-1910**—Gold over silver. 3/4 x 2-3/4" $85.00 (W. Baldwin Collection)

III-97. **Brooch—Art Nouveau**—Gold (Sapphire and pearls) 7/8 x 7/8″ $195.00 (W. Baldwin Collection)

III-98. **Brooch—Art Nouveau**—Mkd. "Sterling front". Star punch trademark. 1 x 1-1/4″ $140.00 (Camille Grace Dealer)

III-99. **Brooch—Art Nouveau**—Sterling front. Star punch back. Replacement pin 1 x 1-3/8″ $140.00 (Camille Grace Dealer)

III-100. **Charm Bracelet—Art Nouveau** —Made with 7 pins and hat pin tops. All sterling except one. $850.00 (Camille Grace Dealer)

III-101. **Locket—Art Nouveau**—Yellow Gold Filled with brilliant. 1-1/4″ Dia. on old Gold Filled chain. $125.00 (Jeanenne Bell Dealer)

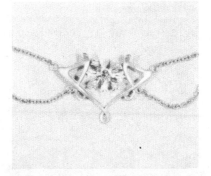

III-102. **Necklace—Art Nouveau**—Gold over brass. 2 baroque pearls and seed pearls and small topaz. Drop 1-3/8 x 1″ $95.00 (Jeanenne Bell Dealer)

III-103. **Match Safe—1880-1910—**
German silver 1-3/4 x 2-3/4" $65.00
(Lucile and Sam Mundorff Dealers)

III-104. **Charms—1890-1910—**Sterling
$15—$18.00 each (Jeanenne Bell Dealer)

III-105. **Pencil—1903 English**
**Hallmark—**Sterling. Turquoise stone is
pushed to reveal pencil. Worn on cord
around the neck or as a fob. 1/2 x 2-1/4"
$32.00 (Jeanenne Bell Dealer)

III-106. **Pencil—1880-1910—**Silver.
Hand engraved monogram and sham-
rocks 3/8 d½ 2-3/4" L. $32.00 (Jeanenne
Bell Dealer)

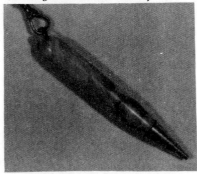

III-107. **Pencil—1890-1910—**on silk
cord with cord. 1/2" Dia. x 2-3/4" L.
$30.00 (Jeanenne Bell Dealer)

III-108. **Pencil—Early 1900's—**Gold
over brass with cord Pencil 4" L. $16.00
(Jeanenne Bell Dealer)

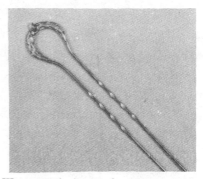

III-109. **Fountain Pin—Early 1900's—** mkd. Engle Pencil Co. N.Y. U.S.A. #26. Nice to hang from silk cord or neck chain. Has 14K Gold Tip. 1/4" Dia. x 3-1/2" L. $22.00 (Jeanenne Bell Dealer)

III-110. **Hairpin—Early 1900's—**Gold Filled. Originally hooked to eyeglasses that rested on the nose. Makes an interesting necklace when attached to neckchain. 2-1/2" L. $22.00 (Jeanenne Bell Dealer)

III-111. **Hairpin—Same as 110—**2-1/2" L $22.00 (Jeanenne Bell Dealer)

III-112. **Eyeglasses—1890-1910—** Tortoise Shell frame. Glass diameter 1-3/8" Length 3-1/4" opened 5". $40.00 (Jeanenne Bell Dealer)

III-113. **Chantelaine—1880-90—**Silver. Pin 3-1/2" x 1-1/2" Note Pad 1-7/8 x 2-1/2" with celluloid pages with days of week—key wind Watch. $475.00 (Jeanenne Bell Collection)

III-114. **Card Case—1880-1910—**Silver. Beautifully engraved. 2-1/2 x 3-3/4" $125.00 (Jeanenne Bell Dealer)

III-115. **Match Safe—1880-1910—** Silver over brass 1-3/4 x 3" $48.00 (Jeanenne Bell Dealer)

III-116. **Brooch/Pendant—1880-1910—**14K Yellow Gold Mtg. Shell Cameo with 2 diamonds 1-3/4 x 2-1/4" $750.00 (Jeanenne Bell Collection)

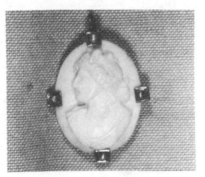

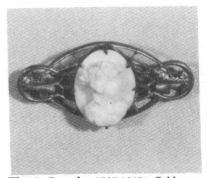

III-117. **Pendant—1890-1910—**14K Yellow Gold with 4 seed pearls and coral cameo. 7/8 x 1-1/8" $250.00 (W. Baldwin Collection)

III-118. **Brooch—1890-1915—**Gold over brass. Coral cameo 1-5/8 x 3/4" $95.00 (Jeanenne Bell Dealer)

III-119. **Brooch/Pendant—Early 1900's —10K Yellow Gold Mtg. Shell cameo $440.00 (W. Baldwin Collection)**

III-120. **Brooch/Pendant—1900-17 —**10K Yellow Gold Mtg. Shell cameo 1-1/4 x 1-1/2" $295.00 (W. Baldwin Collection)

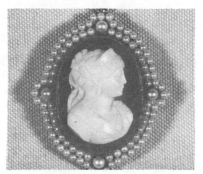

III-121. **Brooch/Pendant**—Early 1900's —14K Yellow Gold Mtg. Stone cameo surrounded by pearls. Done in Victorian style. 1-1/4 x 1-1/2" $1,200.00 (W. Baldwin Collection)

III-122. **Brooch/Pendant**—1900-17 —10K Yellow Gold Mtg. coral cameo 1 x 1-1/4" $350.00 (W. Baldwin Collection)

III-123. **Brooch**—Early 1900's—10K Yellow Gold mtg. Coral cameo 3/4 x 7/8" $225.00 (W. Baldwin Collection)

III-124. **Pendant Necklace**—1908-17— 14K Yellow Gold mtg. Coral cameo with 17" chain. 7/8 x 1" $325.00 (W. Baldwin Collection)

III-125. **Brooch**—Early 1900's— Celluloid cameo. Hook for pin is also celluloid 1-1/2 x 2" $20.00 (Jeanenne Bell Dealer)

III-126. **Brooch**—Early 1900's—Gold Filled. Shell cameo. 1-1/2 x 2" $150.00 (Jeanenne Bell Dealer)

III-127. **Brooch/Pendant—**
**1908-17**—10K Yellow Gold. Shell cameo
1-7/8 x 2-1/2″ $400.00 (W. Baldwin Collection)

III-128. **Brooch—Early 1900's**—Gold
over brass with orchard enameled
flowers with green emerald leaves 2-3/4
x 1-5/8″ $35.00 (Jeanenne Bell Dealer)

III-129. **Locket—1880-1910**—Yellow
Gold Filled 2 x 2-5/8″ $65.00 (Jeanenne
Bell Dealer)

III-130. **Locket—1900-10**—Gold Filled
with enameled flowers 3/4″ Dia. $100.00
(Camille Grace Dealer)

III-131. **Compact—1900-17**—Sterling.
mkd. Elgin American on mesh chain.
Overall length 7-3/4″ Compact 1-5/8 x 2″
$125.00 (W. Baldwin Collection)

III-132. **Locket—1906-14**—Gold Filled.
Given to Kate Hawkins Hooper (Author's
grandmother) by her husband W. E.
Hooper. Value to author $1,000,000;
another like it $85.00 (Jeanenne Bell Collection)

III-133. **Bracelet—1902**—Gold over brass. Victoria on one side of charm; Edward VII on reverse. Coin commemorating Edward's coronation. $150.00 (Jeanenne Bell Collection)

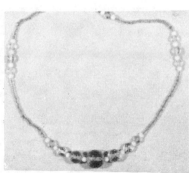

III-134. **Beads—1900-10**—Pink glass faceted beads with clear and white. 16" L. $28.00 (Jeanenne Bell Dealer)

III-135. **Beads—1900-20**—Pressed cut amber beads 18" L. 5/8" Dia. $200.00 (W. Baldwin Collection)

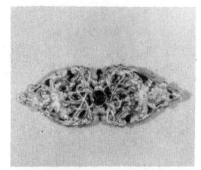

III-136. **Brooch—1890-1910**—Gold Filled with blue stone 2-1/2 x 1" $45.00 (Jeanenne Bell Dealer)

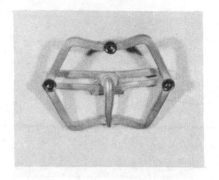

III-137. **Buckle—1890-1910**—Gold over brass with 3 rose cut amethyst colores "stones." Only 1/2 of buckle $8.00 (Jeanenne Bell Dealer)

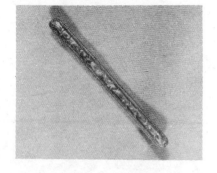

III-138. **Beauty Pin—1900-17**—Gold filled. mkd. E. IRA R & Co. Gold top engraved. 1/4 x 2-1/4" $32.00 (Jeanenne Bell Dealer)

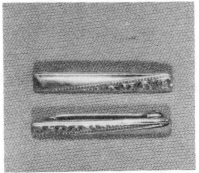

III-139. **Beauty Pins—Pat April 19, 1910 and Oct. 29, 1911**—Gold filled 1-1/4″ x 1/8″ $24.00 pair (Jeanenne Bell Dealer)

III-140. **Brooch—1890-1910**—Gold and tiger eye. 1-3/4 x 3/4″ $45.00 (W. Baldwin Collection)

III-141. **Lavalier—1890-1915**—14K Yellow Gold with enameling and pearls. 25″ chain also has pearl pendant 5/8 x 1-3/4″ $550.00 (Camille Grace Dealer)

III-142. **Lavalier—Art Nouveau**—10K Gold with seed pearls. 3/4 x 1-1/2″ $195.00 (Jeanenne Bell Dealer)

III-143. **Lavalier—1890-1910**—Art Nouveau 14K Gold with Peridot and seed pearls. 1-1/4 x 2″ on new 14K chain. $375.00 (Jeanenne Bell Collection)

III-144. **Lavalier—1890-1917**—14K Yellow Gold with green gold flowers. Small diamond in buttercup mtg. New 14K chain. Drop 1 x 1″ $225.00 (Jeanenne Bell Dealer)

III-145. **Pendant—1880-1900**—18K Yellow Gold with genuine amethyst and pearls 1-1/4 x 1-1/2" $425.00 (Jeanenne Bell Dealer)

III-146. **Lavalier—1890-1917**—10K Yellow Gold drop on 14K chain. Sapphire and pearls 1/2 x 1-1/8" $225.00 (Camille Grace Dealer)

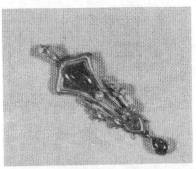

III-147. **Lavalier—1900-17**—14K Yellow Gold with amethyst and pearl. 11/16 x 2" $275.00 (W. Baldwin Collection)

III-148. **Pendant—1910-17**—Gold Filled with pearl 1/2 x 1-1/8" $48.00 (Jeanenne Bell Dealer)

III-149. **Pendant—1916**—10K Gold. Enameling and feathers on Mother of Pearl background. Covered with beveled glass. 1-1/4" Dia. $150.00 (Mignon Stufflebam Collection)

III-150. **Pendant same as 149.** Opposite side

III-151. **Necklace—1900-20**—Gold filled with pink faceted glass "stone." Drop 5/8″ L. Chain 16″ L. $32.00 (Jeanenne Bell Dealer)

III-152. **Brooch—1890-1917**—Sterling. Cloisonne and Basse-Taille enameling. Blue ground and yellow central, white flowers with green stems. 1-1/2″ Dia. $100.00 (Camille Grace Dealer)

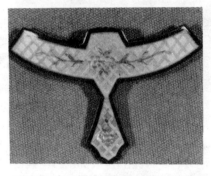

III-153. **Brooch—1890-1915**—Sterling. Enameled iris cloisonne and Basse-Taille 1-1/4 x 1″ white ground with flowers in 3 shades of blue, yellow, and white. $95.00 (Camille Grace Dealer)

III-154. **Scarf Pin—1890-1917**—Hall-marked Sterling with enameling. Pink flowers on white ground. 2-1/8 x 1-5/8″ $95.00 (Camille Grace Dealer)

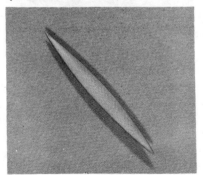

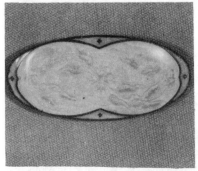

III-155. **Pin—1900-17**—Sterling. Basse-Taille enameling in robin's egg blue. 3 x 1/4″ $48.00 (Jeanenne Bell Dealer)

III-156. **Pin—1900-17**—Cooper. Enameled cloisonne and Basse-Taille 2 x 1″ $75.00 (Camille Grace Dealer)

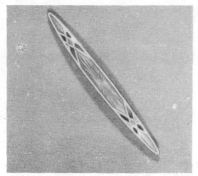

III-157. **Pin—1900-17**—Basse-Taille in white and soft grey. 3-1/4 x 1/4" $55.00 (Jeanenne Bell Dealer)

III-158. **Locket Chain—1910-20**—Silver with enameling. Pale green ground trimmed in black; pink roses. $165.00 (Camille Grace Dealer)

III-159. **Pin—1910-17**—Sterling combining several enameling techniques. Robins egg blue and white with dark blue flowers. 1-1/4 x 1/2" $55.00 (Jeanenne Bell Dealer)

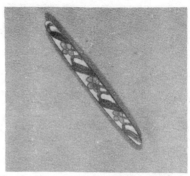

III-160. **Pin—1900-17**—Copper. Enameled with robins egg blue flowers, dark blue and white ground 2-3/4 x 1-1/4" $24.00 (Jeanenne Bell Dealer)

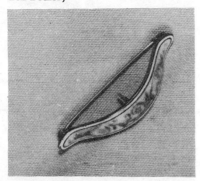

III-161. **Boquet Pin—1900-17**—Hallmarked silver. Enameled. 2" $95.00 (W. Baldwin Collection)

III-162. **Bracelet—1890-1910**—Gold Filled with green stone. Turned so that front and back of chain can be viewed. Note clasp not original. 7" L. $32.00 (Jeanenne Bell Dealer)

185

III-163. **Bracelet—1890-1917**—Gold Filled curb bracelet with heart lock and key (really works) 1-3/4" L. $48.00 (Jeanenne Bell Dealer)

III-164. **Bracelet—Pat. 1905**—Yellow Gold Filled with green and pink gold. Locket on top. Expansion band 3/8" wide Mkd. AAG Co. $48.00 (Jeanenne Bell Dealer)

III-165. **Jointed Bracelet—1890-17**—Yellow Gold Filled. Nicely engraved 1/4" wide. $98.00 (Jeanenne Bell Dealer)

III-166. **Childs Bracelet—1890-1910**—Sterling bangle with 2 hearts. 3/16" $48.00 (Jeanenne Bell Dealer)

III-167. **Childs Bracelet—1880-90**—Sterling bangle hand engraved $48.00 (Jeanenne Bell Dealer)

III-168. **Childs Bracelet—1880-1900**—Yellow Gold Filled. Adjustable. 1/8 x 1/2" wide. $48.00 (Jeanenne Bell Dealer)

III-169. **Childs Bracelet—1880-1910—** Yellow Gold Filled. Flat adjustable band engraved. 1/4" $28.00 (Jeanenne Bell Dealer)

III-170. **Baby Bracelet—1890-1910—** Silver. 1/4" wide $18.00 (Jeanenne Bell Dealer)

III-171. **Bracelet—1890-1917—**Gold Filled mesh with locket. Note snap catch. It is adjustable. Locket 7/8" Dia. Bracelet 1/2 w. x 7-1/2" L. $65.00 (Jeanenne Bell Dealer)

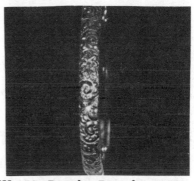

III-172. **Bangle Bracelet—1880-1910—**Gold Filled. 1/4" wide. Beautifully engraved $145.00 (Jeanenne Bell Collection)

III-173. **Jointed Bracelet—1890-1917—**Gold Filled mkd. A.C. Co. 1/2 to 1" wide with amethyst stone $195.00 (Camille Grace Dealer)

III-174. **Jointed Bracelet—Pat. Oct. 6, 1908—**Gold Filled. mkd. S.O.B. Co. Topaz colored stone 3/8 to 1" wide. $150.00 (Camille Grace Dealer)

187

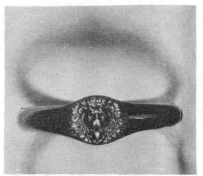

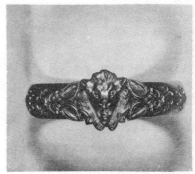

III-175. Jointed Bracelet—1890-
1910—Gold Filled. Lion has pink stone
eyes and brilliant in moutn 3/4 x 1″ wide.
$195.00 (Camille Grace Dealer)

III-176. Jointed Bracelet—1890-
1910—Gold Filled. Lion has ruby eyes
and Peridot in mouth. 3/8 to 1″ wide
$225.00 (Camille Grace Dealer)

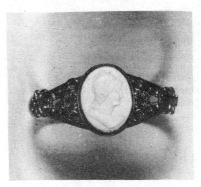

III-177. Jointed Bracelet—1900-
1915—Gold Filled with Topaz colored
stone 1/2 to 1-3/8″ wide. $145.00 (Camille
Grace Dealer)

III-178. Jointed Bracelet—1900-
1915—Gold Filled with cameo 1 x 1-1/4″
$225.00 (Camille Grace Dealer)

III-179. Jointed Bracelet—1900-
1915—Gold Filled with plaque for
engraving 3/8 to 1″ wide. $150.00
(Camille Grace Dealer)

III-180. Jointed Bracelet—1890-
1910—Gold Filled with amethyst stone
5/8″ wide $225.00 (Camille Grace
Dealer)

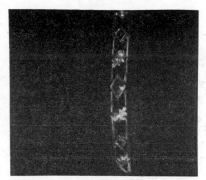

III-181. **Bangle Bracelet—1890-1915**—Gold Filled with faceted pink stone. Enameled leaves and 1 pearl 1/4 x 2-3/4" $75.00 (Jeanenne Bell Dealer)

III-182. **Bangle Bracelet—1890-1910**—Gold Filled for child or small lady. $65.00 (Amanda Bell Collection)

III-183. **Match Case—19810-20**—Silver plated. Mkd. Brun Mill Co. Made in U.S.A. 1-3/4 x 2-1/2" Can be worn on cord around neck or on watch chain. $44.00 (Jeanenne Bell Dealer)

III-184. **Ear Rings—1890-1910**—Moulded amber glass and Gold Filled 3/4 x 1" New 14K wires. $32.00 (Jeanenne Bell Dealer)

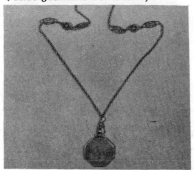

III-185. **Chain and Locket—1910-17**—Sterling. Octagonal locket 1-1/2" chain 44" L. $175.00 (Jeanenne Bell Dealer)

III-186. **Fob—Hallmarked sterling 1901 in England**—Originally worn on watch chain. Makes an interesting piece to wear on a chain around the neck. 1-1/4 x 1-3/4" $38.00 (Jeanenne Bell Dealer)

III-187. **Fob—Hallmarked sterling**—Initial section is 9K gold. 1-1/4 x 1-3/4" $48.00 (Jeanenne Bell Dealer)

III-188. **Fob—1905**—Hallmarked sterling. Note garter surrounding dart target 1" Dia. $38.00 (Jeanenne Bell Dealer)

III-189. **Fob—Art Nouveau**—Gold Filled 1-1/4 x 2" $95.00 (W. Baldwin Collection)

III-190. **Watch Chain with Locket Fob—1900-17**—Gold Filled Mkd. S & BL Co. $68.00 (Jeanenne Bell Dealer)

III-191. **Locket/Fob—1890-1910**—Gold over brass Mkd. B. B. Co. Note Swakia a decorative motif that can be traced to the Egyptians. 1 x 1-1/4" $38.00 (Jeanenne Bell Dealer)

III-192. **Watch Chain with Locket Fob—1880-1910**—Gold Filled. Chain 8-1/2" L. Locket 7/8 x 1-1/4" $70.00 (Lela Reed Collection)

III-193. **Fob—1890-1910**—Art Nouveau influences. Gold filled with blue aqua, and garnet stones. 7/8 x 2-3/4" $65.00 (Jeanenne Bell Dealer)

III-194. **Fob—1890-1910**—Gold Filled with "topaz" stone $28.00 (Jeanenne Bell Dealer)

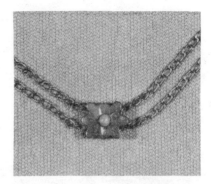

III-195. **Slide Chain—1890-1917**— Yellow Gold Filled Chain with 10K slide. Chain 19" Slide has Garnet and 4 seed pearls $125.00 (Jeanenne Bell Dealer)

III-196. **Slide Chain—1890-1910**—Gold filled. Slide has genuine opal Chain 48" L. $165.00 (Jeanenne Bell Dealer)

III-197. **Slide Chain—1890-1915**—Gold Filled. Slide with pearl. Chain 52" L. $148.00 (Jeanenne Bell Dealer)

III-198. **Slide Chain—1890-1910**— Yellow Gold Filled. Slide has 2 opals and 1 ruby. Chain 52" L. $180.00 (Jeanenne Bell Dealer)

III-199. **Slide Chain—1890-1917—** Yellow Gold Filled. Heavy rope chain 48″ L. Slide has Fleur de Lis Motif. $165.00 (Jeanenne Bell Dealer)

III-200. **Slide Chain—1890-1910—**14K Chain and slide. 1 opal. 48″ L. Chain. $525.00 (W. Baldwin Collection)

III-201. **Three Slides—1890-1917** —Gold. Average 3/8″ $95.00 each (W. Baldwin Collection)

III-202. **Cuff Links—1890-1910—**14K Gold. Sinister looking heads 5/8 x 5/8″ $195.00 (W. Baldwin Collection)

III-203. **Cuff Links—1890-1910—**Gold Filled. Mkd. HA & Co. Note mermaid with flowing hair. 1/2 x 7/8″ $48.00 (Jeanenne Bell Dealer)

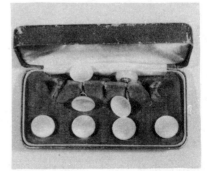

III-204. **Cuff Link Set—1890-1910** —Gold Filled. Mother of Pearl. Cufflinks and collar button made by Kremitz Co. Original box. 5/8″ Dia. $45.00 (Jeanenne Bell Dealer)

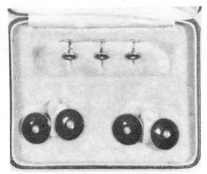

III-205. **Cuff Link Set—Early 1900's**
—Sterling with black enameling and
pearls. Links 5/8″ Dia. $65.00 (Jeanenne
Bell Dealer)

III-206. **Watch Chain—1890-1915**—9K
Cornelian intaglio. Chain 14″. Fob 7/8″
Dia. $450.00 (W. Baldwin Collection)

III-207. **Watch Chain—1890-1920**
—Woven ribbon chain with Gold filled
slide and swivel. Wooden T bar 1/4 x
8-1/4″ $18.00 (Jeanenne Bell Dealer)

III-208. **Watch Chain—1890-1910**
—Gold Filled Mkd. FM Co. 1/2″ wide x
5″ Belt Buckle Fob. $55.00 (Jeanenne
Bell Dealer)

III-209. **Watch Chain—1890-1910**—
Gold Filled 1/2 wide x 4-1/2″ Lions head
has pink stone eyes. $65.00 (Jeanenne
Bell Dealer)

III-210. **Watch Chain—1890-1915**—
Gold Filled. Mesh with fob. 1/2 x 4″ L.
Fob 3/4″ Dia. $55.00 (Lela Reed Collection)

III-211. **Watch Chain—Pat'd June 17 and Aug 12, 1902**—Gold Filled with Citrine in fob. Chain 5-1/2″ L. Picture of back of chain showing mechanism. $65.00 (Jeanenne Bell Dealer)

III-212. **Watch Pin—1900-1920**—Gold Filled 1 x 3/4″ $48.00 (Jeanenne Bell Dealer)

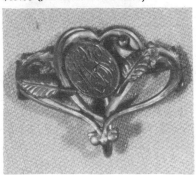

III-213. **Watch Pin—1890-1910**—Gold Filled green and pink gold. 1-1/4 x 1″ $55.00 (Jeanenne Bell Dealer)

III-214. **Watch Pin—1890-1910**—Gold Filled 1 x 1″ $55.00 (Jeanenne Bell Dealer)

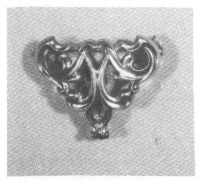

III-215. **Watch Pin—1890-1910**—Gold Filled 7/8 x 3/4″ $48.00 (Jeanenne Bell Dealer)

III-216. **Watch Fob Ribbon—1890-1910**—Gold Filled Fob. 6-1/2″ L. Watch attached to swivel was kept in vest pocket and ribbon and fob hung out. $30.00 (Lela Reed Collection)

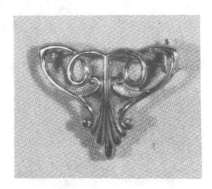

III-217. **Watch Pin—1910-20**—Gold Filled 1 x 1″ $55.00 (Jeanenne Bell Dealer)

III-218. **Watch Chain—1890-1910**—Gold over copper 6-1/2″ L. Note ladies head. $48.00 (Jeanenne Bell Dealer)

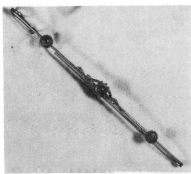

III-219. **Pin—Early 1900's**—Sterling with peacock eye. 7″ L. Used to hold scarf while riding in an automobile. $150.00 (W. Baldwin Collection)

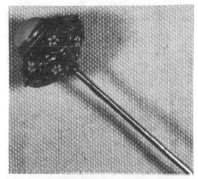

III-220. **Hat Pin—1880-1910**—14K Gold. Persian torquoise with cloisonne enameling 6″ L. Head 3/4″ $150.00 (W. Baldwin Collection)

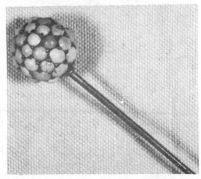

III-221. **Hat Pin—1880-1910**—Gold over brass with persian torquoise 6-1/2″ L. Head 1/2″ Dia. $100.00 (W. Baldwin Collection)

III-222. **Scarf Pin—Early 1900's**—Yellow Gold Filled with 3 blue stones 1/2″ Head. $18.00 (Jeanenne Bell Dealer)

195

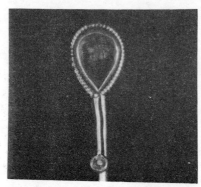

III-223. **Scarf Pin**—1890-1910—Yellow Gold Filled. Shield with amethyst stone 1/2 x 3/4" $22.00 (Jeanenne Bell Dealer)

III-224. **Scarf Pin**—1890-1910—Yellow Gold Filled. Topaz colored stone 1/4 x 5/8" $15.00 (Jeanenne Bell Dealer)

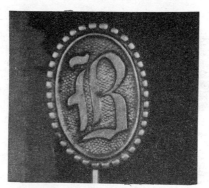

III-225. **Scarf Pin**—1890-1910—Yellow Gold Filled. "B" initial. Head 1/2 x 3/4" $18.00 (Jeanenne Bell Dealer)

III-226. **Scarf Pin**—1890-1910—Yellow Gold Filled 1/4 x 1/2" $15.00 (Jeanenne Bell Dealer)

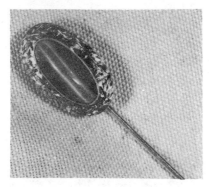

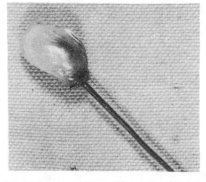

III-227. **Scarf Pin**—1890-1910—Gold. Tiger eye $125.00 (W. Baldwin Collection)

III-228. **Scarf Pin**—1890-1910—Gold with Baroque pearl. Length 3". $135.00 (W. Baldwin Collection)

III-229. **Scarf Pin—1890-1910—**
Sterling. Mother of Pearl. $24.00
(Jeanenne Bell Dealer)

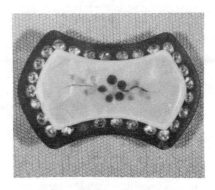

III-230. **Pin—1890-1910—**Celluloid with
hand painted flowers surrounded by
brilliants. $12.00 (Jeanenne Bell Dealer)

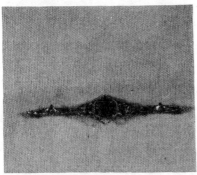

III-231. **Bar Pin—1900-20—**10K White
Gold with aquamarine colored stone.
2-1/4 x 1/2" $125.00 (W. Baldwin Collection)

III-232. **Brooch—1890-1910—**Silver
with amethyst and seed pearls 1-5/8"
$195.00 (W. Baldwin Collection)

III-233. **Locket—1890-1900-**Gold Filled.
Enameled. 3/4 x 1" $125.00 (Camille
Grace Dealer)

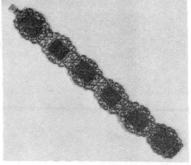

III-234. **Bracelet—1910-17—**Silver over
brass with red moulded glass stones. 1"
wide x 7-1/2" $24.00 (Jeanenne Bell
Dealer)

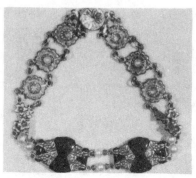

III-235. **Bracelet—1910-20**—Silver over copper with faceted onyx and 3MM pearls. Has a snap catch. 1/2 wide x 7" L. $65.00 (Jeanenne Bell Dealer)

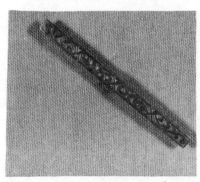

III-236. **Bar Pin—1910-17**—10K Yellow Gold 2-1/4" L. $125.00 (W. Baldwin Collection)

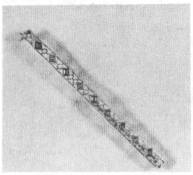

III-237. **Bar Pin—1910-1917**—10K Yellow and green gold with rubies 2-1/4" L. $185.00 (W. Baldwin Collection)

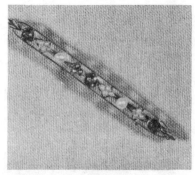

III-238. **Bar Pin-1910-20**—14K Yellow Gold with pearls and amethyst. 2-1/2" L. $225.00 (W. Baldwin Collection)

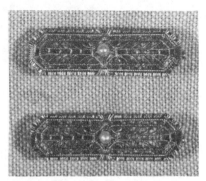

III-239. **Pair of Pins—1910-25**—14K White Gold Fillique with seed pearls. $145.00 (W. Baldwin Collection)

III-240. **Ring—1890-1917**—Silver with gold ornamentation. Imitation cornelian cameo is moulded glass. Drop 1/2 x 7/8" $95.00 (Jeanenne Bell Dealer)

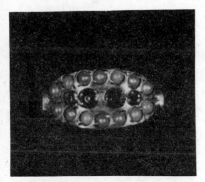

III-241. **Ring—1890-1910**—Gold Filled yellow gold with 14 pearls and 4 garnets. Head 3/4 x 1/4" $48.00 (Jeanenne Bell Dealer)

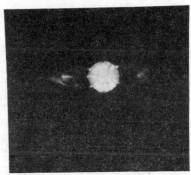

III-242. **Ring—1890-1910**—Gold Filled. Claw mtg. with rose cut brilliant 4 MM. $38.00 (Jeanenne Bell Dealer)

III-243. **Ring—1910-20**—Mkd. Sterling 1/4" wide $32.00 (Jeanenne Bell Dealer)

III-244. **Pendant—1880-90**—Gold over brass with 1" Dia. faceted amethyst colored stone 3 x 3-1/2" worn on black silk cord. $38.00 (Jeanenne Bell Dealer)

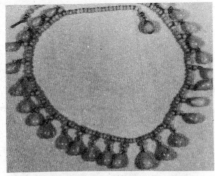

III-245. **Necklace—1890-1910**—Coral and gold. 17" L. $800.00 (W. Baldwin Collection)

III-246. **Necklace—1910-20**—Silver over brass. Cyrstal drops on long 16" chain. Barrell clasp. $32.00 (Jeanenne Bell Dealer)

III-247. **Brooch**—1890-1910—Gold Filled. Mkd. Wedgewood R & F 7/8 x 1″ $100.00 (W. Baldwin Collection)

III-248. **Locket**—Early 1900's—Gold over brass with red "stone." 1-1/4″ Dia. $28.00 (Jeanenne Bell Dealer)

III-249. **Pin for glasses**—Pat'd Feb. 24, 1903; April 26, 1910—Gold Filled Mkd. Kitchum & McDonald N.Y. 1-1/2″ Dia. $18.00 (Jeanenne Bell Dealer)

III-250. **Pendant**—1915-17—10K Mother of Pearl with feathers make bird design. 1-1/2″ Dia. $125.00 (Lucille and Sam Mundorff Dealers)

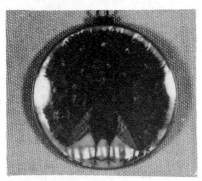

III-251. **Back side of 153**-showing Peacock.

III-252. **Bracelet**—1890-1910—Gold Filled. 1/2″ wide $125.00 (Jeanenne Bell Dealer)

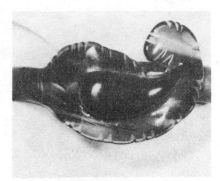

III-253. **Bracelet—1910-25**—Celluliod imitation tortoise 1/2" wide $30.00 (Jeanenne Bell Dealer)

III-254. **Necklace—1880-1917**—Sterling with amethyst. 20" Chain. Drop 1 x 2-1/4" $250.00 (W. Baldwin Collection)

III-255. **Scarf Pin—1910-20**—Yellow Gold with ruby colored stone. 1/4 x 3/4" $18.00 (Jeanenne Bell Dealer)

III-256. **Cuff Links—1890-1910**—Gold Filled with imitation opals. Mkd. Lambourne & Co. Birmingham, England. $55.00 (Jeanenne Bell Dealer)

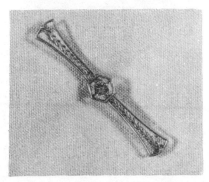

III-257. **Bar Pin—1910-17**—10K Gold with diamonds 2-1/8" L. $195.00 (W. Baldwin Collection)

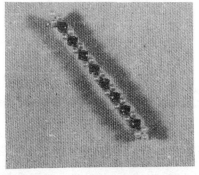

III-258. **Pin—1910-20**—14K Amethyst and pearls. 2" L. $250.00 (W. Baldwin Collection)

III-259. **Bar Pin—1910-20**—14K Yellow Gold with pearls and blue stone. 1-3/4″ wide. $225.00 (W. Baldwin Collection)

III-260. **Watch—1895**—Gold Filled case. Size 16 Elgin Movement $95.00 (Jeanenne Bell Dealer)

III-261. **Watch—1899**-Gold Filled Hunting case-11 jewels with 3 diamond chips. O's. on braided neck cord. $275.00 (W. Baldwin Collection)

III-262. **Watch—1911**—Gold Filled Hunting case Elgin with beautiful white and pink enameled dial. Gold hands. Chain is G.F. with Patent date Sept. 22, 1903. $425.00 (A.B. Noblitt Collection)

III-263. **Watch—1890-1900**—9K Gold English Hallmark. O.F. with Beautifully enameled back. O's. $475.00 (Jeanenne Bell Collection)

III-264. **Watch**—Picture of back of watch in 265.

III-265-Top right—**Brooch**—Circa 1880-90's. Gold with man in the moon carved in moonstone. Crescent set with rose diamonds. L550 $798.00 (A)

III-266-Left—**Brooch**—Circa 1875-90. Caduceus set with cushion shaped rubies and sapphires and rose and cushion shaped diamonds. L715 $1,037.00 (A)

III-267-Center right **Brooch**—Circa 1875-1900. Centered with insect set with a cushion shaped sapphire and rose and cushion shaped diamonds. Crescent is set with half-pearls between single pearl terminals. L605 $878.00 (A)

III-268-Bottom left—**Pendant**—Circa 1860. Gold with royal blue enamelling and diamonds. L1870 $2,712.00 (A)

III-269-Bottom right—**Brooch** Circa 1860. Gold, shell and pearl designed as a spider in a cokleshell. L385 $559.00 (A)

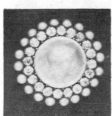

III-270—**Pendant/ Brooch**—Late 19th century—Gold centered with a carved moonstone head of a warrior. Surrounded by old European cut diamonds and seed pearls. T.B. Starr $2,420.00 (A) (Photo courtesy of Sotheby, New York 10-5-83)

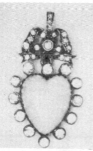

III-271—**Pendant**—Late Victorian. Heart shaped opal embellished with old cut diamonds. L850. $1,233.00 (A) (Photo courtesy of Phillips, London 10-18-83)

III-272—**Watch**—Circa 1890's. Yellow gold fob watch. Back pave set with old cut diamonds. Bezel is also set with diamonds. Bow brooch set with diamonds and centered with collet set ruby. L3,250 $4,712.00 (A) (Photo courtesy of Phillips, London 6-21-83)

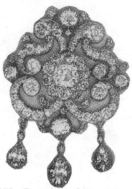

III-273—**Pendant**—Late Victorian. Gold and silver set with old cut brilliants and matching diamond drops and diamond pendant loop. Fitted case. L3,200 $4,640.00 (A) (Photo courtesy of Phillips, London 3-22-83)

III-274—**Bracelet**—Circa 1897. Gold. Made to commemorate the victory of the racehorse "Royal Flush", winner of the Diamond Stakes in the Jubilee year 1897. Center has an enameled plaque of Queen Victoria surrounded by diamonds with a locket below. Flanked by four "Playing Cards". L1,900 $2,755.00 (A) (Photo courtesy of Phillips, London 6-21-83)

III-276—**Brooch**—Late nineteenth century. Gold crescent centered with a sapphire (approx. 1.25cts.). Further embellished with 4 sapphires and several old European cut diamonds. $2,970.00 (A) (Photo courtesy of Sothebys, London 4-10-84)

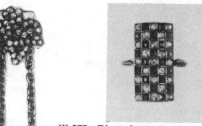

III-275—**Ring**—Late nineteenth century. Gold rectangular head set with a checkerboard pattern of 22 calibre cut rubies and 23 old European cut diamonds. (approx. 55 cts.) $1,760.00 (A) (Photo courtesy of Sotheby, New York 4-10-84)

III-277—**Pendant Watch**—Circa 1910. Platinum and gold open face watch with translucent blue guillouche enameling centered with a rose diamond. The back rim is set with calibre cut emeralds. The front dial bordered with rose cut diamonds. Suspended from a black ribbon sautior with platinum and rose cut diamond ornaments. Dial is signed "Cartier" and the sautior signed "Cartier Paris". $5,500.00 (A) (Photo courtesy of Sotheby, New York 4-10-84)

204

III-278—**Pendant Watch With Brooch**—Circa 1890's. 14K yellow gold with 1 pear-shaped ruby and several old European cut diamonds. $990.00 (A) (Photo courtesy of Sotheby, New York 10-6-83)

III-279—**Earrings**—Circa 1900. 14K yellow gold with purple and white enamel. Each one has an old European cut diamond set in the center. $1,045.00 (A) (Photo courtesy of Sotheby, New York 10-6-83)

III-280—**Brooch**—Circa 1900. Gold and silver set with half-pearls and rose cut diamonds. L352 $511.00 (A) (Photo courtesy of Sotheby's London 4-14-83)

III-281—**Brooch**—Circa 1900. Heart motif with opal and diamonds. L385 $559.00 (A) (Photo courtesy of Sotheby, London 4-14-83)

III-282—**Brooch**—Circa 1900. Gold and silver buckle motif with pale blue enamel set with 14 old mine diamonds. Outer rim bordered by rose-cut diamonds and seed pearls. $3,850 (A) (Photo courtesy of Sotheby's, New York 12-7-83)

III-283—**Bracelet**—Circa 1905. Gold hinged bangle set with cats eye and diamonds. L935 $1,356.00 (A) (Photo courtesy of Sotheby, London 10-6-83)

III-284—**Long Chain**—Circa 1900. Gold chain set at intervals with engraved ivory beads set with cabochon sapphires, rubies, and amethyst (some missing). L825 $1,196.00 (A) (Photo courtesy of Sotheby Parke Bernet & Co. 11-24-83)

III-285—**Brooch**—Circa 1900. Arts and Craft Movement. Gold with 4 round pink tourmalines and 4 freshwater pearls. $990.00 (A) (Photo courtesy of Sotheby, New York 10-5-83)

III-286—**Lavaliere**—Circa 1900. 14K gold with diamonds, seed pearls and 2 pear-shaped sapphires (approx. 1.25 cts). $715.00 (A) (Photo courtesy of Sotheby, New York 10-5-83)

III-287—**Pendant Watch & Chain**—Circa 1900. Platinum with diamonds and enameling. Majestic Watch Co. 18 jewel movement. Necklace spaced with 33 collet-set old European cut diamonds (approx. 2.50cts.). Signed ''Cartier'. $7,150.00 (A) (Photo courtesy of Sotheby, New York 10-5-83)

III-288—**Pendant Watch and Brooch**—Late 19th century. 18K yellow gold with enamel miniature. Patek Philippe movement. Fitted box. $2,000.00 (A) (Photo courtesy of Wm. Doyle Galleries 9-21-83)

III-289—**Pendant/Brooch**—
Circa 1900. Gold set with black
opals and 6 old European cut
diamonds (approx. 1.25 cts.).
$2,090.00 (A) (Photo courtesy of
Sotheby, New York 10-5-83)

III-290—**Buckle**—Circa 1900.
Gold with enameled yellow
flowers and green foliate (some
damage). Engraved on reverse
"Tiffany & Co." $93500 (A)
(Photo courtesy of Sotheby,
New York 10-3-83)

III-291—**Stickpins And Brooch**—Circa 1900. 14K diamond and garnet stickpin signed
"Tiffany & Co."; A gold enamel and moonstone stickpin; two gold and diamond
stickpins with woman's face and a gold enamel, seed pearl and diamond brooch
of a woman's face accented with enamel. $1,760.00 (A) (Photo courtesy of Sotheby,
New York 10-5-83)

III-293—**Lapel Watch And Pin**—Late 19th century. Gold with enamel. Dial is white with blue Arabic numerals. $715.00 (A) (Photo courtesy of Sotheby, New York 9-14-83)

III-292—**Lapel Watch And Pin**—Circa 1890-1910. Yellow gold and silver with rose cut diamonds. $2,700.00 (A) (Photo courtesy of Wm. Doyle Galleries 9-21-83)

III-294—**Bracelet**—Circa 1880-90. Gold and pearls with painted miniature plaques. $425.00 (Photo courtesy of Wm. Doyle Galleries 9-21-83)

III-295—**Sautoir**—Edwardian. Seed pearls with turrent shaped diamond ends and long tassel terminals. Pendant earrings included in original fitted case. L2,800 $4,060.00 (A) (Photo courtesy of Phillips, London 6-21-83)

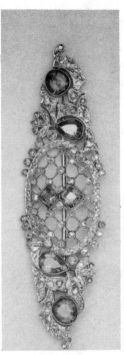

III-296—**Brooch**—Edwardian. Gold set with emeralds and diamonds. L3,000 $4,350 (A) (Photo courtesy of Phillips, London 6-21-83)

III-297——**Bracelet**—Edwardian. Gold flexible with diamond set box links, divided by French cut diamond and calibre emerald baton. L3,400 $4,930.00 (A) (Photo courtesy of Phillips, London 3-22-83)

III-298—**Pendant**—Edwardian. Pearl tassel pendant with diamond cap, calibre emerald hoops and diamond triangular drops. Necklace set at intervals with pearls. Also has a longer, similarly set necklace en suite. L4200 $6090.00 (A) (Photo courtesy of Phillips, London 6-21-83)

III-299—**Pendant**—Edwardian. Yellow gold with blue sapphire and diamond. Fitted case. L2,800 $4,060.00 (A) (Photo courtesy of Phillips, London 6-21-83)

211

III-300—**Brooch**—Edwardian. Gold set with aquamarine and pearls. L3,000 $4,350.00 (A) (Photo courtesy of Phillips, London 10-18-83)

III-301—**Pendant**— Edwardian. Opals and diamond. L950 $1,379.00 (A) (Photo courtesy of Phillips, London 1-24-84)

III-302—**Brooch**— Edwardian. Gold set with cushion shaped mixed cut sapphire. L700 $1,015.00 (A) (Photo courtesy of Phillips, London. 4-26-83)

III-303– **Brooch/ Pendant**— Edwardian. A diamond openwork setting mounted with an oval and triangular opal. L2,500 $3,625.00 (A) (Photo courtesy of Phillips, London 1-24-84)

III-304-**Pendant**—Edwardian. Rose diamond framework set with oval and pear shaped pink tourmalines. L1,300 $1,885.00 (A) (Photo courtesy of Phillips, London 1-24-84)

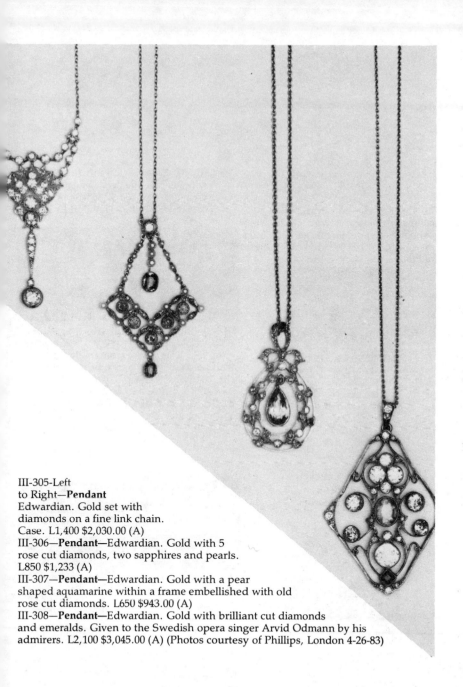

III-305-Left
to Right—**Pendant**
Edwardian. Gold set with
diamonds on a fine link chain.
Case. L1,400 $2,030.00 (A)
III-306—**Pendant**—Edwardian. Gold with 5
rose cut diamonds, two sapphires and pearls.
L850 $1,233 (A)
III-307—**Pendant**—Edwardian. Gold with a pear
shaped aquamarine within a frame embellished with old
rose cut diamonds. L650 $943.00 (A)
III-308—**Pendant**—Edwardian. Gold with brilliant cut diamonds
and emeralds. Given to the Swedish opera singer Arvid Odmann by his
admirers. L2,100 $3,045.00 (A) (Photos courtesy of Phillips, London 4-26-83)

III-310—**Brooch**—Edwardian. Gold pansy with shaped amethysts edged by small diamonds. L1,700 $2,465.00 (A) (Photo courtesy of Phillips, London 10-18-83)

III-309—**Brooch**—Edwardian. Gold with enameled frame set with pearls, rose diamonds and demantoid garnet. Fitted case. L1,300 $1,885.00 (A) (Photo courtesy of Phillips, London 10-18-83)

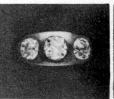

III-313—**Ring**—Circa 1900. Gold gypsy mounting centered with 1 old European cut diamond (approx. .50cts.) flanked by 2 old European cut diamonds (approx. .40cts.) $715.00 (A) (Photo courtesy of Sotheby, New York 10-5-83)

III-314—**Ring**—Circa 1900. 18K gold centered with a 8.3mm natural pearl flanked by one old European cut diamond (approx. 1.75cts.) and another (approx. 1.90 cts.). $6,875.00 (A) (Photo courtesy of Sotheby, New York 10-5-83)

III-312—**Ring**—Circa 1900. Art Nouveau. Gold assymetrical band centered with one old European cut diamond (approx. .85cts.) flanked by 2 old European cut diamonds (approx. .90cts) $1,870.00 (Photo courtesy of Sotheby, New York 10-5-83)

III-315—**Ring**—Circa 1917. Platinum band centered with 1 cabochon emerald (approx. .80cts.) flanked by 2 old European cut diamonds (.90 cts.). $1,870.00 (A) (Photo courtesy of Sotheby, New York 10-5-83)

III-316—**Ring**—Circa 1900. Platinum top-half set with 1 old European cut diamond (1 ct.), 4 old European cut diamonds (approx. 1.80 cts.) and spaced by 8 small old European cut diamonds. Gold shank. $2,090.00 (Photo courtesy of Sotheby, New York 10-5-83)

III-317—**Ring**—Circa 1900. 14K gold gypsy mounting centered with 1 old European cut diamond (approx. .90cts.), flanked by 2 old European cut diamonds (approx. 1.20cts.), Signed "S. Sons" $1,650.00 (A) (Photo courtesy of Sotheby, New York 10-5-83)

214

III-318-Left—**Bracelet**—Art Nouveau. Gold and enamel. Arnould, France. $1,540.00 (A) (Photo courtesy of Sotheby, New York 10-5-83)

III-319— Right—**Bracelet**—Art Nouveau. 14K yellow gold composed of 11 Repousse slides. Each has a lady's head set with a small single cut diamond. American circa 1900. $2,200.00 (A) (Photo courtesy of Sotheby, New York 10-6-83)

III-320-**Clip**—Art Nouveau. Circa 1900. Gold woman's profile set with several old European cut diamonds. $880.00 (A) (Photo courtesy of Sotheby, New York 4-10-84)

III-321- **Pendant/Brooch**—Art Nouveau. 18K yellow gold with green enamel. Woman's headband set with small old European cut diamonds. $1,045.00 (A) (Photo courtesy of Sotheby, New York 10-6-83)

215

III-322—**Locket**—Art Nouveau—14K gold with 1 small old European cut diamond. Reverse has monogram. $1,650.00 (A) (Photo courtesy of Sotheby, New York 10-6-83)

III-323—**Locket/Pendant**—Circa 1900. Gold with lady's head wreath set with 30 small round emeralds and 4 small round diamonds. Her necklace is set with 8 single cut diamonds. Completed by a heavy link chain. $4,675.00 (A) (Photo courtesy of Sotheby, New York 10-5-83)

III-324—**Dragon Fly Pin**—Circa 1910. 18K yellow gold and platinum containing small round diamonds and blue and green enamel. $7,750.00 (A) (Photo courtesy of William Doyle Galleries 9-21-83)

III-325—**Brooch**—Art Nouveau. Silver set with rubies and freshwater pearls. Plique-a-jour enamelling. "Probably designed by Robert Koch." L750 $1,000.00 (Photo courtesy of Phillip Blensstock House 12-15-83)

III-326—**Brooch**—Unusual enameled with female dancer .6cm high. Signed on reverse "May Patridge." Entitled "Flame". L400 $600.00 (Photo courtesy of Phillips, London 11-24-83)

III-327—**Necklace**—Art Nouveau. Gold grape motif of freshwater pearls with emerald pink and green leaves. $1,870.00 (A) (Photo courtesy of Sotheby, New York 12-7-83)

217

III-328—**Dream Set**—Circa 1910. Cuff links, 4 buttons and 3 studs of platinum, mother of pearl and 11 old mine cut diamonds (approx. .50cts.). 14K gold back and posts. $1,045.00 (A) (Photo courtesy of Sotheby, New York 10-5-83)

III-329—**Lavaliere**—Circa 1910. Platinum set with 1 octagonal shaped emerald and 1 pear shaped emerald and embellished with numerous rose cut diamonds and 16 collet set European cut diamonds. $9,350.00 (A) (Photo courtesy of Sotheby, New York 10-5-83)

III-332—**"Jabot" Pin**—Gold minaret design, set with four pale chrysoprase plaques. Embellished with black and white enamel and tulip shaped pearl terminal. Signed "C&A.G." in oval cartouche. Guiliani. L650 $943.00 (A) (Photo courtesy of Phillips, London 6-21-83)

13

III-330—**Wristwatch**—Circa 1914. 18K gold ladies half hunting case with 15K flexible bracelet. 1" diameter. $1,045.00 (Photo courtesy of Sotheby, New York 4-10-84)

III-331—**Wristwatch**—Circa 1919. 14K gold and enamel rectangular man's "Lady Waltham". 1¾" long. $880.00 (Photo courtesy of Sotheby, New York 4-10-84)

III 333-**Powder Box and Lipstick Case**—Circa 1915. 14K gold with platinum and diamond medallions. Embellished with transluscent deep green enamel over a guilloche ground. Tiffany & Co. $1,320.00 (Photo courtesy of Sotheby, New York 12-7-83)

219

III-334—**Lapel Watch**—Platinum with 52 round diamonds weighing approx. 2.75 cts. Tiffany and Co. $1,980.00 (A) (Photo courtesy of Sothebys, New York 9-14-83)

III-335—**Ring**—Circa 1915. Platinum centered with 1 old European cut diamond (approx. 1.50 cts.) and flanked by 2 old European cut diamonds (approx. 1.60 cts.) Further embellished with old European and single cut diamonds. (several missing) $3,300.00 (A) (Photo courtesy of Sotheby, New York 10-5-83)

III-336—**Ring**—Circa 1915. Platinum centered with one briolette diamond in an open work panel embellished with single cut diamonds and several calibre cut emeralds $2,310.00 (A) (Photo courtesy of Sotheby, New York 10-5-83)

III-337- **Diamond and Black Onyx Lapel Watch And Pin**—Circa 1915. The platinum pin containing forty-two round diamonds approx. total 6.00 cts., and the watch containing one hundred round diamonds approx. total 3.00 cts., and three round diamonds approx. total .90 ct., Signed Cartier. $9,000.00 (Photo courtesy of William Doyle Galleries 12-83)

220

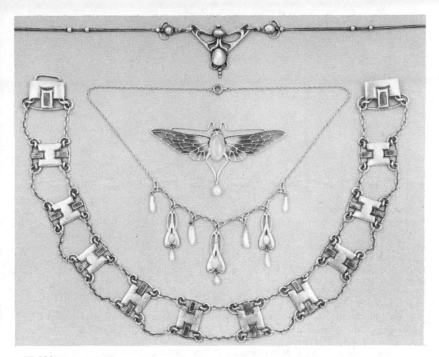

III-338-Top—**Necklace**—Arts and Crafts with blister pearls. In the manner of Edgar Simpson L240 $348.00

III-339-Center—**Pendant**—Gold moth with opal cabochon body and plique-a-jour wings. Pearl drop. 9cm across. Stamped "Jules". L190 $276.00

III-340-Center—**Pendant**—Art Nouveau. 9K gold with opal cabochon and freshwater pearls. 44cm long. L340 $493.00

III-341—**Necklace**—Circa 1902. Silver "Cymric" with blue enameled panels. Probably designed by Archibald Knox. 44 cm. Liberty and Co. L280 $406.00 (Photos courtesy of Phillips, London 11-24-83)

III-342—**Pendant**—'950' with faceted amethysts. 4.50 cm. M.B. & Co. L120 $174.00
III-343—**Pendant**—Arts and Crafts. Moonstone and mother of pearl. 5.50cm long.
By Gaskin. L440 $638.00
III-344-**Pendant**—'950' with mother of pearl and faceted chrysolite. 3.50 cm. M.B.
& Co. L85 $124.00 (Photos courtesy of Phillips, London 11-24-83)

III-345– **Brooch**—Art Nouveau. 15K gold set with mother of pearl and a turquoise
drop. Merrle Bennett & Co. 3.5 cm. L110 $160.00
III-346—**Pendant**—15K gold. Inverted bell shaped set with 3 half pearls and an oval
cabochon turquoise. 4cm. Merrle Bennet & Co. L130 $189.00
III-347—**Pendant**—15K gold centered with an opal cabochon. Drop is also an opal.
3.5 cm. M.B. & Co. L130 $189.00
III-348—**Pendant/Locket**—Gold with blue and green enamels. Glass front and back.
"Probably designed by Archibald Knox". 3.25 cm. Liberty & Co. L130 $189.00
III-349—**Pendant**—9K gold with mother of pearl center and a turquoise drop. 5cm.
M.B. & Co. L120 $174.00 (Photos courtesy of Phillips, London 7-7-83)

III-350—**Brooch**—Gilt metal, snake motif in high relief moulded glass. 4cm. Stamped "RL" & "Lalique". L700 $1,050.00 (Photo courtesy of Phillips, London 7-7-83)

III-351—**Brooch**—925 silver. Peacock feathers set with marcasites and opal cabochons. 4 cm. high. Stamped "TF". Theodor Fahrner. L95 $138.00

III-352—**Pendant**—Art Nouveau. Gold and plique-a-jour. Maidens headband set with rose cut diamonds. Diamond and pearl drop. 4 cm. L400 $600.00

II-353—**Pendant**—'950' with mother of pearl half pearls and translucent blue enamel. Mother of pearl drop. German. Probably designed by Otto Prutsher. Makers mark for Heinrich Levinger of Pforzheim. L180. $270.00

III-354—**Pendant**—Arts and Crafts. Enameled shield shaped 4.50cm. Attributed to C. R. Ashbee. L220 $330.00 (Photos courtesy of Phillips, London 7-7-83)

III-355—**Bracelet**—Arts and Crafts. Set with amazonite cabochons, green-stained chalcedony, rubies, marcasites and amethysts. 20 cm. long. By Sibyl Dunlop. L200 $300.00. (Photo courtesy of Phillips, London 7-7-83)

III-356—**Necklace**—'950' with faceted amethyst. 42 cm. long M.B. & Co. L120 $174.00

III-357— **Necklace**—Arts and Crafts. With enameled panels in green, blue and orange. Baroque pearl. L300 $435.00

III-358— **Brooch**—Art Nouveau. Gold with enameling and pearls. Russian. Makers mark 'A. B. with male head and 56' L140 $200.00

III-359—**Brooch**—'900' owl motif with enameling in brown, violet and yellow. Green paste eyes. Plique-a-jour wings. Holding a pearl. 4.50 cm. Dragonfly makers mark. L250 $365.00 (Photos courtesy of Phillips, London 11-24-83)

III-360—**Necklace**—Art Nouveau. 950 set with mother of pearl and amethyst. Stamped M.B. & Co. L110 $160.00

III-361—**Pendant/Locket**—Sterling with green and white enamelling. Front slides to reveal mirrors within. Makers mark for F. Mahla of Pforzheim. L130 $190.00

III-362—**Pendant Necklace**—Arts and Crafts. With Swiss lapis. Similar in style to the work of Sybil Dunlop L220 $320.00

III-363—**Pendant**—Art Nouveau. Silver with blue, green and orange enamels. 5cm. Stamped ''J.B.B. & Co.'' L65 $95.00

III-364—**Pendant**—Circa 1904, 9K gold with enameled scene. Stamped W. H. H. L120. $174.00

III-365—**Brooch**—Art Nouveau. 900 silver. Hammer texture with 3 Swiss lapis beads. 3.50 cm. across. Marked with L.B. monogram. L55 $80.00

III-366—**Pendant**—Silver with enameling. 7 cm. ''M.B. & Co.'' L70 $102.00 (Photos courtesy of Phillips Blenstock House 12-15-83)

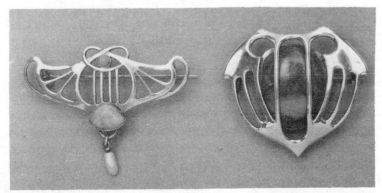

III-367—**Brooch**—Art Nouveau. 9 K gold with turquoise cabochon. 4 cm across. L70 $95.00

III-368—**Brooch**—Art Nouveau. Gold with oval turquoise. L90 $135.00 (Photos courtesy of Phillips Blenstock House 12-15-83)

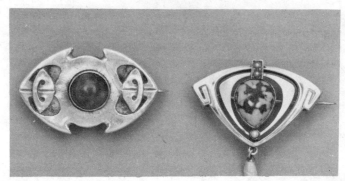

III-369– Brooch—Circa 1903. Silver with marble cabochon center and green/blue enamels. "Liberty & Co." L140 $210.00

III-370– Brooch—Art Nouveau. 9K gold centered with turoquoise. Embellished with seed pearls and a pearl drop. L50 $75.00 (Photos courtesy of Phillips Blenstock House 12-15-83)

III-371–Right—Brooch—Arts and Crafts. Centered with a moonstone cabochon. 5 cm. diameter. L40 $60.00

III-372-Top right—Brooch—Circa 1911. Silver. Santa with sleigh and reindeer. 4.5cm long. Marked "F.H.M.". L20 $30.00

III-373- Top left—Brooch—Arts and Crafts. With moonstone. "In the manner of Gaskin". L40 $60.00 (Photos courtesy of Phillips, London 11-24-83)

III-374--Brooch—18K gold circular with translucent red, green, and blue enamels. 2.50 diameter. Stamped 'H.G.M.' falcon mark. (Rare H.G. Murphy) L350 $493.00 (Photo courtesy of Phillips, London 11-24-83)

## 1920-1930
## THE TIMES

The twenties were years of action and reaction. The word used most to describe this decade is "roaring", but scandalous, shocking, and flaming are also apt adjectives. The world had survived the war, and a feeling of recklessness prevailed.

When the Eighteenth Amendment made alcohol illegal, it became fashionable to break the law. Speakeasies sprang up overnight, and with them came a new "devil may care" society. The forbidden, the sinister, and the shocking had more allure than ever before. It did not take long for organized crime to become involved in bootlegging. Al Capone and his business associates made headlines. Instead of watching this fiasco with distain and disgust, many Americans were fascinated and sometimes even envious. The country's values were turned upside down, and the glitter of money was on top of the heap.

Business was the by-word of the twenties, and business was good. Organizations that combined business lunches with service projects flourished. The Lions, Rotary, and Kiwanis Clubs grew at a phenominal rate. They managed to provide many charitable services that shed a positive light on business. Christianity and free enterprise were combined to everyone's advantage.

In August of 1920 women won the right to vote. This long awaited victory had an emotionally liberating effect, especially on the younger generation. They felt that they were on an equal par with men and should be entitled to all the privileges. They went to barber shops and had their long hair bobbed. Girdles were discarded. Dresses were shortened. Lips were painted. If men could smoke and drink, so could they. The emphasis was on youth, and it was indeed flaming.

This reckless craze was also expressed in the popular dances. The loose and uninhibited steps of the Charleston and the Black Bottom were performed across the nation. Marathons became the rage. Couples danced for days and sometimes weeks to win the prizes these contests offered.

Automobiles had an increasing effect on the American way of life. Fifteen million new cars were registered between

1920 and 1929. As production rose, the prices declined. By 1924 a "Tin Lizzie" could be bought for as little as $290.00 With 470,000 people employed by the automobile industry, the car was becoming a way of life. People who did not even own a bathtub took pride in their new automobile. Travel for pleasure became common. The Sunday drive began to have an effect on church attendance. The older generation was appalled at the freedom the automobile afforded the youth. It initiated a new form of courtship, and condemnation from the pulpit had no influence on its popularity. The older generation was convinced that the world was on the "road" to Hell.

Another innovation was changing the home life—the radio. It had been toyed with by amateurs for a number of years, but when KDKA started broadcasting in November of 1920, the commercial and entertainment value was quickly recognized. Radio manufacturers stepped up production, and sales climbed to almost two million dollars in that year. By 1928 the Montgomery Ward Company Catalogue offered nine pages of radios and radio equipment. Table model prices ranged from $85.75 for a six tube, one dial, battery operated set complete with speakers to $146.00 for an eight tube, one dial model that included antenna equipment and a drum speaker. The more expensive model plugged into a light socket and promised "no more fussing with batteries, hydrometers, acids, water, and equipment." All the new owner needed to do was "plug into the light socket, connect antenna, ground the wire and tune in." Radio tables with matching benches, priced at $9.67, $11.35, and $12.95 were also available. If the customer wanted a handsome cabinet model, it was available in a variety of styles: Spanish ($162.25), Tudor ($196.75), and the Highboy ($203.00). Of course all items could be purchased for a few dollars more on the Easy Payment Plan.

All the companies were offering merchandise on the deferred payment plan. Why wait to own a new car or radio when for only a few dollars down and a few dollars a month it could be enjoyed now? More and more people adopted this philosophy even though it added to the cost of the item. It was so easy to take advantage of these Easy Payment Plans that many homes were completely furnished on credit.

With the work day reduced to eight hours, there was more time for attending movies and sporting events, listening to the radio, or reading. New magazines were started, and the number of professional authors increased from 7,000 in 1920 to 12,000 by 1930.

Movie attendance continued to increase. Going to the movies at least once a week became an intricate part of life for millions. Movie palaces were built to provide a volumptuous atmosphere for viewing the Kings and Queens of Hollywood. Viewers felt as if they knew the stars personally. When Valentino died in 1926, over 100,000 stood in line to pay their last respects.

Radio and newspapers had a positive effect on sports. Professional players had an opportunity to become instant celebraties. It was a short step from the sports' arena to Hollywood. Babe Ruth, Jack Dempsey, and Gene Tunney were but a few of the many who capitalized on their fame by making movies.

What the country needed was a national hero. When C.A. Lindbergh took off from Roosevelt Field, New York, the flight was covered by radio and newspapers, even though his chances of reaching his destination were slim. America went wild with jubilation when thirty three and one-half hours later he arrived in Paris, tired and triumphant. He was welcomed home with a hero's honors including a ticker tape parade in New York City.

Everybody loves success stories. After hearing how average people made fortunes in the stock market, the general public was eager to try its luck. Housewives shaved money from their household allowance to invest. Instead of putting the money into savings' accounts, people bought stocks, hoping to make their fortune. But on October 24, 1929 the bubble burst. The market went under, carrying with it the hopes, dreams, and fortunes of thousands of people.

The Thirties began on a somber note. After the gaiety of the twenties, it was a nightmare. Alan Jenkins described it in his book "The Thirties". "This was the depression, the slump, deeper than anyone could have imagined, after the Twenties bull market and the 1929 crash; the first middle class poverty that American had ever known, the worst years America went through not excluding two world wars."

In the weeks following the crash, there was hope that conditions would improve. The President refused to admit to the nation just how bad things really were. When it became apparent that the economy was not improving but actually getting worse, the country realized that something had to be done. Government leaders were adamently against Americans being put on the "dole", but no one had any ideas about what could be done to relieve the situation.

Then came F.D. Roosevelt and his "new deal". No one really knew what this new deal was, but almost anything would be better than the one they had. Roosevelt won the election by a landslide vote. True to his word, he immediately began to implement new government programs. These programs became known to the people by their initials. The N. R. A. regulated working hours and wages; the C. C. C. employed young men to work in areas of conservation; the P. W. A. financed the programs of the W. P. A. People were employed to do everything from building bridges to entertaining. The nation was working its way out of the economic crisis. Roosevelt's new deal was the right deal.

During this time of economic uncertainty, the radio offered a delightful form of escape. By tuning into Amos n Andy people could forget their troubles and laugh. Other comedy favorites were George Burns and Gracy Allen, Fibber McGee and Molly, Edger Bergan and Charlie McCarthy, Jack Benny and Bob Hope. The Lux Radio Theatre brought drama into the living room. For those who loved music there was Kate Smith. In the mind's eye the listener visualized the performers. These mental pictures became so real that it sometimes was quite a shock to be confronted with an actual photograph of the star. By 1935 there were more than thirty million radios. The Sears Roebuck Catalogue for that year shows that prices had dropped. It pictured "the most advanced battery operated radio in the world" complete with tubes, batteries, and antenna for only $39.95. It boasted that this radio had a weatherband and worldwide reception. A smaller AC-DC table model was priced at $18.95, and an AC electric radio in a beautiful cabinet was only $31.50. These new low prices made it possible for more and more homes to have this wonderful form of amusement. The radio was changing the living habits of America. Schedules were altered to insure time to listen to favorite programs.

Movies were more popular than ever. A double feature complete with newsreel was only a dime, a small price for being transported into a make believe word of glamor, sophistication, and adventure. Stars such as Joan Crawford, Greta Garbo, Jean Harlow, and Mae West were the epitomy of sex appeal and glamour. Clark Gable, James Cagney, Robert Taylor, and Tyrone Power caused hearts all over the country to skip a beat whenever they appeared on the screen. Fred Astaire, Ginger Rogers, Bing Crosby, Judy Garland, Mickey Rooney, and Shirley Temple sang and danced their way into the hearts of America.

In a society sadly in need of money, the rich held a fascination all their own. Playboys and debutantes were big news. Papers were filled with descriptions of coming out parties and social events for these select few. The December 27, 1937 issue of Life Magazine included the article "A Day in the Life of a Debutante." Through a series of photographs the readers were taken through a typical day that began with breakfast in bed and included exciting activities such as sitting for society page photographs, selecting her coming-out dress (a mere $300.00), and checking off names of eligible bachelors in Juliana Cuttings famous book. "Because her party was small," stated the article, "with only 300 guests and costing $5,000, only a fraction of the Cutting list was used." A popular definition of a debutante was: A bare back with lots of "green backs."

In the latter years of the decade, a new sound played to a new beat emerged. The sound was "Big Band"; the beat was swing. The new pied pipers were Benny Goodman, Glenn Miller, Jimmy Dorsey, and Artie Shaw. With this new style came jive talk and jitterbugging. A new generation had emerged.

By the end of the decade America had a new hope, technology. People felt that through science, engineering, and technology the world would become a better place in which to live. DuPont was developing new materials such as nylon and polytherene. Laboratories were experimenting with sulphur drugs and antibodies. In 1939 The World's Fair opened in New York. It was filled with displays that pointed to a future bright with hope.

## 1920's-1930's

### FASHION IN CLOTHING AND JEWELRY

The fashions of the twenties were as erratic as the times. Everything was fast-paced and changing; this was reflected by the fluctuating styles. Hem lines yo-yoed up and down; waistlines disappeared and then re-appeared at the hip line; hairstyles went from long to short, then back to shoulder length—all this in ten short years.

After the war women experienced an exhilerating feeling of liberation. This feeling was expressed most profoundly by the clothing they wore. Fashion took on a boyish look. The bust was ignored, the figure was sublimated, and dresses became short sacks. By 1925 the hemline was at the knee and sometimes even above it. Hair was cropped off in what was commonly referred to as a "bob." In some styles the back was cut short, but a little length was left at the side to be plastered to the cheek in "spit curls." Cloche hats snugly fit the head so these whisps of hair were the only proof that any existed.

Girls who adhered to the modern styles were known as "flappers." An amusing description of a "Flapper Jane" appeared in the September 9, 1925 edition of The New Republic Magazine.

Jane isn't wearing much, this summer. If you'd like to know exactly, it is; one dress, one step-in, two stocking, two shoes. A step-in, if you are 99 and 44/100 ths percent ignorant, is underwear—one piece, light, exceedingly brief but roomy. Her dress, as you can't possibly help knowing if you have even one good eye and get around at all outside the Old People's Home, is also brief. It is cut low where it might be high, and vice versa. The skirt comes just an inch below her knee, overlapping by a faint fraction her soiled and twisted stockings. The idea is that when she walks in a bit of breeze, you shall now and then observe the knee (which is not rouged—thats just newspaper talk) but always in an accidental Venus-surprised-at-the-bath sort of way. This is a bit of coyness which hardly fits in with Jane's general character.

Jane's haircut is also abbreviated. She wears of course the newest thing in bobs even closer than last year's shingle. It leaves her just about no hair at all in the back, and 20 percent more than that in the front about as much as is being worn this season by a cellist (male); less than a pianist, and much much less than a violinist. Because of this new style, one can confirm a rumor heard last year: Jane has ears.

232

*The corset is as dead as the dodo's grandfather; no feeble Publicity pipings by the manufacters, or calling it a "clasp around" will enable it, as Jane says, to 'do a Lazarus.' The petticoat is even more defunct. Not even a snicker can be raised by telling Jane that once the nation was shattered to its foundation by the shadow-skirt. The brassiere has been abandoned, since 1924. While stockings are usually worn, they are not a sine-qua—nothing doing. In hot weather Jane reserves the right to discard them, just as all the chorus girls did in 1923. As stocking are only a frantic, successful attempt to duplicate the color and texture of Jane's own sunburned slim legs, few but expert boulevardiers can tell the difference.*

*These which I have described are Jane's clothes, but they are not merely a flapper uniform. They are the style of 1925, Eastern Seaboard. These things and none other are being worn by all of Jane's sisters and her cousins and her aunts. They are being worn by ladies who are three times Jane's age, and look ten years older; by those twice her age who look a hundred years older. Their use is so universal that in our larger cities the baggage transfer companies one and all declare they are being forced into bankruptcy. Ladies who used to go away for the summer with six trunks can now pack twenty dainty costumes in a bag.*

Many people shared this disdain for modern attire. The Literary Digest of November 21, 1925 informed that "admittance to the audience with the Pope was recently denied to 32 women and girls because they were not properly clothed." The Hebrew Union of Orthodox Congregations also passed a "resolution condemning the scant garb of women." These had little effect on fashions. They were worn until they were no longer amusing.

The arts were having an increasingly important effect on design. The popularity of the Russian Ballet had brought with it a profusion of bright colors. Art movements such as Cubism, Favasium, and Futurism influenced fabric designs making geometric prints popular.

Jewelry was used to compliment the dress and soften the effect that short hair had on the features. Dangling earrings, long ropes of beads, and a multitude of bracelets all added to the razzle-dazzle of the outfit. Everything that glittered or dangled captured the imagination. Crystal and rhinestones became fashionable.

There were necklaces to adorn any neckline. Beads combining crystal and jet were dramatic and therefore fashionable (see page 258). An illustrated jewelry catalogue for 1923 lists "fine faceted novelty beads" in a choice of imitation jet, blue sapphire with crystal rondel, imitation jet with crystal rondel, transparent ruby, and aquarmarine with crystals. The beads were 34 inches long, and the tassels added another four (4) inches. Prices ranged from $1.50 to $3.00. Today they would cost from $28.00 to $46.00.

Amber beads were popular. A twenty (20) inch necklace of genuine amber in a "clear light color" was priced at only $9.00, but a twenty four (24) inch Bakelite bead necklace in the "old amber color" was the same price. Evidently the new Bakelite was highly desirable.

There was an infinite variety of jewelry on the market. An article in Country Life, December 1926, comments on this:

> Ten years ago the conventional jeweled pin at the height of fashion was the straight bar pin, for it was best suited to the needs of the softer blouse and of the frocks which often had V necklines flanked by turned-back collars. Now we see more circles and ovals and use of pearls, as a plain pearl necklace is correct with almost any simple daytime dress. Also, the small plain hat has created the need for jeweled hat ornaments, which were not necessary when hats had more trimming, such as feathers and flowers.
>
> It may also be supposed that this restraint imposed on jewels for daytime by wearing of sports clothes has had something to do with the elaborateness of jewels worn for the late afternoon and evening. We see in the holiday displays more wide jeweled bracelets than those of slender one-stone width, and when the latter are worn they are most often worn in numbers.
>
> Doubtless, too, the prosperity of the present time has something to do with the great variety seen in jewelry. To harken back to the history of civilization, we find always in periods of prosperity jewelry becomes more varied and more specialized in its uses, for people can afford different types for different needs.

By 1927 women were beginning to tire of the masculine look. When Lavin unveiled her new designs for feminine dresses made of soft materials, they were a welcome change. Greta Garbo also had a softening influence. Her starring role in "The Woman of Affairs" caused women to wear slouch hats and to let their hair grow longer.

Designers began to have an impact on clothing for the average woman. Madeline Veornet, Leanne Lavin, and Coco Channel were designers whose creations were known and admired by American women. Reproductions of Channel's jewelry collection adorned her creations. Designers were branching out into all fields of personal adornment. The Deliniator of April 1928 makes this growing influence quite clear.

*But what have the dressmakers to do with jewelry? Nothing—any more than they have to do with perfume, or powders, gloves or shoes, or hats, bags, flowers or lingerie; but all these—and a great many things besides—they now make and sell because they have found that everything that a woman puts on or uses on her body while she is wearing one of their gowns, enormously affects the chic of the gown. That is why any woman who buys a Vionnet gown wants Vionnet lingerie; or any woman who buys Lanvin sports suit wants the hat that goes with it; or any woman who believes Channel can make a smart gown is equally convinced she can make the smart perfume to accompany it. And now, when she buys her dress, she buys, at the same time and place, the jewels to complete it.*

*Since the dressmakers have thus summarily taken the designing of jewelry into their own hands, two expected developments have taken place; first, the jewels bear a much closer relation to the gown that formerly; and second, they are not genuine.*

*Once—not so long ago—no lady worthy of the name would have been caught dead or alive, wearing imitation jewelry. To-day even the ladies who have their safety vaults full of genuine stones, have also their complete regalias of imitation jewelry—jewelry so gargantuan and blatant that there is not the smallest pretense that it is genuine. Indeed, that is just where the fun and the chic of the new jewelry comes in. It doesn't consist in a string of pearls so tiny and so meticulously perfect that they really might be real, but in a yard or so of "emeralds" of a size that no real emeralds ever could be; or a yard of "diamond" bracelets up the arm such as the Empress of all the Russians never had. That's the new jewelry!*

*And all this the dressmakers of Paris have brought about. They have made their perfumes the smartest in the world, beating the perfumers at their own game; and now they bid fair to beat the jewelers at theirs. For no jeweler in the world, not all the Cartiers and Tiffanys combined, could turn out jewelry of the stupendous proportions that ladies demand to-day. After all, there is only one Culliman in all the world, and to-day thousands of women are clamoring for their Culliman.*

Designers created special jewelry for "bathing costumes". There were "painted and waterproofed wooden balls for necklaces, bracelets and earrings!" The article stated, "some people will wear them and no doubt look excessively chic."

It took awhile for this new Paris trend on combining jewelry and clothing designs to filter down to the average woman. But by 1936 the concept was so highly accepted that the Sears Roebuck Catalogue featured dresses that came complete with accessories. A "hand smocked dress with matching bracelet and clips" was advertized as the "fashion of the hour" ($3.98). The bracelet was described as a "lovely carved bracelet". The clips were of the same color and material. Another "4 star jubilee feature" was a "satin back crepe dress of Cleanese with handmade scroll trim". A "stunning pin, bracelet and buckle" came with it. The advertisement stated thay were "beautifully carved". They were all most likely made of Bakelite.

A look at a Montgomery Wards Catalogue for Fall 1928-29 gives some interesting insight regarding the average American woman's dress on the eve of the stock market crash. The "featured fashions" were direct from New York and Paris. Hemlines had already begun to drop below the knee. Silhouettes were long with accent on the hip line. Silk crepe, canton crepe, and silk georgette were popular materials. They came in intriguing colors such as marron glace (cocoa), Monet (bright) blue, English (dark) green, Chiente (deep) red, and Claret red. The most expensive dress in the catalogue was $24.98. Many styles ranged in price from $9.98 to $15.98. There were even a few dressy dresses in the $5.98 to $6.98 price range.

Wrap coats with fur trim were in fashion. They were all shown with side buttons at the hip line. Raccoon coats were popular. Montgomery Wards Catalogue described them as "the youthful raccoon fur coat which you see on every college campus and at every sports or social gathering of the fall and winter." The price was $265.00.

The Montgomery Ward 1928-29 Catalogue included twenty pages of jewelry. The "latest novelties in necklaces" were a crystal, peach, topaz, or sapphire colored stones (similar to the one on page 205); a 16" length of composition beads interstrung with gilt beads and a central ornament (1 x 1-1/4") in either sapphire blue, amber, rose, or light green colored glass (98 cents); and "to complete the smart outfit- indestructable pearls, a full 56" long (98 cents).

Pearls were by far the most popular necklace in the 1920's. The perfecting of the cultured pearl caused the price of Oriental pearls to decline but not enough to enable the average working girl to buy them. For her there were the "reproduction" or "indescructible" pearls. The Montgomery Wards Catalogue pictured them in many prices and sizes. A strand of pearls with "a beautiful opalescent hue, carefully matched in color and perfectly graduated in size" was guaranteed not to break, crack, peel, or discolor and was priced at only $9.95. For the more budget minded customer a 24" length of imported French pearls was priced at $.98.

Pearls were always considered to be in good taste. An essential accessory for a woman's wardrobe, they are worn with both day and evening dresses. The 60" rope was advertised to be "a favorite with our customers." Other standard lengths were 15", 18", 24", and 30".

Many "new rhinestone ornaments" were pictured in the catalogue. A rhinestone flexible bracelet about 5/8 x 6-1/2" with a white metal back was $1.00. An oval cameo pin about 1-1/2 x 1-3/4" with three rhinestones on each side was $.79. Belt buckles and shoe ornaments in the modern style were the most pictured rhinestone ornaments.

Synthetic stones were highly advertised. The man-made sapphires and rubies were set in 10, 14, and 18 Karat filligree mountings. Let this be a warning, a stone can be in a lovely 18K gold mounting obviously made in the twenties and still be synthetic. They were advertised to have "all the brilliance, all the hardness of genuine mined stones—the same rich color and the same sparkling luster." Prices ranged from $4.98 to $13.75.

Birthstones were very popular. Most were placed in white gold filligree rings, but they were also available in lavalieres and pins. A filligree "Birthmonth Bar Pin" in 10K white gold with a "small round stone" was priced at $1.98. Today it would bring 30 to 50 times that. Almost all the Birthmonth jewelry was in white gold becaused it resembled platinum, which was so popular at the time.

The dramatic look of onyx in a white gold mounting made it a favorite for rings. They were available in 14K gold and usually included a diamond set in the onyx. One ring pictured in this combination was "enhanced by the decorative raised pierced setting that holds the diamond ($12.75)." A more Decco looking dinner ring described as an "artistic 14K white solid gold ring with genuine black onyx and genuine diamond with an oval cut center" was priced at $6.98. Again it would easily be worth 20 times that amount today.

Styles in wedding rings were changing. The gold wedding band had been replaced by one of platinum engraved with orange blossoms of flowers. For the first time matching wedding and engagement rings were available. The J.R. Woods & Sons Catalogue for 1927 states: "This usually appeals to the prospective bridegroom and insures the sale to him of the wedding ring. Many times the wedding ring can be picked out at the same time as the engagement ring and laid away until just before the marriage. Also at the time it is quite possible to tell the customer about the returning custom of men's wedding rings which should match the brides. Wide-awake jewelers often make three sales instead of one."

By 1928 these "wide-awake" jewelry companies were combining the wedding ring and the engagement ring into a bridal set. The Montgomery Wards Catalogue pictured four priced from $29.85 (an 18K white gold engraved band, matching engagement ring set with a one eighth carat diamond) to $166.35 (a solid platinum set that had a 3/8 carat diamond).

In the twenties the emphasis was on youth. Everyone wanted to be young. The easiest way to hide the years was to cover them with cosmetics. Elizabeth Arden and Helena Rubenstein capitalized on the craze and became leaders in the industry. Lips were painted a la Clara Bow. Powder and rouge became necessities. "In the year 1929 every American woman bought more than one pound of powder and eight rouge compacts. There were 1,500 brands of face cream and 2,500 different perfumes."[12]

Catalogues pictured "smart new compacts." They were available in round, rectangular, and octagonal shapes, and each had its' own little chain handle. The white metal cases were engraved and most had emaneled plaques (see page 227). Inside the compact was a mirror and a place for powder and rouge. Refills could be purchased in most stores.

By looking through the Montgomery Ward Catalogue for 1931-32 it is very apparent that something had happended to the economy. Prices had dropped drastically! The most expensive dress "direct from the New York opening" was only $3.94. Quite a difference when compared to the $24.98 price in the 1928-29 catalogue.

The catalogue also pictured longer dresses. Throughout the decade the hemline gradually lowered. In 1931 it was at mid-calf; by the fall of 1933 it had dropped to between the calf of the leg and the ankle.

The biggest influence on fashion in the thirties was Hollywood. People escaped their problems for a few hours by going to the movies. There they were exposed to the newest in fashion, bigger than life on the silver screen. In 1933 Adrian, a fashion designer for Hollywood, stated, "Motion Pictures are becoming the Paris of America. There, when women see the stars in pictures they can see them as their fashion guides."[13]

Clothing retailers were quick to realize the tremendous influence that the stars had on the American women. The Montgomery Ward 1931-32 Catalogue featured "styles worn at Hollywood First Nights". Next to their lovely "Sun Down frock of luxurious silk canton crepe with graceful shoulder bows of transparent velvet" ($4.74) was a picture of Claudette Colbert "exotic Paramount star" and an invitation to see her in her newest film "Death Takes A Holiday." With coats advertised to be "Hollywoods' favorite Models" was a picture of Helen Twelvetrees also a Paramount star. Another advertisement assured that "Hollywood favors smartly tailored sports coats." It featured Marlene Dietrich as "Paramount Pictures tailored queen. See her in 'Song of Songs'."

The 1935-36 Sears Roebuck Catalogue featured "autographed fashions worn in Hollywood by the stars". The advertisement for a "lovely smocked dress ($3.98)" claimed to be "a fashion in the wardrobe of the exquisite Hollywood star, Adrienne Ames. Each dress bears her autographed label." In the section that advertised collars, stars such as Ann Southern and Marion Nixon were shown wearing their "autographed fashions". The hat section pictured six hats ($1.69—$1.98) modeled by their namesake stars. Who could resist the urge to buy one after seeing how smart it looked on the star?

Movie fashions became big business. An article about the Modern Merchandising Bureau in New York City appeared in the January 1937 issue of Fortune Magazine. It explained that "the work of the Bureau consists of providing retail shops with models of hats and dresses worn by the stars of current films, but it is a good deal more complicated than it sounds. First of all, the Bureau has to study the stills of coming attractions and figure out what styles are going to be

240

popular. Then it has to arrange with a manufacturer to have them made up before the picture is released. And finally it has to supply retail shops with advertising that mentions the movie from which the model was taken and the theatre at which it is playing."

In April of 1937 National Business published "a 12,000 Mile Style Parade" by Edgar Lloyd Hampton. He commented on the fact that Hollywood was the "world's style capital" and that young American designers were creating movie fashions that were changing the clothing habits of the nation.

First on the list we might mention the 'sex dress,' that close fitting gown which caused so many automobile accidents back around 1930. It established a vogue for the tight-fitting dress and influenced the styles of the entire world. To a yet greater degree has the movie influenced the youthful styles of clothes, and for 'girls of every age.'

A specific example of a definitely-creted new style ws the High-Tie which they put around Clara Bow's waist a dozen years ago, sweeping the flappers of that period into an entirely new vogue. Paris later modified this tie into a narrow girdle involving the waistline of everything from a street suit to an evening gown, and the world forthwith adopted it as its own.

Another example, and it caused our ultra-fashionables to shudder when it appeared upon our streets, around 1924, was a little hat which the younger movies stars wore pushed back against their foreheads. Yet within a year the smartest thing in the Paris fashion plates was a hat cut close across the forehead and pushed clear back against the hairline. Of this type of hat the movies created two distinctive designs—the small hat, and the brimless hat—and the camera was responsible for both, because the camera is unalterably opposed to brims. The electrician can do nothing with a face concealed beneath a drooping brim.

Slacks were a Los Angeles invention. Yet no merchant anywhere took them seriously. So the manufacturer put them on beautiful movies stars—with the studios cooperating—and gave the photographs to the press. As one manufacturer laughingly put it: 'They looked so darned cute that every woman wanted them.'

That many of these styles should turn into world vogues is equally apparent. For never in history has a group of people been so much admired and so persistently imitated as the movie stars. These stars appear on the screen wearing the most elaborate and harmonious garbs that genius can conceive and cash produce.

Hollywood stars were used to advertise a variety of products. A Doublemint Gum advertisement in the May 1939 issue of Good Housekeeping pictures Joan Blondell and Dick Powell, "two great Hollywood stars". It states that "they are happily married and have two children." Joan Blondell is said to have originated the hairstyle she is wearing in the picture. "It ties in a small curly cluster at the back of the neck." The advertisement stressed that "in Hollywood the chewing of delicious Doublemint Gum is a popular pastime, and, ladies, note the lovely face contours of attractive Joan Blondell. Many Beauty Specialists find that the excerise of chewing Doublement Gum vigorously several times a day, while gently lowering and raising your head, helps to keep that youthful chin line admired by all."

The word chic became the byword of the 1930's. It was used to describe anything that was "in." "Chic" was the ultimate compliment. Glamourous, swanky, slinky, and stunning were other adjectives that vividly described the mood staged by Hollywood.

Glamourous Jean Harlow was the envy of women everywhere. She made the slinky bias cut dress popular, and it was worn to proms, weddings, and coming-out parties. Women loved the chance to be feminine again. Backs were rediscovered, and dresses with "intriging open spaces" in the back became fashion news.

In 1935 Helen Koues wrote this fashion report for Good Housekeeping Magazine:

> Our new silhouette again shows full skirts over smooth hips for day and evening wear. Full sleeves for the day, with loose-backed fingertip coats, fitted short coats, and capes—long capes to the floor, short capes to the hips—all with the simplicity that is both feminine and new. Sailor hats are with us again. And taffeta for morning, noon, and night in patterns varying from tiny strawberries to great modern splashes of color. The evening clothes were never lovelier, never more feminine; ruffles, great sashes, taffetas, and nets; or the scarves of the mysterious East find occidental use. And so women once again, although she flies a plane or runs a motor, goes back to feminine wiles and Furbelaws; but she remains attuned in action to a swiftly moving world in which she plays an ever increasing part in the affairs of men.

Out of the emphasis placed on modern styles by the Exposition des Arts Decoratifs in Paris came the Neo-modern School of Dress Designers. According to an article in The Deliniator of October, 1936 they created clothes that were "logical and inevitable for modern life" and gave them "arresting perfection by harmony, line and fabric". Alix Schiaparelli, Robert Piquet, and Marcel Rochas were named as creators in the new school. Several of their designs for Butterick Patterns were illustrated. One of the dresses had a "swinging hemline fourteen inches off the floor, broad shoulders and a slim waistline". It featured the "new, young, alert silhouette" that was popular. A long dress with "sculptural lines that follow the supple body of the modern woman" was pictured. Its "glistening cire satin falls in the unbelted princess line and the bodice is slit and clasped together with a bowknot clip," stated the article. The coat featured was described as having "princess lines to follow the structure of your body to the waistline and then flare away from your long slender legs". (Did they assume that all women had long slender legs?) The "fulness of the sleeves and wide revers" were said to "give breadth to the top of the coat above the belted waistline".

Because the economy was depressed and money was tight, the important part jewelry could play in revitalizing an old outfit was stressed. Even though the Montgomery Ward Catalogue of 1931-32 featured fewer dresses and lower prices than in 1928-29, their jewelry section had been expanded. A new dress might cost two or three dollars, but an old one could be dressed up with a new 56″ length of "unbreakable imitation pearls" for only 29 cents.

The emphasis was on costume jewelry. Evidently Montgomery Ward had a high concept of costume jewelry. Their 1931-32 catalogue advertised that "the smartest and most attractive of new costume jewelry creations" was made of genuine rock crystals combined with "sparkling genuine diamond centers". The "richness and beauty" of the stones were "further enhanced by the delicate tracery of pierced designs". These Lalique type jewels were set in both 10 and 14 Karat white gold. The 14K pendant was $21.75; a 14K ring $14.85; and a 10K bracelet was $16.50. Today these pieces would cost twenty times that amount.

For those who could not afford diamonds the "new smart silver jewelry with real "stones" provided a flashy look. The "real stones" were "genuine marcasites", and their glitter provided the glamorous look dictated by Hollywood designers. The jewelry had a slightly heavier look than that of the previous decade. The long dangling rectangular earrings and necklaces were definitely in the style now referred to as Art Decco. A necklace on a 15″ chain with ear drops and bracelet to match, made of sterling silver and set with marcasites, was priced at $4.48.

Marcasites were also used to surround other stones. Genuine Chrysoprase (jade green), genuine onyx (black), and genuine cornelian (burnt orange) were set in sterling silver and "studded with sparkling real marcasites". These were very popular, and a good many examples are still in existence today. A complete set consisting of a necklace, ear drops, bracelet, and gold ring sold for $7.98. Today the same set would cost in excess of $300.00

If a piece of jewelry was done in the new modern style, this fact was always brought to the attention of prospective buyers. "Another example of pleasing modernism in genuine stone set jewelry" was the "hand carved genuine stones linked with a washed gold sterling silver chain." They were available in a choice of Rose Quartz, Amethyst Quartz, and Jade. The pendants sold for $2.48, and the bracelets were $5.98. Throughout the decade the term modernistic was used to describe the styles now referred to as Art Deco.

Not everything was designed in the modernistic style. Several pieces of jewelry listed as "the kind grandmother wore," were illustrated in the 1935-36 Sears Roebuck Catalogue. The advertisement stated, "Antique designs are new again. Modernized into up-to-the minute accessories. Natural gold color metal with just a trace of black enameling outlining the engraved designs will give a rich added touch to most any costume and has the appearance of much more expensive jewelry." These modernized antique designs could be ordered in bracelets, dress clips, brooches, or button earrings. They could never be mistaken for Victorian pieces. Even with the black enameling they still looked very Decco.

In the September 1934 issue of Country Gentleman, Ruth Hogeland noted that "the quaint old victorian fashions of using lovely slim ladylike hands with frilled cuffs as ornaments has reached to the costume jewelry field. Now we have beautifully carved composition ones in white or bright colors, serving as clips. They come singly or in pairs." The materials and colors used for these pieces assures that they will never be mistaken for Victorian.

Rhinestones continued to be popular throughout this time period. The 1935-36 Sears Roebuck Catalogue called them the "most necessary, useful costume accessories for the fall and winter season". They offered "the newest creations direct from the leading New York Stylists". The designs were "reproduced from high priced models", and the rhinestones were "set in white platinum-like metal" that was "rhodium finished to prevent tarnishing". Another advertisement made it quite clear that "rhinestones can be worn with any costume—for daytime or evening".

The Sears Roebuck Fall and Winter Catalogue for 1936-37 noted that "nothing adds to the costume more than a rhinestone ornament. Adding a brilliant buckle or clip to a dress gives it an entirely new appearance. Sears offers the newest styles, most modern designs, copied from expensive Paris creations. Only the finest rhinestones are used. They are set in highly polished metal mountings, closely resembling platinum." A flexible bracelet, button earrings, a belt buckle, and dress clips were illustrated. Each piece was $.95. Rhinestones were truly the jewelry for the masses.

"Massiveness is an important note in jewelry," stated an article in Collier's for November 11, 1933. "A bracelet set with great square-cut topazes may be echoed by two square topazes that make a ring heavy as a mans. Clips, worn singly or in pairs, to ornament a hat, a bag or to drape a neckline, are larger than ever."

Clips were a very versatile accessory. They could be worn on the dress, hat, or hand bag. Consequently, they became a necessity for the well groomed woman. The Independant Woman stated in November, 1937, "Clips are always good. Newest are the large gold ones, either plain or set with jumbo-sized chunks of bright stones. These clips need not be expensive—just so long as the effect is good."

Costume jewelry designs are indeed an indicator of what has captured the minds, hearts, and imagination of the people. In the 1920's the discovery of King Tut's tomb made it fashionable to wear jewelry bearing his likeness. Many Egyptian motifs were incorporated into Art Decco designs. When Franklin D. Roosevelt became President of the United States, he and his family became the favorite subject for newspaper and magazine articles. Even his Scotch Terrier, Fala, was photographed. By 1935 women were wearing pins in the shape of a Scottie. The Sears Roebuck Catalogue for that year featured three variations of the "Scottie Dog Pin": one about 2″ long with a black carved head in a choice of dull gold or silver color (48¢); another was a "carved design on pressed wood" in an "Ivory-Tan color, size 1-3/4 x 1-1/2″ (10¢); the third was an enameled in natural colors, size 1-1/2 x 1″ (19¢).

Women were intrigued by things from the Orient. Lounging pajamas with an oriental look were worn for entertaining at home. Jewelry made in China, and stones imported from the Orient became very fashionable. Some good examples of this type of jewelry can be found on page 275.

The economy had an effect on ring designs. Smaller diamonds were placed in illusion settings to give them a larger look. In the twenties wedding bands were often encircled with diamonds, but in the thirties the diamonds were only set across the top. Business Week, September 10, 1938, said that diamond imports had been small because jewelers were selling from stock. The article was optimistic because "jewelers are luring the customers back into their shops again with other come-ons. Feminine fashion this year is of course, the jewelers delight. The ladies are supposed to wear their hair pulled up on their heads this year, and this exposed a large expanse of neck and ear for the jewelers to cover. They're concentrating on such pre-1900 items as pendant earrings, big necklaces, jeweled combs, barrettes, hair-clips, and even (God forbid) tiaras. Gold jewelry set in semi-precious stones, which haven't been around in a number of years, is back on their shelves. And so is flower jewelry."

# ART DECO

There is much discussion and confusion concerning Art Deco. Generally it is a term applied to a decorative style of the twenties and thirties. But the term was never used during the time in which the style was popular, thus adding to the confusion.

Perhaps the confusion as to what constitutes Art Deco can be attributed to the many varied influences that combined to produce the style. The Russian Ballet, Cubism, King Tut, the Bauhaus and the Paris Exposition all contributed to the collage that became known as Art Deco.

As in most period styles, the seeds of the style were sewn in the previous decade. When Dieghilev's Russian Ballet Company made its debut performance in Paris in 1910, it won the hearts and imagination of all Europe. The bold colors in the scenery and costumes designed by Leon Balst signaled a liberation of color for the "pastel" world. By the twenties his bright emerald greens, vivid reds, and "shimmering" blues, along with his stenciled patterns and luxurious fabrics had become incorporated into all fields of fashion and design.

Through the set designs of the Ballet Russes, many people were exposed for the first time to "Modern Art". Cubism and its offspring—orphism, neoplastecism, fauvism, and futurism —provided the geometric lines and abstract designs for Art Deco style. The new art oxpressed a psychology of design for people living in a modern world, a world filled with action and speed.

When Howard Carter discovered the opening to a tomb in Egypt on November 26, 1922, little did he realize the impact it would have on modern fashion. When the discovery was officially announced three days later, it was publicized throughout the world. Never had there been such a discovery! Newspapers were filled with descriptions of the many ancient objects made of gold. The riches of the young king were almost beyond belief.

By the time the burial chamber was opened in February, 1923, King Tut and his world had already influenced fashion and design. Women were wearing Tut hats and jewelry bearing his likeness. Stones used in King Tut's jewelry—lapis lazuli, cornelian, chaldecony—became popular. Egyptian motifs such as the falcon, vulture, and scarab were seen on everything from belt buckles to pendants. At first these unusual materials and designs were used in copies of the ancient articles, but it was not long before they were assimilated in to the Art Deco style.

Art Deco takes its name from the International Exposition des Arts Decoratifs which was held in Paris in 1925. Nations from all over the world were invited to participate with the stipulation that they submit only those exhibitions executed in new modern designs. Any designs based on styles of the past or that incorporated those styles were strictly forbidden.

The November 1925 International Studio Magazine reported on the exhibit. Their opening paragraph gives an insight to the style of the exposition:

> When Cezanne uttered his historic dictum that all form could be reduced to the cone, the cylinder, and the cube, the cornerstone was laid for a movement which had its fullest expression in the International Exposition des Arts Decoratifs in Paris. Cezanne's esthetique, the credo of modern art, was developed simultaneously with the age of scientific research and the glorification of the machine. Both of these are determining factors in the development of the new decor. It was, however, due to Cezanne's pronouncement that we substituted the philosophy of the angle for the curve, that we came to see that the intersection of two planes might be as beautiful as the relation of two colors, and that beauty was as existent in mere mass and proportion as in ornamented shapes. It is due to this that we have learned that designs whose inspirations are the clean lines of the machine may be quite as beautiful as those deriving from animal, human or flower forms. To have absorbed consciously or not this esthetique is a necessary prequisite to an enjoyment and appreciation of the new note for which the International Exposition des Arts Decoratifs stood sponsor.

For hundreds of years sources from the past had provided inspiration for designs. The time had come for something new. "Gone are the time honored motives of the lotus and the fleur de lis, the Doric column and the Gothic arch. In their place we are asked to see as beautiful and decorative, angles and geometric designs; instead of ornamentation, flat surfaces and proportioned masses. Gone is all carving and superimposed decoration; interest and variety must depend upon the application of color and flat design, or the quality of beauty existing in the unadorned material."[14]

The exposition also provided tangeable evidence of the

many influences on modern design. "In the modern decor there are evidences of the Wiener Werkstaede, Munich Succession, Swedish and Polish peasant art, English Pre-Raphaelitism and French Cubism," stated the International Studio. It described the expostion as "looking like nothing so much as a Picasso abstraction".

The article acknowledged the importance of the Exposition and stated, "With the Exposition des Art Decoratifs a new style is established to take its place with the historic periods. To the Renaissance, the Jacobean, the Georgian, The Rococo and the Colonial is added the modern. It can no longer be said to be in a state of experimentation representing isolated examples by the more venturesome of the designers. It is a concerted movement representing the fruit of many minds and many years' experience. For the first time there is revealed to the public the spirit and achievement of the whole modern decorative art movement, in the form of architecture, interior decoration, furniture, the arts of the silversmith, the jeweler, the worker in metals, and the designers of textiles and wallpapers." The Exposition became the focal point for the new modernistic designs. They gained world acknowledgment. In the years that followed, the style became more defined.

Knowledge of all these varied influences on the Art Deco style shatters the veil of confusion and makes it easy to identify. Today almost anything done in the Art Deco style is very collectible. Because of this demand, jewelry can be quite expensive. That is not to say that bargains cannot be found. They can, especially in costume jewelry. Examples of the Art Deco style can be found on pages 268-273.

### Emerald

Emeralds have been popular since before the time of Cleopatra, but their rich green color made them especially desirable for the jewelry of the 1920's and 30's. The gem is at its best when used in the rectangular or square step cut that is also known as the emerald cut. It was well suited to the geometrical shape of Art Deco jewelry designs.

The emerald is part of the beryl group of colored stones. Prized for its medium light to medium dark green color, in larger sizes it is sometimes more expensive than a diamond of the same size. All genuine emeralds have inclusions referred to by gemologists as a "jardin". Often stones of the most desirable color also contain the most inclusions. These are more desirable than a pale stone with little "jardin".

The most beautiful emeralds come from Columbia. They are so esteemed that the finest emeralds from any location are known as Columbian emeralds. Other deposits are mined in Brazil, Rhodesia, Australia, South Africa, and India. In the United States emeralds are found in North Carolina, Maine, and Connecticut.

Man has always been fascinated by the emerald. In ancient times it was believed that gazing at an emerald would restore eyesight. Many wore it because they believed it would heighten intelligence and help them to save money. Today it is a favorite birthstone for people born in May, hopefully bringing them success and love.

## Ruby

Rubies both genuine and synthetic were widely used in the 1920's and 30's. Their bold red color helped create the dramatic effect that was so much in demand.

The ruby is part of the corundum group of colored stones. To be termed a ruby it must have a transparent red or purplish red hue. The lighter red stones are known as pink sapphires. "Pidgeon's blood" red is the most desirable color and is identifiable by a slight blue cast in the pure red stone. These and other rubys are known as Burmese, regardless of where they are mined. Ruby deposits are found in Burma, Thailand, Ceylon, and Africa. In the United States they are mined in Montana and North Carolina.

Biblical references attest to the high value placed on the ruby throughout the ages. A large ruby is sometimes more valuable than a diamond of comparable size. The ruby's hardness makes it a practical stone with a multitude of uses.

Fortunate is the person born in July because the ruby is the birthstone for that month. Wisdom, wealth, and health are but a few of the many blessings that are believed to belong to the wearer of this lovely gem.

## Marcasites

In the 1920's and 30's the average woman could add glitter

and glamour to her life by wearing marcasites. Their reflective sparkles adorned pins, earrings, necklaces, bracelets, clips, and buckles.

The "stone" known as marcasite is actually pyrite (PIE-rite). There is a mineral named marcasite, and, although it is similar in appearance, it is not suitable for jewelry. This case of mistaken identity is now commonly accepted. The iron sulphide, pyrite is cut into small pointed or rounded facets to create "marcasites". Since their luster is metallic, their brilliance comes from light reflecting off the facets.

Marcasites were a fashionable substitute for diamonds as early as the 1700's. They were always mounted in silver as were the diamonds of that period. In the mid 1800's they once again came into favor. The fashion waned until the glittering mood of the twenties revived it again.

Within the last year marcasite jewelry has risen sharply in price. Better marcasites are set in and not just glued. Of course, the metal the "stones" are in and the design of the piece are also factors that greatly influence price. There are many new marcasite pieces on the market. Buying from a reputable dealer who will guarantee in writing the age of the piece, is the best assurance for the new collector.

Many good examples of marcasite jewelry can be found on pages 269-276.

### Ivory

Ivory, one of the oldest materials used for ornamental purposes, has been recognized throughout the history of civilization for its beauty and value. In the 1920's a resurgence of interest in African carvings brought with it a renewed interest in ivory.

As most people know, ivory is the tusk of the African Elephant. But many do not realize that the tusks of the hippopotamus and walrus are also classified as ivory. Elephant ivory is distinguishable by its "cross hatched" or "engine turned" look when viewed under magnification. The other ivorys have wavy grain lines. Once the ivory has been carved into bracelets, necklaces, and earrings, it is very hard to distinguish its origin.

The so-called vegetable ivorys, the coroze nut from South America and the doum-palm nut from Central Africa, are often mistaken for genuine ivory. They are used to make beads and smaller items. A way to distinguish between vegetable and animal ivory is listed in the "Is it Real?" section of this book.

Ivory tends to yellow with age, but according to expert dealer Edward J. Tripp, this only adds to its value. It can be bleached, but this takes away value and beauty. He also cautions against subjecting ivory to extreme changes in temperature that could cause cracking or splitting. Since ivory is porous and is easy to stain, care should be taken to keep it away from anything that might discolor it.

## Bakelite

Jewelry made of bakelite was popular during the 1920's and 30's. This new plastic was invented in 1909 by Leo Hendrick Baekeland (1863-1944). He came up with the resin while trying to develop a new type of varnish.

Bakelite is a phenolic plastic and can be moulded or cast. Jewelry items are moulded. The name Bakelite is a trade name for the Bakelite Corporation. The same mixture is known as Durez when made by the Durez Companay and other names when manufactured by other companies.

# IV. The Jewerly—1920-1930's

IV-1. **Lavalier—1915-25**—10K Yellow Gold with sapphire and baroque pearl 1-32/8 x 1-1/2″ Original 14″ chain. $195.00 (Jeanenne Bell Dealer)

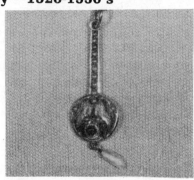

IV-2. **Lavalier—1915-25**—10K Yellow Gold with amethyst and seed pearls. 1-1/2 x 1-3/4″ $235.00 (Camille Grace Dealer)

IV-3. **Lavalier—1915-25**—Gold Filled with genuine opal and baroque pearl on new gold filled chain 3/8 x 1-1/2″ $95.00 (Jeanenne Bell Dealer)

IV-4. **Lavalier—1915-20's**—10K White Gold with aquamarine and pearls. 5/8 x 1-3/4″ L. $150.00 (Camille Grace Dealer)

IV-5. **Lavalier—1910-20's**—14K Yellow and green gold with rubies and pearls. 1-3/8 x 1-1/2″ $295.00 (Camille Grace Dealer)

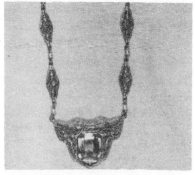

IV-6. **Necklace—1920's**—10K White and yellow gold with blue stone and pearls. 15″ L. Drop 1-3/8 x 1″ $245.00 (W. Baldwin Collection)

IV-7. **Necklace—1920**—Silver filligree with blue stones in drop. 1 x 1-1/2" Chain is 16" L. $75.00 (Jeanenne Bell Dealer)

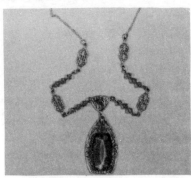

IV-8. **Necklace—1920's**—Silver over brass. Large blue glass drop. Some blue enameling. Drop 1-1/4 x 2" Chain 25" L. $78.00 (Jeanenne Bell Dealer)

IV-9. **Necklace—1920's**—Sterling filligree with black onyx drop 3/4 x 1-1/8" $65.00 (Jeanenne Bell Dealer)

IV-10. **Necklace—1920's**—Sterling filligree on new 16" chain. Paste stones. 3/4 x 1-1/2" $58.00 (Margaret Sorrell Collection)

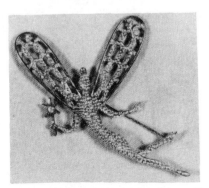

IV-11. **Brooch—1920**—Sterling with rhinestones. Tinkerbell. 3-1/8 x 2-1/2" $100.00 (Camille Grace Dealer)

IV-12. **Brooch—1915-20's**—14K Yellow gold with peridot and enameling. Could just have easily gone in the 1890-1917 period. 1-3/8 x 3/4" $195.00 (W. Baldwin Collection)

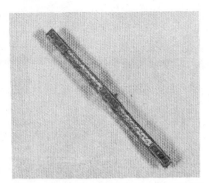

IV-13. **Bar Pin—1915-20's**—10K White and Yellow gold with synthetic sapphired. 2-1/4″ L. $175.00 (W. Baldwin Collection)

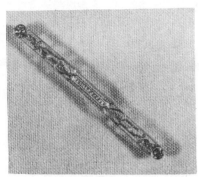

IV-14. **Bar Pin—1910-20's**—10K Yellow and white gold with pearls and peridot 2-3/8″ L. $175.00 (W. Baldwin Collection)

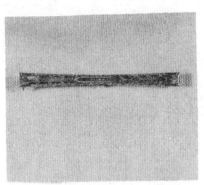

IV-15. **Bar Pin—1920's**—14K White gold filligree 2″ L. $145.00 (W. Baldwin Collection)

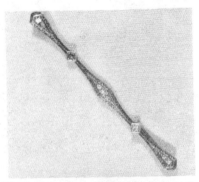

IV-16. **Bar Pin—1920's**—Sterling and Brilliants 2-1/2 x 1/8″ $32.00 (Jeanenne Bell Dealer)

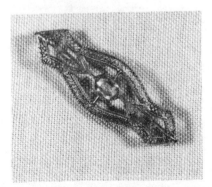

IV-17. **Bar Pin—1915-20's**—10K Yellow Gold filligree with pink stone. 1-1/2 x 5/8″ $145.00 (W. Baldwin Collection)

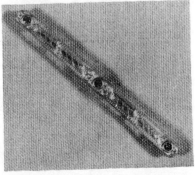

IV-18. **Bar Pin—1915-20's**—Yellow and white gold filligree with synthetic sapphire. 2-1/2″ $175.00 (W. Baldwin Collection)

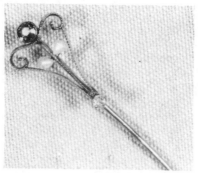

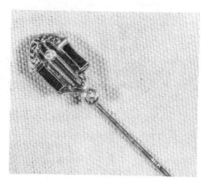

IV-19. **Scarf Pin—1905-20's**—Gold with amethyst, pearl, and 1 diamond $95.00 (W. Baldwin Collection)

IV-20. **Scarf Pin—1915-20's**—White gold. 2 sapphires, 1 diamond. $95.00 (W. Baldwin Collection)

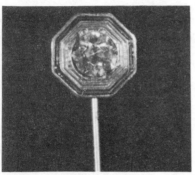

IV-21. **Scarf Pin—1915-20's**—White metal with brilliant and dark blue enamel trim. 3/8″ Dia. $28.00 (Jeanenne Bell Dealer)

IV-22. **Necklace—1920-30—24″** Celluloid chain with drop of clear plastic and simulated jet cameo. Oval. 2-1/4 x 3″ $30.00 (Jeanenne Bell Dealer)

IV-23. **Necklace—1920-30**—Chain with drop of clear plastic with imitation jet cameo of plastic. 2 x 2-1/2″ Chain is 28″ L. $30.00 (Jeanenne Bell Dealer)

IV-24. **Necklace Pendant—1920's—** Celluloid with colored flowers 1-3/8 x 1-6/8″ (Kate Throneberry Collection) $32.00

IV-25. **Necklace—1920's**—Celluloid 1/2 x 2-1/2″ $18.00 (Jeanenne Bell Dealer)

IV-26. **Necklace—1920's**—Silver chain with celluloid imitation ivory. 18″ L. $24.00 (Jeanenne Bell Dealer)

IV-27. **Necklace—1920-30**—Silver over brass. Opaque green "stone" with imitation pearls. 18″ L. $28.00 (Jeanenne Bell Dealer)

IV-28. **Ear Rings—1920-30**—Gold over brass filligree with imitation coral flowers 5/8 x 1-3/4″ $24.00 (Jeanenne Bell Dealer)

IV-29. **Pair of Pins—1920's**—Gold over brass mtgs. Paintings on porcelain. Reflect Florida land boom of the 1920's. 1″ Dia. $65.00 pair. (Jeanenne Bell Dealer)

IV-30. **Beads—1920-30**—Faceted and hand knotted. Marked "Made in Austria" 59″ L. $58.00 (Jeanenne Bell Dealer)

257

IV-31. **Necklace—1920-30**—Gold over brass with imitation pearls. 32″ L. $22.00 (Jeanenne Bell Dealer)

IV-32. **Pendant Necklace—1920's**—Silver over brass chain with clear and green glass. Drop had design etched into back. 1 x 1-5/8″ Overall length is 31″ $68.00 (Jeanenne Bell Dealer)

IV-33. **Beads—1920-30**—Faceted crystal beads 16″ L. x 1/2″ Dia. $38.00 (Jeanenne Bell Dealer)

IV-34. **Necklace—1920's**—crystal Drop 1 x 2″. Necklace length 18 1/2″ $85.00 (W. Baldwin Collection)

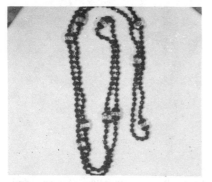

IV-35. **Beads—1920's**—Faceted Jet and Crystal. Hand knotted. 54″ L. $125.00 (Jeanenne Bell Dealer)

IV-36. **Necklace—1920's**—Faceted crystal glass drop on silver plated chain. 16″ L. $58.00 (Jeanenne Bell Dealer)

IV-37. **Beads—1920-30**—Gold over brass clasp. Jet beads. 17″ L. $75.00 (Jeanenne Bell Dealer)

IV-38. **Glasses and Chain—1920's**—mkd. 1/10 12K GF. chain barrell mkd. Kitchall McDougall, Montclair, N.J. $48.00 (Jeanenne Bell Dealer)

IV-39. **Eyeglass Longnette—1915-25**—14K Gold. Diameter of glass 1-1/2″. $250.00 (W. Baldwin Collection)

IV-40. **Same as 39** opened.

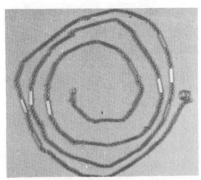

IV-41. **Chain—1915-20's**—10K Yellow Gold (heavy) 25″ L. $369.00 (Jeanenne Bell Dealer)

IV-42. **Pin Locket—1920-30**—Gold over copper with Basse-taille enameling. Green ground with pink flowers 1-1/2 x 2-1/2″ $35.00 (Jeanenne Bell Dealer)

IV-43. **Necklace—1920-30**—Hand carved bone. Approximately 9-1/2 MM. $38.00 (Jeanenne Bell Dealer)

IV-44. **Necklace—1925-30's**—Plastic used to imitate carved ivory. 16″ L. $16.00 (Jeanenne Bell Dealer)

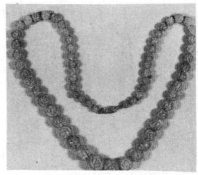

IV-45. **Necklace—1928-30's**—Glass, amethyst, and crystal. 15″ L. $55.00 (W. Baldwin Collection)

IV-46. **Necklace—1920's**—14K Clasp, carved coral flower beads. 17″ L. $350.00 (W. Baldwin Collection)

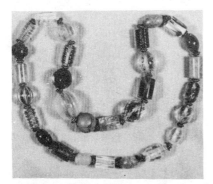

IV-47. **Necklace—1920-30's**—Beads of cornelian, amethyst, rose quartz, rock crystal, jade, torquoise, peking glass. Hand carved. 21″ L. $500.00 (W. Baldwin Collection)

IV-48. **Bracelet—1920-30**—Silver over brass clasp. Faceted black and crystal beads with opaque glass beads 7″ L. $9.00 (Jeanenne Bell Dealer)

IV-49. **Locket—1920-30's**—Gold Filled. 2″ Dia. $55.00 (Anne Noblitt Collection)

IV-50. **Pair Buckle Pins—1915-30**—Sterling Silver with pearls. 1 x 1-3/8″ $100.00 (W. Baldwin Collection)

IV-51. **Garter Buckles—1920's**—14K 1 x 1-1/2″ $150.00 (W. Baldwin Collection)

IV-52. **Garter Buckles—1920's**—14K 1 x 1-1/2″ $150.00 (W. Baldwin Collection)

IV-53. **Necklace—1930's**—Gold over white metal. Place for 2 pictures. (See 54 opened.) 2 x 1-3/4″. Chain 16″ L. $38.00 (Jeanenne Bell Dealer)

IV-54. **Bracelet—1930**—Same motif as 53. 2 x 1-3/4″ Chain 6″ L. $32.00 (Jeanenne Bell Dealer)

IV-55. **Lavalier—1920-30**—10K Yellow Gold with peridot. 3/4" Dia. $195.00 (Camille Grace Dealer)

IV-56. **Brooch—1920-30**—Gold over brass 3 x 2-1/2" $18.00 (Jeanenne Bell Dealer)

IV-57. **Necklace—1925-30's**—Plastic with rhinestones on original hand woven cord 39" L. 1-3/8 x 2" $58.00 (Jeanenne Bell Dealer)

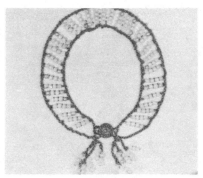

IV-58. **Necklace—1920-30**—Gold over brass with imitation pearls and coral 1-1/4 x 16" L. $24.00 (Jeanenne Bell Dealer)

IV-59. **Button—1920's**—White metal and fabric 2-1/4" Dia. $15.00 (Jeanenne Bell Dealer)

IV-60. **Buckle—1920's**—Bakelite with enameled metal head. This is 1/2 of buckle. 2-3/4 x 2-1/2 $24.00 (Jeanenne Bell Dealer)

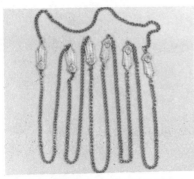

IV-61. **Necklace—1920's**—Gold over brass chain with King Tut. 52″ L. with 6 Tuts. 3/4 x 1-1/8″ $38.00 (Jeanenne Bell Dealer)

IV-62. **Pin—1925-30**—Mkd. 10K. Egyptian motif with marbelized glass scarab and baroque pearls 2 x 1-1/4″ $145.00 (Camille Grace Dealer)

IV-63. **Pin—1920-30**—Copper over base metal. Egyptian motif. 1-1/4 x 1-1/2″ $18.00 (Jeanenne Bell Dealer)

IV-64. **Cross—1920-30**—Ivory. Hand carved on silk cord. 1-3/4 x 2-1/2″ $68.00 (Jeanenne Bell Dealer)

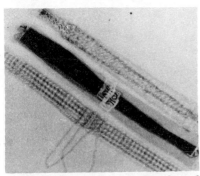

IV-65. **Watch Bands**—Top: pearls and imitation Sapphire. Pat'd 2-7-22. Middle: Ribbon Watch Band. Bottom: Imitation pearls mkd. 1/10 14K G.F. Pat'd Nov. 9, 1926 FELCO. $12-15 .00 (Jeanenne Bell Dealer)

IV-66. **Watch Chain—1920's**—White metal. Slipped on to belt and allowed watch to fit in pocket. 7″ L. $28.00 (Jeanenne Bell Dealer)

IV-67. **Baby Necklace—1915-20's—**
Yellow Gold Filled with new gold filled
chain. $28.00 (Jeanenne Bell Dealer)

IV-68. **Locket—1915-20's—**Gold over
brass with original black ribbon. 1/4 x 2"
$38.00 (Jeanenne Bell Dealer)

IV-69. **Necessary—1915-20's—**Sterling.
Place for Rouge, Powder, and Coins.
2-3/8 x 3-3/8" $200.00 (W. Baldwin Col-
lection)

IV-70. **Necklace—1920's—**Gold over
brass with celluloid cameo 1 x 1-1/4"
$12.00 (Jeanenne Bell Dealer)

IV-71. **Brooch/Pendant—1915-25—**10K
Wedgewood 1-1/8 x 7/8" $300.00
(Camille Grace Dealer)

IV-72. **Brooch/Pendant—1920-30—**900
silver with shell cameo and marcesites
1-1/4 x 1-1/2" $165.00 (W. Baldwin Col-
lection)

IV-73. **Brooch/Pendant—1915-20's** —800 silver. Nicely done shell cameo. 1-1/4 x 1-3/4" (Camille Grace Dealer) $195.00

IV-74. **Brooch/Pendant—1915-20's** —10K Yellow and green gold with pink coral cameo. 1-1/2 x 1-3/4" $350.00 (Jeanenne Bell Dealer)

IV-75. **Brooch—1920's**—Mkd. "Sterling made in England" Glass cover over plastic figure with shining blue background. 1-1/2" Dia. $38.00 (Jeanenne Bell Dealer)

IV-76. **Necklace—1920's**—Silver over brass. Glass "stones" with white cameo heads. 15" $28.00 (Jeanenne Bell Dealer)

IV-77. **Necklace—1915-20's—10K** white gold with some yellow gold. Shell cameo and pearls. 1/2 x 5/8" original chain. $195.00 (Jeanenne Bell Dealer)

IV-78. **Brooch/Pendant—1920—10K** Yellow Gold mtg. Shell cameo. 1-3/8 x 1-3/4" $400.00 (W. Baldwin Collection)

IV-79. **Brooch—1915-20's—**10K Yellow gold, pink coral cameo 1-1/4 x 1-5/8" $295.00 (W. Baldwin Collection)

IV-80. **Brooch/Pendant—1915-20's** —10K yellow gold mtg. Shell Cameo. 1-1/4 x 1-5/8" $295.00 (Jeanenne Bell Dealer)

IV-81. **Brooch/Pendant—1915-20's** —14K yellow gold. Coral cameo. 1-1/2 x 1-5/8" $350.00 (Camille Grace Dealer)

IV-82. **Brooch/Pendant—1915-20's** —14K coral cameo 1-1/2" Dia. $400.00 (W. Baldwin Collection)

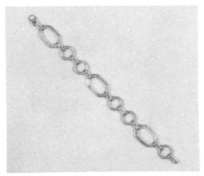

IV-83. **Bracelet—1920's—**Silver with engraved designs. 5/8 x 6-1/2" $32.00 (Jeanenne Bell Dealer)

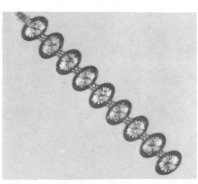

IV-84. **Bracelet—1920's—**Copper with black enameled ground and pink, green, orange, yellow, and white flowers. 1 x 7" $28.00 (Jeanenne Bell Dealer)

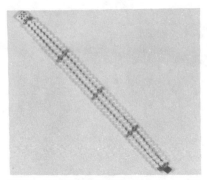

IV-85. **Bracelet—1920's**—Sterling Fittings with 3 rows of imitation pearls strung on sterling chain. 7″ L. $35.00 (Jeanenne Bell Dealer)

IV-86. **Bracelet—1915-20's**—Silver filligree with topaz stone 3/8″ wide. $85.00 (Anne Noblitt Collection)

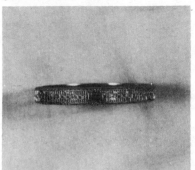

IV-87. **Child's Bracelet—1915-20's**—White metal with glass ruby. Hinged Bangle 1/4″ wide. $38.00 (W. Baldwin Collection)

IV-88. **Hinged Bracelet—1920's**—Silver plate filligree with pink glass "stone." 5/8″ wide $75.00 (Jeanenne Bell Dealer)

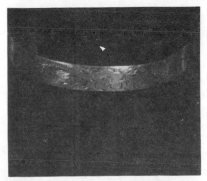

IV-89. **Hinged Bracelet—English hallmark 1921**—Sterling 3/8″ wide. Heavy. $95.00 (Jeanenne Bell Dealer)

IV-90. **Hinged Bracelet—1920-30**—Gold Filled with wedgewood type center. 3/4″ wide $65.00 (Jeanenne Bell Dealer)

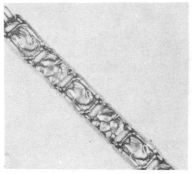

IV-91. **Bracelet—1920-30's**—830 silver. mkd. Georg Jensen 7/8″ wide x 7-1/4″ L. $600.00 (W. Baldwin Collection)

IV-92. **Bracelet—1930**—Silver over brass 1″ wide Bangle. $38.00 (Jeanenne Bell Dealer)

IV-93. **Hinged Bracelet—1930's**—Gunmetal with imitation cut steel design. 1″ wide with safety chain. $24.00 (Jeanenne Bell Dealer)

IV-94. **Pair of Hinged Bracelets—1920-30's**—White metal with black enameling and silver ornamentation. 1/2″ wide. Oval shape. $80.00 pair. (Jeanenne Bell Dealer)

IV-95. **Brooch—1920-30**—Gold over brass with colored "stones." 3-1/2 x 2-3/4″ $18.00 (Jeanenne Bell Dealer)

IV-96. **Necklace—1920-30**—Imitation Marcasite. 43″ L. including orignal ribbon (see IV-97)

IV-97. **Matching Belt—1920-30—** Adjustable 5/8" wide x 35" L. Set: $65.00 (Jeanenne Bell Dealer)

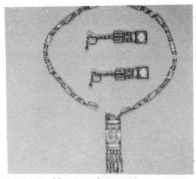

IV-98. **Necklace and Ear Rings—1920-30—**Sterling with lead crystal Baguette. One tassle hangs in front and one in back. 23" L. Note clasp location. Ear Rings 1/2 x 2-1/2" $150.00 (Jeanenne Bell Dealer)

IV-99, **Necklace—Art Deco—** Plastic with Marcasites on original cord complete with slide. Cord 35" L. Drop 1-1/2 x 3" $60.00 (Jeanenne Bell Dealer)

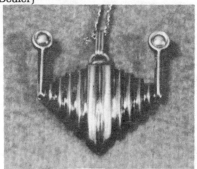

IV-100. **Brooch/Pendant—Art Deco—** 1/12 10K Gold filled. 1 x 1-1/4'' overall. New Gold Filled chain. $30.00 (Jeanenne Bell Dealer)

IV-101. **Necklace—Art Deco—**Sterling with hemetite and marcasites. 16" L. Center drop 3/4 x 1-1/2" $225.00 (W. Baldwin Collection)

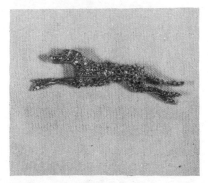

IV-102. **Pin—1930's—**Sterling. Marcasites. Greyhound showing popular speed motif of Deco style. 2-1/4 x 5/8'' $75.00 (W. Baldwin Collection)

269

IV-103. **Necklace—1925-30's**—Jade Green Bakelite drop with imitation marcasite on dog. New sterling chain. 1-3/4 x 1-1/2" L. $38.00 (Jeanenne Bell Dealer)

IV-104. **Pin—1930's**—White metal. Lizard design with imitation marcasites. Red glass eyes. 2-3/4" L. $28.00 (Jeanenne Bell Dealer)

IV-105. **Brooch—1930's**—Silver over base metal. Imitation marcasites. 2-1/8 x 1-5/8" $18.00 (Jeanenne Bell Dealer)

IV-106. **Bow Pin—1920-30's**—Silver mtg. with marcasites and torquoise center stone. 1-7/8 x 3/4" $85.00 (Jeanenne Bell Dealer)

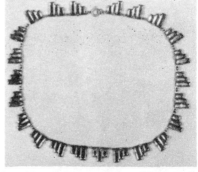

IV-107. **Ear Rings—1920's**—Deco. Silver with marcasites 1-1/2". L. $80.00 (Jeanenne Bell Dealer)

IV-108. **Necklace—Deco**—Silver over brass. Mkd. Czechoslovakia. Emerald colored glass baugettes. 1/2 x 16" L. (see 109)

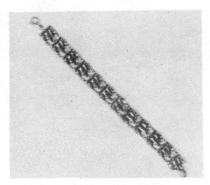

IV-109. **Matching Bracelet**—(see 108) 7″ L. $75.00 Set (Jeanenne Bell Dealer)

IV-110. **Locket—1930's**—Silver. Black enameling on original chain with marcasites 30″ L. $200.00 (Camille Grace Dealer)

IV-111. **Pendant—1930's**—Mkd. Sterling Germany. Marcasites and Chrysoprase surrounded by black enamel. 7/8 x 1-1/2″ L. $175.00 (Camille Grace Dealer)

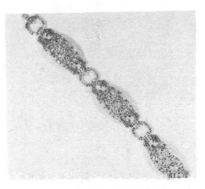

IV-112. **Bracelet—1930's**—Silver and marcasites Mkd. "Made in France" 7/8 x 7-1/2″ $250.00 (Camille Grace Dealer)

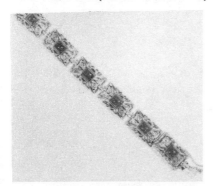

IV-113. **Bracelet—1930's**—Mkd. Sterling Germany. Marcasites with Chrysoprase 3/4 x 7-3/4″ $180.00 (Camille Grace Dealer)

IV-114. **Necklace—1930's**—Sterling with hematite and marcasites 7/8 x 1-3/4″ Drop. Chain 15″ L. $145.00 (Camille Grace Dealer)

271

IV-115. **Cigarette Case—1930's**—Silver with Marcasites 3-3/8 x 2-7/8″ $550.00 (W. Baldwin Collection)

IV-116. **Brooch—1930's**—Sterling. Marcasites $45.00 (Camille Grace Dealer)

IV-117. **Brooch—1930's**—Silver over white metal chrysoprase and Marcasites. 2 x 1-5/8″ $98.00 (Camille Grace Dealer)

IV-118. **Brooch—1930's**—Silver with marcasites and aquamarine colored stone 2 x 1″ $145.00 (Camille Grace Dealer)

IV-119. **Necklace—1920-30**—Sterling. Lapis and Marcasites. Chain 18″ L. Drop 7/8 x 2″ $150.00 (W. Baldwin Collection)

IV-120. **Necklace Drop—1930's**—Silver mtg. Shell cameo with marcasites. 3/4 x 1″ $125.00 (Camille Grace Dealer)

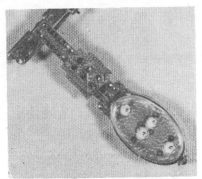

IV-121. **Pin Watch—1920-30's—**935 Silver with Marcasties. Watch is beautifully enameled with pink flowers "C. Bucherer." 1-3/16 x 2-3/4" $695.00 (W. Baldwin Collection)

IV-122. Back view of watch in IV-121

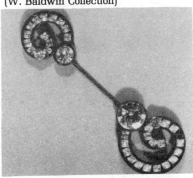

IV-123. **Hat Ornament—1930's—**Plastic with rhinestones. 1 x 3-1/4" L. $18.00 (Jeanenne Bell Dealer)

IV-124. **Necklace—1930's—**Silver over brass with blue glass and small black rondells strung on wire. Drop 1-3/4 x 1-1/4" overall length 15-1/2" $38.00 (Jeanenne Bell Dealer)

IV-125. **Necklace—1930's—**Small hand cut black bead strand woven together 3/4" wide x 15" L. $38.00 (Jeanenne Bell Dealer)

IV-126. **Necklace—1930's—**40 strands of small hand cut beads. Lapis blue color. Note clasp. Approximately 2 x 18" L. $65.00 (Jeanenne Bell Dealer)

273

IV-127. **Brooch—1930's**—Sterling. Chrysoprase. 1-3/4″ Dia. $100.00 (W. Baldwin Collection)

IV-128. **Pin Watch—1930's**—14K Gotham Swiss Watch. 1-1/2 x 2-1/8″ overall. $575.00 (W. Baldwin Collection)

IV-129. **Necklace—1920-30's**—Yellow Gold over brass. Imitation lapis stone 22″ L. $38.00 (Jeanenne Bell Collection)

IV-130. **Necklace—1930**—Oxidized metal with large blue glass "stones" and small ones in colors of pink, green, topaz, and brilliant 1-1/2 x 2-1/2″ $20.00 (Jeanenne Bell Dealer)

IV-131. **Brooch and Ear Ring Set— 1930's**— White metal painted navy blue with blue glass "stones." Brooch 2-1/4 x 3″ Ear Ring 5/8 x 1-5/8″ $30.00 Set. (Jeanenne Bell Dealer)

IV-132. **Necklace—1930**—Gold over brass chain with cornelian and pearls. Chain 19″ L. $48.00 (Kate Throneberry Collection)

IV-133. **Pin—late 1930's**—Sterling. Dutch girl with umbrella 1-5/8″ L. $42.00 (Peggy Carlson Collection)

IV-134. **Pin—1920-30**—Mkd. China with hand carved cornelian stone 2-1/8 x 7/8″ $80.00 (Camille Grace Dealer)

IV-135. **Pin—1920-30's**—Silver over copper. Mkd. China hand carved lapis stone 2-7/8 x 1-1/4″ $98.00 (Camille Grace Dealer)

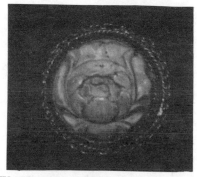

IV-136. **Ring—1920-30's**—Gold over copper, mkd. "China", hand carved. Torquoise stone 7/8″ Dia. $85.00 (Camille Grace Dealer)

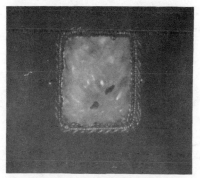

IV-137. **Ring—1920-30's**—Gold over copper, mkd. "China". Hand carved rose quartz 5/8 x 3/4″ $85.00 (Camille Grace Dealer)

IV-138. **Clip—1930's**—Brass with Mother of Pearl. 2-3/8 x 3-3/4″ $24.00 (Jeanenne Bell Dealer)

275

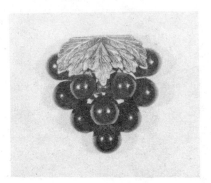

IV-139. **Clip—1930's**—Gold over brass leaves and clip with Bakelite grapes. 2 x 2" $22.00 (Jeanenne Bell Dealer)

IV-140. **Clip—1930's**—Deco. Sterling with onyx and Marcasites. 5/8 x 1" $34.00 (Jeanenne Bell Dealer)

IV-141. **Dress Clip—1930's**—Oxidized metal with green, red, topaz, and blue stones. 1-3/4 x 2" $22.00 (Jeanenne Bell Dealer)

IV-142. **Pin—1930's**—Mkd. "Sterling Denmark". Attributed to Georg Jenson a Danish sculpturer. 1-1/8 x 7/8" $95.00 (Camille Grace Dealer)

IV-143. **Brooch—1930's**—Mkd. Sterling 1-7/8 x 1-1/2" $95.00 (W. Baldwin Collection)

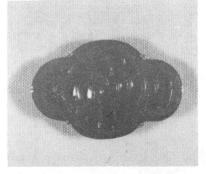

IV-144. **Brooch—1920-30**—Mkd. Sterling Germany. Cornelian. 1-7/8 x 1-1/4" $90.00 (W. Baldwin Collection)

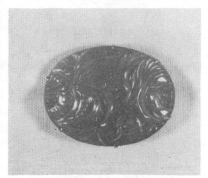

IV-145. **Brooch—1920-30**—Mkd. Sterling Germany. Chrysoprase stone 1-5/8 x 1-3/4" $85.00 (W. Baldwin Collection)

IV-146. **Locket-1920-30's**—Gold Filled. Mkd. S. B. & Co. 2 red stones surrounded by clear stones. 1-5/8" Dia. $55.00 (Jeanenne Bell Dealer)

IV-147. **Locket—1925-30's**—Gold Filled. Mkd. F & B 1" Dia. $48.00 (Jeanenne Bell Dealer)

IV-148. **Strap Holder—1920-30**—Silver over brass. Green enameling on links of chain. $28.00 (Jeanenne Bell Dealer)

IV-149. **Ear Rings—1920's**—Faceted crystal with new 14K wires. 3/8 x 1/2" L. $38.00 (Jeanenne Bell Dealer)

IV-150. **Ear Rings—1930's**—Gold Filled Mtg. Agate dropes. New 14K gold post. 1-7/8" L. $45.00 (Jeanenne Bell Dealer)

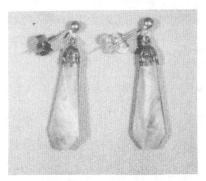

IV-151. **Ear Rings—1930's**—Gold Filled mountings with marblized green glass drops. New gold post. 1-5/8″ L. $22.00 (Jeanenne Bell Dealer)

IV-152. **Ear Rings—1925-30's**—Gold Filled. Blue marblized glass. 1 x 1-7/8″ $45.00 (Jeanenne Bell Dealer)

IV-153. **Ear Rings—1920-30**—Gold Filled. Mkd. Czechoslovakia. Blue moulded glass. 1 x 2″ L. $48.00 (Jeanenne Bell Dealer)

IV-154. **Ear Rings—1930-40**—Gold Filled. 3/4″ Dia. $28.00 (Jeanenne Bell Dealer)

IV-155. **Ear Rings—1920-30's**—Gold over brass with imitation lapis. Mkd. Czechoslovakia. 5/8 x 1-3/4″ L. $58.00 (Jeanenne Bell Dealer)

IV-156. **Brooch—1930's**—mkd. "Sterling Silver German" Enameled flower with marcasites. 2 x 1-3/4″ $100.00 (Camille Grace Dealer)

IV-157. **Brooch—1930's**—Gold over brass with amethyst colored glass stones. 2-1/2 x 3" $28.00 (Jeanenne Bell Dealer)

IV-158. **Brooch—1920's**—Sterling Denmark with enameling 1-1/4" Dia. $75.00 (W. Baldwin Collection)

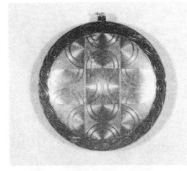

IV-159. **Compact—1925-30's**—White metal with navy blue enameling. Mkd. Evans. 2-3/8" Dia. $65.00 (Jeanenne Bell Dealer)

IV-160. **Back of IV 160 Compact**

IV-161. **Compact—1930's**—White metal with soft yellow and black enamel. Mkd. Evans. Place for Rouge and Powder. 2-1/4" Dia. $85.00 (Jeanenne Bell Dealer)

IV-162. **Vanity Case—1920's**—White metal with enameled plaque. 2-1/8 x 3-1/2" $45.00 (Jeanenne Bell Dealer)

279

IV-163. **Vanity Case and Coin Holder**—One identical to this in Montgomery Ward 1928-29 Catalogue. White metal with enamel plaque 2-1/2 x 2-1/8″ $48.00 (Jeanenne Bell Dealer)

IV-164. **Necessary—1920-30**—Beautifully enameled to wear on finger. Separatge lipstick. 2-1/8 x 2-1/4″ $125.00 (Camille Grace Dealer)

IV-165. **Belt Buckle—1930's**—Cut steel 2-1/2 x 1-7/8″ $48.00 (Jeanenne Bell Dealer)

IV-166. **Belt Buckle—1930's**—Cut steel 2-3/4 x 1-3/4″ $48.00 (Jeanenne Bell Dealer)

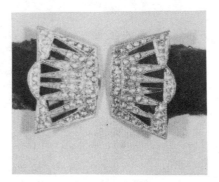

IV-167. **Belt Buckle—1930**—White metal mkd. "B" Rhinestones. 2-1/2 x 1-3/4″ $24.00 (Jeanenne Bell Dealer)

IV-168. **Brooch—1920's**—Gold over brass. Venetian glass mosaic. Done in older style. 1-1/2 x 1-1/8″ $55.00 (Jeanenne Bell Dealer)

IV-169. **Bracelet—1920's**—Gold over brass with cream colored celluloid inset. 3/4″ wide $24.00 (Jeanenne Bell Dealer)

IV-170. **Beads—1920's**—Cherry amber graduating from 8 MM to 1/2″ 23″ L. $550.00 (W. Baldwin Collection)

IV-171. **Necklace—1920-30's**—Gold Filled on 28″ G.F. Chain Drop 1-1/4 x 2″ L. $28.00 (Jeanenne Bell Dealer)

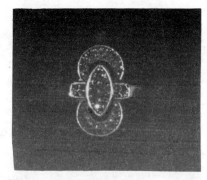

IV 172. **Ring—1930's**—Mkd. "Sterling Germany." Marcasites 3/4 x 1″ $125.00 (Jeanenne Bell Dealer)

IV-173. **Ring—1930's**—Sterling. Marcasites 1 x 1/2″ Some damage so only $95.00 (Jeanenne Bell Dealer)

IV-174. **Ring—1930's**—Mkd. Silver. Marcasites beautifully done. 1/2 x 3/8″ $145.00 (Jeanenne Bell Dealer)

IV-175. **Ring—1930's**—Sterling. Hemetite surrounded by Marcasites 1 x 1-1/8" $145.00 (Jeanenne Bell Dealer)

IV-176. **Ring—1930's**—Mkd. Sterling Germany. Onyx with marcasites. Head 5/8 x 1" $125.00 (Jeanenne Bell Dealer)

IV-177. **Ring—1930's**—Sterling with marcasites and enameling. 7/8 x 1-1/4" $250.00 (Camille Grace Dealer)

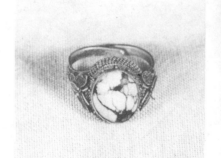

IV-178. **Ring—1930's**—Silver. mkd. "China" with torquoise 3/4" Dia. $95.00 (Lucille and Sam Mundorff Dealers)

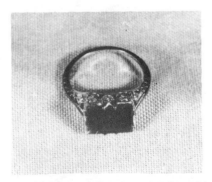

IV-179. **Ring—1920's-30's**—14K White Gold filligree with synthetic ruby. Head 3/8 x 7/16" $295.00 (W. Baldwin Collection)

IV-180. **Ring—1930's**—Silver. Marcasites and cornelian. 3/4 x 1-1/8" $140.00 (Lucile and Sam Mundorff Dealers)

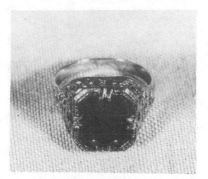

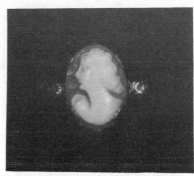

IV-181. **Ring—14K White gold filligree with almadine garnet.** $295.00 **(W. Baldwin Collection)**

IV-182. **Ring—1920-30—**1/30 14K R.G.P. Shell Cameo and 2 white stones 1/2 x 5/8″ $48.00 (Jeanenne Bell Dealer)

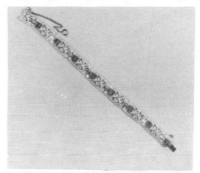

IV-183. **Bracelet—1930-40—**Bakelite 1-1/0″ wide hinged $28.00 (Jeanenne Bell Dealer)

IV-184. **Bracelet—1920-30—**Rh. finished white metal 1/21 x 7″ $65.00 (Jeanenne Bell Dealer)

IV-185. **Clip Lorgnette—1920-30's—**White metal. Dress clip lorgnette wilth rhinestones $225.00 (Camille Grace Dealer)

IV-186. **Same clip as 185—**Opened.

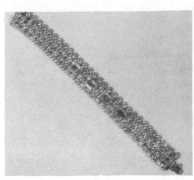

IV-187. **Tie Tack-1930's**—Gold over white metal. Snake motif. 3/4" Dia. $12.00 (Jeanenne Bell Dealer)

IV-188. **Bracelet—1925-35**—Rhinestones with blue baugette stone. Nicely done 3/8 x 7" L. $55.00 (Jeanenne Bell Dealer)

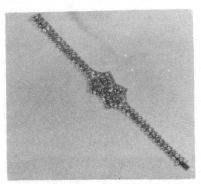

IV-189. **Bracelet—1920-30**—Rhinestones set in bow motif 1" wide x 6-3/4" Long. $48.00 (Jeanenne Bell Dealer)

IV-190. **Belt Buckle—1920-30**—Cut steel with velvet inserts. 2-1/2 x 3" $35.00 (Jeanenne Bell Dealer)

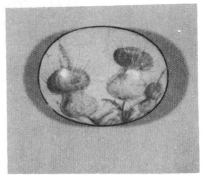

IV-191. **Pin—1930-40**—Wood. Hand painted. To wear on beach. 2 x 1 1/2" $12.00 (Jeanenne Bell Dealer)

IV-192. **Brooch—1920-30**—Sterling bezel with nicely done shell cameo. 1-1/4 x 1-5/8" $155.00 (Jeanenne Bell Dealer)

IV-193. **Wrist Watch—1920's**—Sterling case and bracelet. Movement marked ABRA-watch Co. Geneva 6 J. 2 adj. $95.00 (Jeanenne Bell Dealer)

IV-194. **Wrist Watch—1920's**—Mkd. Rolled Plate white gold. Movement Mkd. Solomon Watch Co. Swiss. 6 jewels-2 adj. $85.00 (Jeanenne Bell Dealer)

IV-195. **Wrist Watch—1930's**—14K Gold Filled case. Movement mkd. Helbrose Watch Co. 7 jewels-Swiss. Celluloid and leather watch band, $80.00 (Jeanenne Bell Dealer)

IV-196. **Locket—1930-40**—Gold over brass on new Gold Filled chain 1 x 1-1/4" $32.00 (Jeanenne Bell Dealer)

IV-197. **Bracelet—1930-40**—Gold over brass. Hinged bangle with safety and black enameling. 1" wide $75.00 (Jeanenne Bell Dealer)

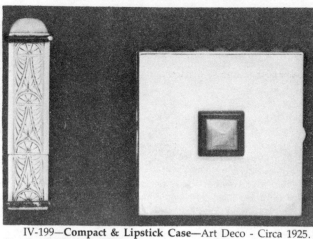

IV-199—**Compact & Lipstick Case**—Art Deco - Circa 1925. Gold, Jade and Lapis. Berlioz-Leroy, Paris-Cannes. $1,980 (A) (Photo courtesy of Sotheby's New York 12-7-83)

IV-198—**Necklace**—Circa 1920. Platinum openwork set with old European cut diamonds and 2 pear shaped sapphires (approx. 9cts.). The chain is set with 49 collet-set diamonds (approx. 5cts.) The pendant is detachable. Black, Star & Frost Co. $9,900 (A) (Photo courtesy of Sotheby's New York 4-10-84)

IV-200—**Brooch**—Circa 1920. Platinum and gold set with 2 carved jade leaves spaced by scroll motifs embellished with round and single cut diamonds. $715.00 (A) (Photo courtesy Sotheby's, New York 10-5-83)

IV-210—**Brooch**—Art Deco- Black enameled with alternating old brilliant cut diamonds & black Oriental pearls. L5,500 $7,975.00 (A) (Photo courtesy Phillips, London 1-24-84)

IV-202—**Brooch**— Circa 1920. Platinum centered with a lapis lazuli cameo of a soldier with helmet. Embellished with old European cut diamonds. $1,980.00 (A) (Photo courtesy of Sotheby's, New York 10-5-83)

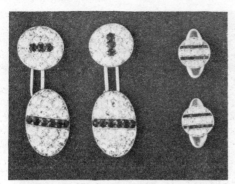

IV-203—**Cufflinks & 2 Studs**—Circa 1920. Gold and platinum set with rubies and old mine diamonds. $2,310.00 (A) (Photo courtesy of Sotheby's, New York (10-15-83)

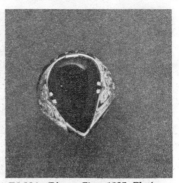

IV-204—**Ring**—Circa 1925. Platinum centered with 1 cabochon ruby (approx. 14cts). Leaves set with 10 marquise-shaped diamonds, 12 baguettes, 24 single cut diamonds and 18 calibre cut rubies (many missing) $2,530.00 (A) (Photo courtesy Sotheby's, New York 10-5-83)

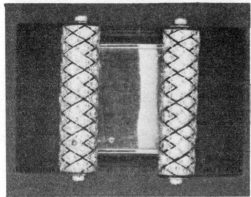

IV-205—**Bracelet**—Art Deco. Circa 1925. Gold and Platinum with black enamel and diamonds. Cartier, Paris. $6,600.00 (A) (Photo courtesy Sotheby, New York 10-19-83)

IV-206—**Double Clip Brooch**—Art Deco. White gold with circular, step cut and kite shaped aquamarines and diamonds. Le Roy et Fils. L1,600 $2,320.00 (A) (Photo courtesy Phillips, London 10-18-83)

IV-208—**Bracelet**—
Circa 1925. Platinum
pierced mounting
set with round and
old European cut
diamonds and 37
calibre cut sapphires.
$3,850.00 (A)

IV-209—**Lavaliere**—
Circa 1920. Platinum
kite shaped mount
centered with 1
marquise-shaped
diamond (1.20cts.)
and 2 old European
cut diamonds (ap-
prox. 1ct.) Also
embellished with 9
smaller old Euro-
pean cut diamonds
and calibre-cut
rubies. $2,860.00 (A)
(Photos courtesy
Sotheby's, New
York 10-5-83)

IV-207—**Double Clip Brooch**—Art Deco.
White gold with diamonds by Cartier.
L5,400 $7,830. (A) (Photo courtesy
Phillips, London 1-24-84)

IV-210—**Brooch**—Art Deco. Gold hoop with emeralds and sapphires with smaller hoops of diamonds in between. L2,000 $2,900.00 (A) (Photo courtesy Phillips, London 4-20-83)

IV-211-Right—**Bracelet**—Art Deco. White gold square arched panels set with diamonds and citrine. L3,000 $4,350. (A) (Photo courtesy Phillips, London 1-24-84)

IV-212-Far right - Bracelet — Art Deco. White gold set with numerous brilliants and decorated with green paste cabochons and onyx. L7,800 $11,310 (A) (Photo courtesy of Phillips London 1-24-84)

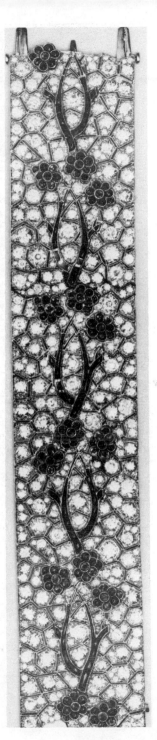

IV-213-Left—**Bracelet**—
Art Deco. Gold with
center diamond approx.
3.5cts. Panels set with
diamonds and ''French''
cut sapphire batons.
L7,000 $10,150 (A) (Photo
courtesy of Phillips, London 6-21-83)
IV-214-Center—**Bracelet**—
Circa 1925. Gold with
black enamel and
diamonds.      L4,180
$6,061.00 (A) (Photo
courtesy Sotheby, Parke,
Bernet and Co. 10-6-83)
IV-215-Right—**Multi-
Colored Stone Bracelet**—
White gold containing
lapis, onyx, carnelian,
amethyst, citrine, jade
with one hundred and
thirty six assorted small
round diamonds approx.
total 5 cts. $16,000.00
(Photo courtesy of Wm.
Doyle Galleries, New
York 9-21-84)

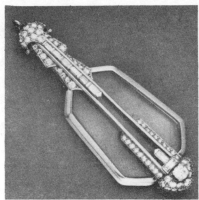

IV-216—**Lorgnette**—Art Deco. Circa 1925. Platinum set with diamonds. $2,475.00 (A) (Photo courtesy of Sotheby, New York 12-7-83)

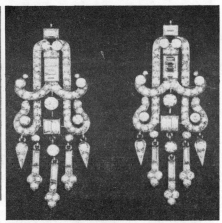

IV-217—**Earrings**—Circa 1925. White gold Girandole design decorated with round and baguette diamonds (lacking fittings). L3,080. $4,466.00 (A) (Photo courtesy of Sotheby Park Bernet, London 12-15-83)

IV-218—**Wristwatch**—Art Deco. White gold set with alternating lines of small brilliant cut diamonds and French cut onyx. Matching shoulders on a bracelet set with onyx plaques and diamonds. L2,600 $3,770 (A) (Photo courtesy of Phillips, London 9-20-83)

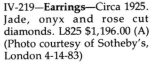

IV-219—**Earrings**—Circa 1925. Jade, onyx and rose cut diamonds. L825 $1,196.00 (A) (Photo courtesy of Sotheby's, London 4-14-83)

IV-221—**Wristwatch**—Circa 1920, 9K gold octagonal case. Rolex nickel level movement, 15 jewels, white enamel dial with Roman numerals. English hallmarks. 1¼'' diameter. $1,760 (A) (Photo courtesy of Sothebys, New York 4-10-84)

IV-220—**Earrings**—Circa 1925. Jade, onyx and diamond. Drops are carved jade. Links are composed of rose cut diamonds. Top hoop is onyx. L495 $718.00 (A) (Photo courtesy of Sotheby's, London 5-12-83)

IV-222—**Pocket Travel Watch**—Black enameled case. "Zenith" 6 cm L170 $198.00 (Photo courtesy of Phillips, London 11-23-84)

IV-224—**Traveling Watch**—Circa 1929. Silver case with black enamel lacquered with bird. 3.50cm 'Le Captive' by Dunhill L160 $232.00 (A) (Photo courtesy of Phillips, London 11-24-83)

IV-223—**Traveling Watch**—Art Deco with simulated black onyx and marcasite bands. 4 cm L180 $261.00 (Photo courtesy of Phillips, London 11-23-84)

IV-226—**Wristwatch**—Art Deco. Gold and diamond. Signed and numbered. Cartier. Fitted Case. L5,000 $7250.00 (A) (Photo courtesy of Phillips, London 6-21-83)

IV-225—**Compact**—Circa 1926. Art Deco. Silver with enameling. 8.5cm x 6.5cm. L140 $203.00 (A) (Photo courtesy Phillips, London 11-24-84)

IV-227—**Brooch**—Art Deco. White gold pave set with old cut and rose cut diamonds. Calibre cut sapphires (some synthetic) set in Grecian key design. L1,900 $2,755.00 (A) (Photo courtesy of Phillips, London 3-22-83)

IV—228**Watch Clip** Art Deco. Oblong dial with black Roman numerals within an asymmetric black enamel border. Individually numbered. By "Cartier". L980 $1,421 (A) (Photo courtesy of Phillips, London 6-21-83)

42

IV-229—**Brooch**—Art Deco. Carved rock crystal vase with a floral bouquet of diamonds, rubies, emeralds and sapphires. Individually numbered. L2,600 $3,770.00 (A) (Photo courtesy of Phillips, London 6-21-83)

IV-230—**Bracelet**—Art Deco. Three rows and two rows of coral beads. Mitre shaped diamond divider and clasp. In fitted case by ''Cartier''. L2,400 $3,480.00 (A) (Photo courtesy of Phillips, London 3-22-83)

IV-231—**Miniature Traveling Clock**—Pink guillouche enameling with white enamel dial and rose cut diamond hands. Grey agate base. Original case. By ''Cartier''. L1,200 $1,740.00 (A) (Photo courtesy of Phillips, London 3-22-83)

IV-232— **Wristwatch**—Circa 1935. 18K man's two toned gold. Bacheron & Constantin, Geneve. Circular nickel lever movement #414241. Three adjustments. 17 jewels, bimetallic compensation balance, silvered matte dial with gold arabic numerals. 14K brickwork strap. $1,320 (A) (Photo courtesy of Sothebys, New York 4-10-84)

IV-233—**Wristwatch**—Circa 1936 - 18K man's Patek Philippe & Co. Retailed by Tiffany & Co. Nickel lever mount, bi metallic compensation balance, 18 jewels, 3 adjs. 1½'' long. $1,650 (A) (Photo courtesy of Sothebys New York 4-10-84)

IV-234-Left—**Ring**—Circa 1920. Plat. mounting set with 3 old European cut diamonds and 27 small old European cut diamonds. (1 missing). $1,320.00 (A)

IV-235- Right—**Brooch**—Circa 1930. Plat. mounting alternately set with 6 square cut sapphires and 9 old European cut diamonds. (approx. 1.50 cts.) Marcus & Co. $1,540 (A) (Photos courtesy of Sothebys, New York 12-7-83)

IV-237—**Necklace**—Circa 1930. Art Deco 5.3mm - 8.4mm jade beads (93) with a carved jade budda seated on a lapis base mounted in a platinum and 18K white gold Further embellished with one oval shaped cabochon emerald, 3 fancy shaped carved emeralds and blue enamel. $7,700 (A) (Photo courtesy of Sothebys, New York 12-7-83)

IV-236- **Bracelet**—Circa 1937. Platinum and white gold centered with one large cabochon emerald with Arabic inscription. Buckle motif set with 184 diamonds (approx. 10 cts.) and 48 calibre-cut emeralds. $14,300 (A)

IV-238—**Brooch**—Art Deco. Circa 1930. Plat. set with rubies, sapphires, emeralds and black onyx. Oriental style bird on a flowering branch. Branches highlighted with black enamel. $9,350 (A)

IV-239-Left—**Ring**—Circa 1930. Plat. centered with
a row of 7 square cut sapphires bordered by small
round diamonds. Marcus & Co. $2,310.00 (A)
IV-240-Right—**Brooch**—Circa 1930. Plat. openwork
mounting centered with oval black opal (approx. 5.50
cts.). Embellished with diamonds. Marcus & Co.
$3,850 (A) (Photos courtesy of Sothebys New York
12-7-83)

IV-241- **Brooch**—Circa 1930. Stylized bunch of
grapes set with cabochon rubies and rose cut and
brilliant cut diamonds. L935 $1,356.00 (A) (Photo
courtesy of Sothebys, London 12-15-83)

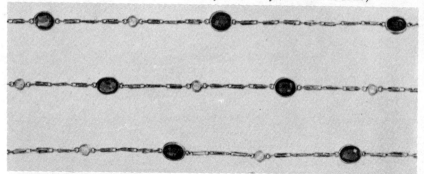

IV-242—**Necklace**—Circa 1930. Platinum chain 56'' long decorated with 30 rubies
and 29 small diamonds. $4,125.00 (A) (Photo courtesy of Sothebys, New York
4-10-84)

IV-243—**Brooch**—Circa 1930. Plat. with
oval crystal centered with a carved opal
depicting a group of grape harvesters. On
each side is a platinum band set with
calibre cut sapphires and old European cut
diamonds. Wadderien. $4,400 (A) (Photo
courtesy of Sothebys, New York 12-7-83)

IV-244—-**Ring**—Circa 1930. Plat. band
of stepped design centered with a row of
square cut emeralds bordered by rows of
diamonds and emeralds. $3,850 (A)

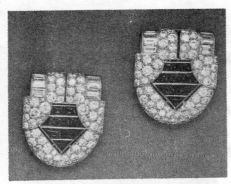

IV-245- **Clips**—Circa 1930. Plat. with arrow motif of 16 calibre-cut rubies. Further embellished with four baguette diamonds (approx. 2 cts.) 12 smaller baguettes and 4 square cut diamonds (totalling approx. 2.20 cts.) $8,800.00 (A)

IV-246- **Brooch**—Circa 1930. Plat. "Arc-De-Triumphe" motif topped by a half-moon shaped diamond (approx. 1.50 cts.) and further set with a total of approx. 4.20 carats of diamonds. Cartier, Paris. $10,450.00 (A)

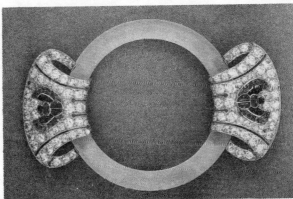

IV-247— **Brooch**— Art Deco. Plat. with center ring of crystal flanked by pave set diamond scrolls decorated with Egyptian style beetle motifs set with rubies, emeralds and black onyx. Fitted box stamped J. Chaumet, Inc. France. $11,500.00 (A)

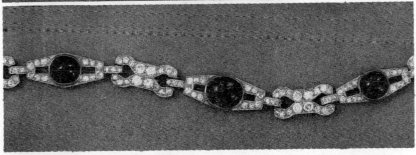

IV-248—**Ring**—Platinum centered with a cushion shaped ruby (approx. 8.12 cts.) surrounded by small round diamonds. $17,050.00 (A)
IV-249—**Necklace**—Circa 1930. Plat. choker set with 9 cabochon rubies (approx. 23 cts.) and 316 old European-cut diamonds (approx. 9.15 cts.). $24,200 (A)

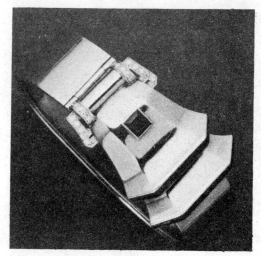

IV-250– **Bracelet**—Circa 1937. 14K gold bangle with bell shaped clip (detachable) set with 1 square-shaped ruby, 26 calibre-cut rubies and 26 single cut diamonds. By Cartier. $4,400 (A) (Photo courtesy Sotheby, New York 10-6-83)

IV-251–Top—**Ring**—Circa 1935. Platinum centered with 1 emerald cut aquamarine (approx. 40 cts.) with 12 round diamonds and 16 calibri cut synthetic rubies. $4,400 (A)
IV-252-Bottom—**Earclips**— Circa 1935. Platinum set with 8 oval shaped rubies (approx. 8 cts.) and 40 baguette diamonds (approx. 2 cts.) $5,225 (A) (Photo courtesy of Sothebys, New York 10-5-83)

# 1940-1950's

## The Times

The forties dawned on a world filled with "Wars and rumors of war". Most Americans did not want to become involved in these foreign entanglements. However, as the European situation changed, people began to think that the United States should give aid to Great Britain. Any indecisiveness about involvement was shattered on December 7, 1941 when the Japanese bombed Pearl Harbor. Shocked and indignant, the country united to fight the enemy.

Everyone pulled together to ease the work load created by the war. Ships, planes, guns, shells, and a million other items were needed to win. There was work for everyone. Almost 18 million women worked outside the home. They discovered they could do jobs that had been traditionally assigned to men and do them well. Many women did volunteer work in blood banks and canteens. Others planted victory gardens and raised a large portion of their food. These activities made them feel like working partners with the men in uniform.

Teenagers gained a more important role in society. With men off to war and women away at work, they were called upon more often. Some were lured away from school at age 14 by high paying factory jobs. In September 1943 McCalls Magazine published an article about the "4-4 Plan." It told of the success many cities had experienced with a program that encouraged teenagers to attend school four hours and work four hours. "The academic program was arranged for these students so that none of the essentials were omitted—." Teenagers without regular jobs did odd jobs and babysitting.

People were earning more money than ever before, but there was little to spend it on. The war had caused shortages in everything from gasoline to sugar. Rationing coupons and points became a part of American life. The slogan "use it up-wear it out-make it do" was enacted daily by people who wanted to do their part in the war effort. Money was needed to win the war, and the public responded by putting its money into War Bonds.

When the war ended August 14, 1945, the people celebrated by ringing church bells, kissing strangers, blowing
whistles, and partying. At last their friends and loved ones
would be coming home. Congress had prepared for the home-
coming by passing the G.I. Bill of Rights. This program provided funds to make the veteran's assimilation back into society
easier. Money was made available for going back to school,
buying a house, or going into business.

In retrospect most people would agree that the fifties were
indeed fabulous. But what they choose to forget is that these
were the years in which America learned to live with fear.
Postwar events had shattered all hope of world peace. Only a
few months before the new decade began, it was learned that
the Russians also possessed "the bomb". People went on with
their lives and continued to dream their dreams, but lurking
in the back of their minds was the haunting fear of annihila-
tion.

The American dream of home ownership led to an exodus
from the city and into the suburbs. The housing industry
mushroomed. Subdivisions seemed to pop up overnight in
places where cows once grazed. New schools were built to
educate the products of the post war "baby boom". Shopping
centers were built to accommodate the needs of these "bed-
room" communities.

The American dependency on the automobile continued to
grow. Father needed a car to get to work, and mother had to
have a way to get the children to dancing lessons and little
league practice. The Sunday drive continued to be popular
even though it often included a ride past the latest home-built
bomb shelter. The automobile and the suburbs became as
much a part of the American way of life as "mom and apple
pie".

For the youth of America the fifties were a great time in
which to be alive. Middle class affluency had provided them
with money to spend. The record industry boomed. A new
rhythm, entirely different from the big band sound, was
emerging. It was based on rock, rhythm, and soul.

In the South white radio stations refused to "air" these
records so the white youth listened to the "colored" stations.
They liked what they heard. The songs of Little Richard and

Fats Domino were different. That's what the new generation wanted. A new dance was needed to fit the new beat. The Bop became popular overnight.

Elvis Presley had this new sound and beat. Teenagers went wild over his records. Within months they were at the top of the charts. Adults were convinced that the girating hips of this new idol would lead teenagers down the wrong path. In fact, many believed that rock and roll was the work of the devil.

In the late 50's the Hoola Hoop had hips all over America girating. Almost everyone who could stand and wiggled tried it. Literally millions were sold.

Television was creating a whole new life style. Family schedules were centered around favorite T.V. shows. One town even experienced a water shortage when Milton Berle paused for a commercial because everyone chose this time to go to the bathroom. Most stations did not start telecasting until late afternoon, but some new T.V. owners were content to look at a test pattern. Shows such as "I Love Lucy, Your Show of Shows, Dragnet, Ed Sullivan," and "Your Hit Parade" were worth the wait. It was new. It was fun. It was fabulous.

# THE FASHIONS IN CLOTHING AND JEWELRY

The war in Europe had far reaching effects on the fashion industry. With France engaged in the war, American designers had to rely on their own expertise to capture the American woman's fancy. The September 8, 1941 Time Magazine stated, "U.S., couturiers, last week and this, unveiled for the first time the American woman package-in-the-U.S." The styles were not as dramatic or "seductively named" as the ones originating in Paris, but the American designers presented "good wearable, saleable clothing. The chief trends of this ingenuity show in slender skirts with slits or 'back drops' which fall much lower behind than in front; 'front peplums' give fullness to tight skirts; the 'deep armhole cut' and 'soft shoulder'."

The United States' declaration of war brought many changes in the American way of life. A War Production Board was formed to regulate production of goods and insure that war needs would be met. Fashions were designed to use as little material as possible. At the same time no dramatic changes were made so that last season's clothes would still be fashionable. The Office of Price Administration suggested that the American housewife make this pledge: "I will buy carefully. I will take good care of the things I have. I will waste nothing." This was quickly paraphrased to "Eat it up. Wear it out. Make it do. Do without". and it became the motto of the war years.

There were shortages in everything from cotton dresses to hosiery. Women used leg make-up instead of nylons. When stores were fortunate enough to receive shipments, there were always more customers than stockings. Bloomingdales in New York solved this problem by allowing customers to buy two pair of stockings with each War Bond purchased. According to Business Week, February 20, 1943, Bloomingsdales sold all 3,000 pairs within 40 minutes, and War Bond sales "totaled $39,000".

The jewelry industry was also experiencing its share of shortages. The September 5, 1942 Business Week reported: "Sales are at high level, but present bread-and-butter stock

McCall's, Sept. 1943

303

can't be replenished. The most serious shortage is metals. The supply of silverplate and of inexpensive jewelry made from base metals is now strickly limited to inventories that manufacturers and retailers have on hand. There will be no more when these are exhausted. Sterling silver has been widely used to replace the baser and scarcer metals." Consequently, if a piece of jewelry is marked 1/20 12K on Sterling or G.F. on S.S., it was probably made during these years.

The War Production Board also limited use of imported silver. "Under the recent W.P.B. crackdown, manufacturers can continue to use up their stocks of imported silver—purchased mostly at around 35¢ an ounce—until Oct. 1. After that they must use domestic silver, which costs over twice as much, or nothing. War industrial requirements will gobble up whatever silver is obtained as a result of arrangement providing for a 45¢ price for good neighbor producers."[15]

The article noted "important shortages other than metals are cultured pearls, imported from Japan and the Dutch East Indies, and high grade imitation stones which have, in the past come chiefly from Central Europe. The bulk of the trade's largest suppliers—watch manufacturers, makers of silverplate and sterling, and the biggest volume producers of costume jewelry already are wholly or partially engaged in war work for which they are particulary suited virtue of highly precision equipment and staffs of skilled metalworkers."[16]

In spite of these limitations jewelry sales continued to soar. Business Week, April 17, 1943, explained it this way: "With the workers unable to spend their bulging bankrolls on automobiles, refrigerators or silk shirts, jewelry sales (including silver, watches, and clocks) last year hit an all time high of $790,000,000 showing a 30% increase over 1941 and considerable gain over the biggest previous year."

The article also told of more restrictions placed on metals:

Conservation order M-162 prohibited use of platinum and its counterpart, iridium, used as the hardening agent in platinum alloy. Platinum is needed now as a catalyst in producing nitric and sulphuric acids for munitions plants; it is widely used in chemical, electrochemical, and electrical fields as well as in the dental industry. Platinum clad metals are used to prevent metallic contamination of food and vitamins products in critical stages of processing . . .

Also out is rhodium (conservation order M-95), which is used to prevent tarnish in silver products and give them a light plating. And manufacturers are restricted in the use of silver itself, WPB's M-199 allows them 50% of the amount used in either 1941 or 1942 whichever was greater. This allowance must be cut even farther, what with silver being used as a substitute for tin in soldering, for nickel plate, copper, and stainless steel in lining chemical vats and aviation and electrical equipment particularly bus bars for conducting current in electrolytic plants.

In short the use of only two of the jewelers basic materials is wide open—precious stones which can be marketed only in settings of precious metals, and palladium, a platinum metal which the conservative jewelry trade has been reluctant to adopt because it is new to the industry. Deprived of platinum, manufacturers are at last turning to palladium, using unrestricted ruthenium rather than iridium as the hardening agent in its alloy.

Bader and Co. Inc. of Newark, N.J. the world's largest dealer in the platinum metals (palladium, platinum, iridium, rhodium, ruthenium, osmium) has assured jewelers that palladium is an adequate substitute for platinum, and the International Nickel Co. of Canada, LTD., which produces palladium as a byproduct of nickel, is hopefully looking to the jewelry industry to absorb its stockpile, which has long been a drug on the market.

Jewelers, finding no consumer resistance to palladium, show signs of adopting it for postwar marketing of rings, pins, and watches. Consumers cannot distinguish it from platinum, don't mind its being slightly lighter in weight (about the same as a 14 carat yellow gold). The current market value is about 70% that of platinum—OPA's Maximum Price Regulation 309 establishes ceilings at $35 per troy ounce for platinum, $24 for palladium.

Once the palladium backlog is absorbed, current production may not provide a supply sufficient to exclude platinum from an expanding postwar market since platinum is somewhat more plentiful. But now that trade prejudice has been overcome, palladium promised competition for the traditionally treasured white metals.

In September 1944, order L-45 was rescinded eliminating these restrictions on gold and platinum. The jewelers were jubilant! The federal excise tax on jewelry had been raised from 10% to 20% in April, and it was hoped that the easing of restrictions might stimulate sales.

With women performing jobs formally done by men, some basic changes in wardrobes were necessary. The American woman was quick to realize that slacks were the answer. "Starting with the defense industries in England and then hopping the Atlantic, slacks have spread from the purely sports category to all fields of female activity—from air raid work to dressy evening lolling," commented the New York Times Magazine in March, 1, 1942. "It is not great novelty this year to see women hurrying about Manhattan in them during the week, and on a recent Sunday two East Seventies types were seen tramping up the ultra-bourgeois street, Madison Avenue, in flannel trousers and tennis shoes. The sale of slacks in department stores is estimated to be about ten times greater than it has ever been before at this time of year, and dress designers working on new collections are including all sorts of versions of the pants movement, from something strictly for harems to boy's tights cut off just below the knee."

The April 13, 1942 Time Magazine states: "U.S. women by the millions have renounced skirts in favor of slacks. . . . Not since Mrs. Amelia Bloomer created an international uproar in 1849 by appearing in public in voluminous Turkish trousers had such a feminine trouser sensation swept the country. High-school girls in Brooklyn's big Abraham Lincoln High School struck for the right to wear slacks. In Detroit Mayor Edward Jefferies grudgingly admitted that a female employee of the city, forced by priorities to bicycle to work, might do her job in slacks. Pants made good sense for wartime. Lieut. Commander Roy R. Darron ordered women employed in the machine shops of the Alameda Naval Air Station in California to wear pants to work."

There was an alternative for the women who did not want to wear pants—culottes. "Thousands of girls nowadays are doing the marketing, going to first-aid classes, garden-club meetings, and their war jobs on two wheels instead of four," noted Colliers, May 9, 1942. "Well fashions usually more or less express the times in which they appear. The bicycle boom means culottes in a big way. They seem the best answer to what-to-wear-while-pedaling."

Clothing sizes were being standarized. During the late 1930's W.P.A. workers had been used by the Department of Argriculture's Bureau of Home Economics to "measure 147,000 children and 15,000 women".[16] Boy's clothes were the first to receive the fruits of this effort. Sizes were gauged by height and hip measurement instead of the unsatisfactory yardstick of age. Sears Roebuck was the first to apply the information to womens clothing. In 1943 they came out with "36 different sizes in 6 classifications (ranging from junior scale to stout)."[17] Women could find their correct size by measuring their waist, bust, hips, and length.

After the war women had money to spend, and spend it they did. According to an article in Colliers, December 15, 1943:

American women are crazy over jewelry. They spend a billion three hundred million a year on it. The young girls are buying tiny jeweled pins to fasten on demure velvet neckbands. One store reports a brisk sale of butterfly cutouts for a suntan, or initials will be cut in the anklet. The dealers say those combs edged with imitation gold, so popular even a year ago for holding back a page-boy bob, don't sell so much any more; but with fourteen-carat tops, at eighteen dollars a pair for the small ones, they can't be kept in stock. Gold barrettes to hold the hair out of little girls eyes sell for eleven dollars apiece. Gold bobby pins are seven-fifty a pair—gold snowflakes to screw on, of course, are extra. Sterling silver bicycle clips, at five dollars a pair are another popular item. They're good for holding up sweater sleeves—or clipping in slacks legs for that slim, ballet look.

To see what the trend is, you don't have to go into fine jewelry shops. All you have to do is to walk into that old copycat, the five-and-ten. There you'll see sophisticated sunbursts, and dome-shaped earrings and bracelets, replicas of the costly gold ones that are popularly studded with chips of turquoise, diamond and ruby. Elegant, not gaudy, is the world.

Costume jewelry became big business. Many designers switched to the costume jewelry industry during the depression. Their expertise cause the industry to blossom.

In 1946 Providence, Rhode Island, was the costume jewelry capital of the United States. Coro Incorporated, with 2,000 employees and sales of $16,000,000, was headquartered here. This undisputed leader in the industry was founded in 1902 as Cohn and Rosenberger. Later the company was renamed using the first two letters of each name. Coro's high priced line was sold under the name of Corocraft.

Costume jewelry was produced in all price ranges. Trifari, Drussman & Fishel was the style leader. Their jewelry was priced from $10.00 and up. R.M. Jordan was a leader in the medium priced jewelry: $1.00 to $20.00. Monet was known for its tailored jewelry, and Forstner was the leading producer of the popular snake chains.

307

In December 1946 Fortune Magazine noted "the twenties and early thirties were dominated by modernistic patterns, sleek and severe, while the past half dozen years have seen an inundation of Renaissance elegance and Victorian fancy—scroll motifs, flower sprays, sunbursts, nosegays. This trend is continuing with increasingly delicate designs and a strong return of white finishes after the wartime reign of gold. Paris is featuring invisible mountings and flexibility—which increases the shimmer and may increase the interest."

By 1947 Western Wear started to make the news. The lady responsible for this new attire was Marge Riley. Born in South Dakota, Marge spent time on a ranch in Wyoming. Her love for the west led her to design clothes for herself and later others. In 1948 her shops were doing a "six figure" annual business. She designed clothes for Joanne Dru, Roy Rogers, and Gene Autry. An outfit ranged in price from $370.00 to $750.00. Marge's dream was to massproduce Western Clothes the average person could afford.

Dior created the biggest fashion sensation of the decade when he presented his "New Look" in 1947. Women had grown tired of the narrow skirts and squared shoulders of the war years. Dior offered a new feminine look with long (12" off the floor) full skirts, small waist, and rounded soft shoulders. It was a welcomed change!

Nylon was also a welcomed addition to the wardrobe. It has been on the market in the form of stockings, parachutes, and toothbrushes for years, but new developments in weaves and dyes made it the perfect "wash and wear" fabric. How liberating! No longer was a gal dependent on an iron for that fresh look. Nylon also made the perfect petticoat for the "new look". Stiffened nylon called crinolin became part of every woman's wardrobe in "the fifties".

The jewelry used to compliment this new style was huge. It took on larger proportions, just as it did in the 1860's when skirts were widened. Massive rings were so in style that Life Magazine featured a full page of them in April 1952.

Huge earrings were also popular. Look Magazine, May 31, 1955, included an article on "Whopper Earrings". The newest styles were "bigger than silver dollars". Look jokingly called them "ear muffs—summer style". Large pearl buttons, "gold saucers," and bouquets of flowers were a few of the many motiffs.

308

In the mid-fifties, short shorts caused quite an uproar. They were cool, great looking on the right figure, and sure to receive attention. The August 1, 1955 Newssweek included this "short" delemma:

> Some congressman took a dim view of the female knee. A lady who wore shorts in the visitor's gallery, they argued, was hardly a lady. What's more, she impaired the dignity of the House and distracted its members. They asked William (Fishbait) Miller, the doorkeeper, to bar anyone over 10, of the female persuasion who appeared in shorts.
>
> The Senate, on the other hand—older and perhaps less susceptible—was entirely unconcerned by the spectacle. If a lady, even one over 10, wanted to wear shorts in the Senate gallery, she was welcome to do so.
>
> Last week, as Washington sweltered in a heat wave well beyond its normally unbearable summer temperature, the unofficial House rule became a 'silly season' issue. Offended and annoyed by the ban on shorts, a number of women had complained to their congressmen, who looked into this violation of 'constitutional rights.' They found that the Senate maintained its dignity and its equanimity in the presence of bare knees—and the House rule was rescinded.

By 1956 short shorts had become a permanent part of the fashion scene. Most people wondered "What next?" The question was answered by the Chemise. Men could not understand why women would want to wear these "sacks". Jack Nabley of the Chicago Daily News called it "a tent looking for a desert to light on". But women liked them. More importantly (to the manufacturers), they bought them. Even Marilyn Monroe added a few to her wardrobe. "If the sack is truly a crime, as some critics allege, there are some accessories after the fact—accessories such as gloves and hats, and stockings and shoes, costume jewelry and furs," stated the May 5, 1958 Newsweek. It also described the proper accessories for the new Chemise. The relatively plain style required much accessorizing. Jewelry was very important. "The chemise hiked sales 10 percent for Coro, Inc., biggest of the fashion jewelry manufacturers. Hot items: Ropes (of heavy beads), bibs (of several parallel strands), bracelets, and chemise-length (from earlobe to shoulder) earrings."[18]

# V. The Jewelry—1940-50's

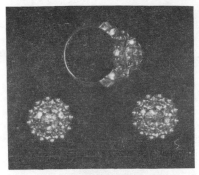

**V-1. Ring and Ear Rings—1940—10K**
Gold Filled with aquamarine colored stone 5/8'' Dia. $195.00 (Jeanenne Bell Dealer)

**V-2. Bracelet—Late 1930-40's—**Plastic section strung on 2 elastic bands. Alternating black and amber colors. Design is incised moulding from the back and painted blue, green and gold. 1-1/4" W. $48.00 (Jeanenne Bell Dealer)

**V-3. Pin and Ear Rings—Early 1940's—**Plastic with design incised in moulding in back and painted. Pin 1-1/8 x 1/2" Ear Rings 3/4 x 3/4" $18.00 Set. (Peggy Carlson Collection)

**V-4.** Ear Rings—1945—White metal, Antiqued Keyhole motif. 1 x 2" $12.00 (Mary Holloway Private Collection)

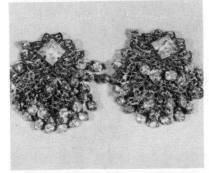

**V-5.** Ear Rings—1945—White metal with rhinestones 1-1/4 x 1-5/8" $18.00 (Mary Holloway Collection)

**V-6.** Ear Rings—Early 1940's—Copper with sterling screws. 1 x 1" $12.00 (Mary Holloway Collection)

V-7. Ear Rings—1945—White metal and rhinestones 3/4 x 1″ $22.00 (Mary Holloway Collection)

V-8. Necklace—1940's—Gold on copper. Drop has green marblized stone with imitation amethyst and pearls. Drop 1-3/4 x 2-1/4″ $28.00 (Jeanenne Bell Dealer)

V-9. **Locket—1940's**—Gold over sterling heart with millitary insignia on Mother of Pearl. New Gold Filled chain. Locket 5/8 x 1″ $32.00 (Jeanenne Bell Dealer)

V-10. **Pin—1940's**—Sterling with gold wash. Anchor motif was patriotic symbol during the war. 3/4 x 1-1/4″ $22.00 (Peggy Carlson Collection)

V-11. Bracelet—1940's—Gold Filled with silver wings insignia. 5/8″ hinged with safety $75.00 (Jeanenne Bell Dealer)

V-12. **Bracelet—1940's**—Gold Filled mesh. mkd. Whiting & Davis Co. 1″ wide. Top design 1-1/4 x 1-1/2″ $58.00 (Jeanenne Bell Dealer)

V-13. **Bracelet—1940's**—Sterling marked "Truant Sterling" Blue "stones" are plastic. 3/4 x 7-1/2" L. $42.00 (Jeanenne Bell Dealer)

V-14. **Bracelet—Early 1940's**—Silver. Heart has jump spring opening. Note plainness in comparison to the one from the 1890's. 7" L. $38.00 (Peggy Carlson Collection)

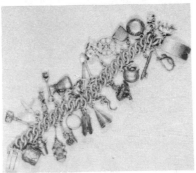

V-15. **Charm Bracelet—1943-45**—Sterling with 26 sterling charms. $295.00 (Mary Holloway Collection)

V-16. **Bracelet—1940's**—Silver with pig skin inserts. 3/4 x 7-3/4" $38.00 (Peggy Carlson Collection)

V-17. **Bracelet—1940's**—10K Yellow Gold with 3 synthetic blue sapphires. 3/8 x 7" L. $250.00 (Jeanenne Bell Collection)

V-18. **Child Bracelet**—Sterling Hallmark. Adj. 1/4" Heavy. $38.00 (Jeanenne Bell Dealer)

V-19. **Hinged Bangle—1940's**—Gold Filled. Beautiful 3/4" wide $165.00 (Anne Noblitt Collection)

V-20. **Childs Bracelet—1940's**—Sterling with yellow and pink gold. Locket 1" Dia. Mkd. "Lusitern-Sterling 1/12 12K G.F. on Sterling" $38.00 (Jeanenne Bell Dealer)

V-21. **Childs Bracelet—1940's**—Yellow Gold Filled with pink and green gold. Expansion type with locket. 3/4" Bracelet 1/2" wide. $38.00 (Jeanenne Bell Dealer)

V-22. **Bracelet—1940's**—Gold over white metal. Hinged Bangle with safety. 3/4" wide. $38.00 (Jeanenne Bell Dealer)

V-23. **Bracelet—1940's**—White metal. Hinged bangles with safety chain. 1-1/4" wide. $38.00 (Jeanenne Bell Dealer)

V-24. **Bracelet—1940's**—Gold over brass with 3 strands of imitation pearls. Clasp 1-1/4" Dia. $10.00 (Jeanenne Bell Dealer)

V-25. **Brooch—1940's**—Mkd. "1/20-12K G.F. Iskin Jewelry" Pink, yellow, green gold with a shining finish. Blue stones. Original Box. $38.00 (Jeanenne Bell Dealer)

V-26. **Childs Bracelet—1940's**—Gold Filled on Sterling 6-1/2" L. $28.00 (Jeanenne Bell Dealer)

V-27. **Necklace and Ear Rings—1940's**—Mkd. "1/20-12K G.F. Art" Original box. Necklace can be worn as a pin. Ear Rings have screw backs. $45.00 (Jeanenne Bell Dealer)

V-28. **Necklace and Ear Rings—1940's**—Gold over white metal. Mkd. "Leo Glass" Topaz colored "stone", original box. Original price $12.95. Now $48.00 (Jeanenne Bell Dealer)

V-29. **Necklace and Ear Rings—1940's**—Silver finished white metal with amethyst color stones. Original box with original price of $5.00. Pretty enough to wear out tonight: $55.00 (Jeanenne Bell Dealer)

V-30. **Pin and Ear Rings—1940's**—Mkd. "1/20 12K G.F. on Silver Carl-Art Inc. Providence, R.I." In original box. Original price $21.50 Now: $95.00 (Jeanenne Bell Dealer)

V-31. **Pin and Ear Rings—1940's**—1/20 12K G.F. M & S Co. Pin 1-3/8 x 1-1/4″ Ear Rings 1/2 x 1″ $45.00 (Peggy Carlson Collection)

V-32. **Necklace and Brooch—1940's**—Mkd. "Pr. St. Co. 1/20 12K G.F." Original box tagged "Nancy Lee." Red stones. Original price $24.00 Now $80.00 (Jeanenne Bell Dealer)

V-33. **Necklace and Bracelet—1940's**—Mkd. "1/20 12K on Sterling" Original box with price tag marked $18.95 Amethyst stones. $98.00 (Jeanenne Bell Dealer)

V-34. **Brooch—1940's**—Gold over silver with pearls 2-1/2 x 7/8″ $95.00 (W. Baldwin Collection)

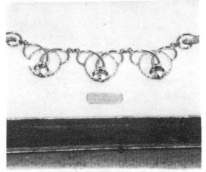

V-35. **Necklace—1940's**—Box marked "1/20 10K G.F. on Sterling" Aquamarine stones. Lovely chain necklace $48.00 (Jeanenne Bell Dealer)

V-36. **Ear Rings—1940's**—Gold over sterling mtgs. Hand carved cinnibar drops 1-1/2″ L. $65.00 (Jeanenne Bell Dealer)

316

V-37. **Ear Rings—1940's**—Gold over white metal with shell cameos on new 14K gold wires. 3/4 x 1-1/2" L. $85.00 (Jeanenne Bell Dealer)

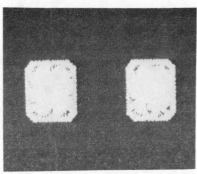

V-38. **Ear Rings—1940's**—Sterling mtgs. with hand carved ivory in original box. 3/4 x 1" $80.00 (Jeanenne Bell Dealer)

V-39. **Necklace Cross-1940's**—Mkd. "1/20 12K G.F. on Sterling" 3/4 x 1-1/8" Original box and chain. $48.00 (Jeanenne Bell Dealer)

V-40. **Pin with Cross—1940's**—Gold over brass. Victorian hand holding cross. Hand 1-1/2 x 1/2" Cross 3/4 x 1/2". Cross should be hanging down. $24.00 (Jeanenne Bell Dealer)

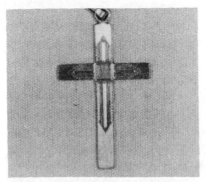

V-41. **Cross—1957**—1/20 12K G.F. 1 x 1-3/4" $24.00 (Mary Holloway Collection)

V-42. Locket—1940's—Yellow Gold Filled Heart 3/4 x 1" $28.00 (Jeanenne Bell Dealer)

V-43. **Locket—1940's**—Yellow Gold Filled 5/8″ Dia. $28.00 (Jeanenne Bell Dealer)

V-44. **Locket-1940's**—Yellow Gold over brass. 7/8 x 1″ $22.00 (Jeanenne Bell Dealer)

V-45. **Locket—1940's**—Yellow Gold Filled heart. 3/4 x 1″ $28.00 (Jeanenne Bell Dealer)

V-46. **Locket—1940's**—Yellow Gold Filled. On original 18″ chain. Mint condition. $38.00 (Jeanenne Bell Dealer)

V-47. **Locket—1940's**—1/20K G.F. Mother of pearl top with gold cross. Original box and chain. $32.00 (Jeanenne Bell Dealer)

V-48. **Locket—1940's**—Yellow Gold Filled Heart. 1 x 1-1/4″ $28.00 (Jeanenne Bell Dealer)

**V-49. Necklace—1940's—**10K Yellow, pink and green gold with aquamarine stone on original chain. Drop 3/4 x 1-1/4" $265.00 (Jeanenne Bell Dealer)

**V-50. Brooch—1940's—**Gold Filled 1-3/4 x 2-1/4" $15.00 (Jeanenne Bell Dealer)

**V-51. Brooch/Pendant—1940's—**925 silver. Shell cameo 1-3/8 x 1-3/4" $150.00 (W. Baldwin Collection)

**V-52. Brooch/Pendant—1940—**Silver over copper mtg. with shell cameo. 1-1/4 x 1-1/2" New 20" Sterling chain. $95.00 (Jeanenne Bell Dealer)

**V-53. Necklace—1940's—**Gold over brass 1-1/4 x 1-7/8" Chain 28" L. onyx and pearl. $60.00 (Lucile and Sam Mundorff Dealers)

**V-54. Brooch—1940's—**Yellow Gold Filled with topaz colored stone. 1-1/4 x 1" $32.00 (Camille Grace Dealer)

V-55. **Compact and Brooch—1940's—** mkd. "Sterling by Cini" Compacts with matching necklaces were also popular. Compact 4″ Dia. Brooch 2-1/2 x 2-3/4″ $175.00 (Lucille and Sam Mundorff Dealers)

V-56. **Necklace and Ear Rings—1940's** —Copper with enameling. $38.00 (Peggy Carlson Collection)

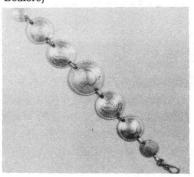

V-57. **Watch Chain—1943-44—**Made of coins from Australia, New Zealand, 7-1/2″ $42.00 (Jeanenne Bell Dealer)

V-58. **Watch Pin—1940's—**Gold Filled with pink and green gold with glossy finish 1-1/2 x 1″ $45.00 (Jeanenne Bell Dealer)

V-59. **Watch Pin—194's—**Gold over sterling 2-1/2 x 3/4″ $38.00 (Jeanenne Bell Dealer)

V-60. **Cigarette Case—1940's—**Mkd. Evans. Beautifully enameled 4-3/8 x 3-1/4″ $125.00 (Camille Grace Dealer)

V-61. **Cigarette Case—1940's**—Gold over brass mkd. Evans. Top is mother of pearl with enameling. 3 x 4″ $125.00 (Camille Grace Dealer)

V-62. **Pin—1940's**—Gold Filled. Spells "Amanda" These name pins were very popular. A common misconception is that they were made of 10K gold wire. Not true 2-3/8 x 1/2″ $28.00 (Amanda Bell Private Collection)

V-63. **Brooch—1940's**—Sterling 1-3/4 x 1-1/2″. This style brooch was advertized in the "Brecken Book," of jewelry in 1947. "Minute design Pierced Brooch $5.75". Now $55.00 (Camille Grace Dealer)

V-64. **Necklace**—Sterling with rhinestones. Arlene Francis made this motif famous when she wore it on T.V. show "Whats My Line?" $32.00 (Jeanenne Bell Dealer)

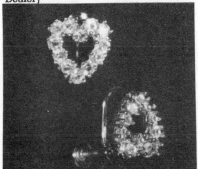

V-65. **Ear Rings—1950's**—Sterling. Rhinestones. Same motif as 67 in original box. 1/2 x 1/2″ $32.00 (Jeanenne Bell Dealer)

V-66. **Bracelet—late 1940's early 50's**—Gold Filled. Mkd. "Coro" each flower has a pearl center. 3/4 x 7-1/2″ $48.00 (Jeanenne Bell Collection)

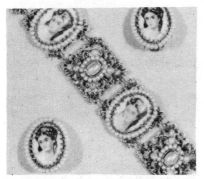

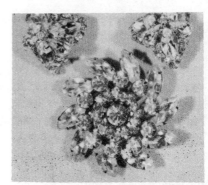

**V-67. Bracelet and Ear Rings-1940's-50's**—Yellow gold over brass. Transfer on porcelain accentuated with hand painted details. Pearls strung on wire. Bracelet 1 x 7" Ear Rings 3/4 x 1" $65.00 (Mary Holloway Collection)

**V-68. Brooch and Ear Rings—1949-52**—White metal with rhinestones. Brooch 2" Dia. Clip Ear Rings 1 x 1" $38.00 (Mary Holloway Collection)

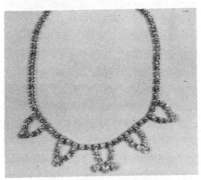

**V-69. Necklace—1940-50**—Silver over brass. Rhinestones. Mkd. Garne Jewelry. $48.00 (Jeanenne Bell Dealer)

**V-70. Necklace—1940-50**—Rhinestones. mkd. "D'vera, N.Y." $48.00 (Jeanenne Bell Dealer)

**V-71. Necklace—1940's—Rhinestones** $44.00 (Jeanenne Bell Dealer)

**V-72. Brooch—1950's—Rhinestones 2"** Dia. $35.00 (Jeanenne Bell Dealer)

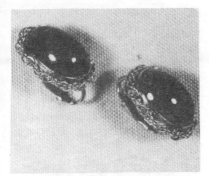

**V-73. Ear Rings—1940's—14K Gold with colored garnets. Clips. 3/4 x 7/8" L.** $295.00 **(W. Baldwin Collection)**

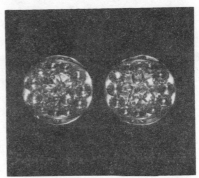

**V-74. Ear Rings—1952**—Copper. mkd. "Gert Barkin. New Hope, Pa." 3/4" Dia. $18.00 (Peggy Carlson Collection)

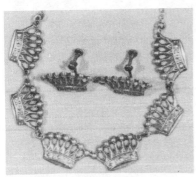

**V-75. Necklace and Earrings—1940's -50**—Sterling. Crowns each marked sterling. 7/8 x 5/8" $65.00 (Jeanenne Bell Dealer)

**V-76. Pin—1950's**—Black enameled metal. Mkd. "Weiss" Berries are red stones with green stone tops. 1-1/2 x 1/4" $25.00 (Jeanenne Bell Dealer)

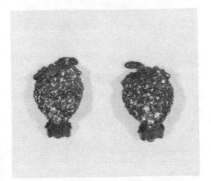

**V-77. Matching Ear Rings with V-79**—Strawberrys. $10.00 (Jeanenne Bell Dealer)

**V-78. Pin and Ear Rings—1940's—Gold Filled with Mother of Pearl. Pin 2-3/8 x 1-7/8" Ear Rings 7/8 x1-1/4" $35.00 (Anne Noblitt Collection)**

**V-79. Brooch—1940-50**—Rhinestones
Mkd. "Weiss" 2-5/8 x 1-3/8″ $48.00
(Anne Noblitt Collection)

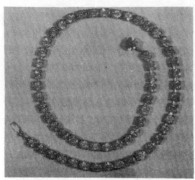

V-80. **Necklace—1950's**—Rhinestones
14″ L. $28.00 (Jeanenne Bell Dealer)

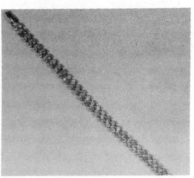

V-81. **Bracelet—1950**—2 rows of rhinestones 6-1/2″ L. $28.00 (Jeanenne Bell
Dealer)

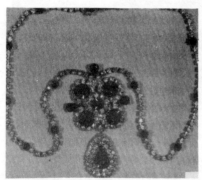

V-82. **Necklace—1950's**—Rhinestones
and imitation blue sapphire. Each stone
nicely set. $85.00 (Jeanenne Bell Dealer)

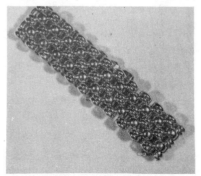

V-83. **Bracelet—1950's**—Marked
"Made in Switzerland plaque orl 20
microns" with safety 1″ wide $195.00
(Jeanenne Bell Collection)

V-84. **Brooch/Pendant—1940-50**—Gold
Filled. Transfer on porcelain accentuated by hand painting and surrounded
by pearls. 1-3/4 x 2-1/8″ $55.00
(Jeanenne Bell Dealer)

**V-85. Ear Rings—1940-50**—Mkd. "Limoge, France" clip backs. $48.00 (Jeanenne Bell Dealer)

**V-86. Bracelet—Late 1950's**—Mkd. "Sterling England" 6 old masters, each 5/8 x 1". Bracelet 7" L. Original box states "This bracelet is hand painted in oils." $95.00 (Peggy Carlson Collection)

**V-87. Brooch/Pendant**—Matches 86. 1-7/8 x 2-3/8" $85.00 (Jeanenne Bell Dealer)

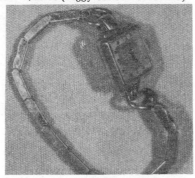

**V-88. Wrist Watch—1940's**—14K Yellow Gold. Movement marked Hamilton-911-17 Jewels $295.00 (Jeanenne Bell Dealer)

**V-89. Brooch—1940's**—14K Gold with Shell Cameo. 1-3/8 x 1-3/4" $325.00 (W. Baldwin Collection)

**V-90. Ear Rings—1950's**—Sterling. Siam motif with Niello enameling 5/8 x 1" $28.00 (Jeanenne Bell Dealer)

V-91—**Clips**—Circa 1940. Gold and platinum set with 12 emerald cut citrines, 20 square cut citrines and 20 round diamonds. Cartier, London. $4,400 (A) (Photo courtesy of Sotheby, New York 12-7-83)

V-92—**Clip & Earrings**—Circa 1940. 18K pink gold. The brooch has 10 round diamonds and 14 round cabochon rubies; the earclips have 18 round diamonds and 20 round cabochon rubies. $1,430.00 (A) (Photo courtesy of Sotheby, New York 12-7-83)

V-93—**Bracelet**—Circa 1938. 18K pink gold with 144 ruby cabochons and 135 round diamonds. (approx. 5cts. total) $8,250 (A) (Photo courtesy of Sotheby, New York 12-7-83)

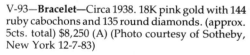

V-94—**Wristwatch**—Circa 1940—18K gold Patek Phillippe & Co. Geneve, nickel lever movement, 18 jewels, adjusted to 5 positions, mono-metallic compensation balance, silvered and matte dial, arabic and baton numerals. Dial and movement signed. 1⅜" diameter. $990.00 (Photo courtesy of Sotheby, New York 4-10-84)

V-95—**Wristwatch**—Circa 1940. 18K rectangular man's Patek Phillippe & Co., Geneve tonneau nickel lever movment, 3 adjustments, 18 jewels. Signed Tiffany on movement and case. 18K brickwork strap. Diameter 1¾". $3,025.00 (A) (Photo courtesy of Sotheby, New York 4-10-84)

V-96—**Clips & Earrings**—Circa 1940s. 14K yellow gold set with sapphires and citrines. Signed "Tiffany". $1,100.00 (A) (Photo courtesy of William Doyle Galleries 9-21-83)

V-97-Left—**Ring**—Circa 1940. Gold with 8 round fancy greenish to brownish grey-yellow natural color diamonds, 16 calibre cut cabochon rubies and 18 round and single cut diamonds. $2,750 (A)

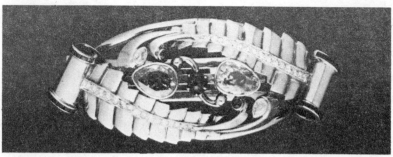

V-98—**Brooch**—Circa 1940. Yellow and pink gold leaf motif embellished with rubies and diamonds. $1,320.00 (A) (Photo courtesy of Sotheby, New York 10-5-83)

V-99—**Bracelet**—Circa 1940. Pink and yellow gold bangle centered with 1 pear shaped diamond (approx. 2.25 cts.) and 1 pear shaped diamond (approx. 1.80 cts.). Embellished with 2 small pear shaped diamonds and numerous small round diamonds and calibre cut rubies. $3,685.00 (A) (Photo courtesy of Sotheby, New York 10-5-83)

V-100—**Brooches**—Circa 1940. Pink gold studded with 124 round and single cut diamonds (approx. 4 cts.) and 8 round and oval shaped cabochon rubies. $1,650.00 (A) (Photo courtesy of Sotheby's, New York 12-7-83)

V-101—**Brooch**—Circa 1940. Gold maple leaf set with fancy colored sapphires and citrines in shades of green, yellow and burnt orange. Verdura. $2,860.00 (A) (Photo courtesy of Sotheby's, New York 12-7-83)

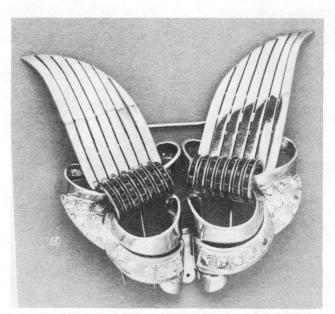

V-102—**Double Clip Brooch**—Circa 1940. Platinum with calibre cut rubies and old European cut diamonds. $2,475.00 (A) (Photo courtesy of Sotheby's, New York 12-7-83)

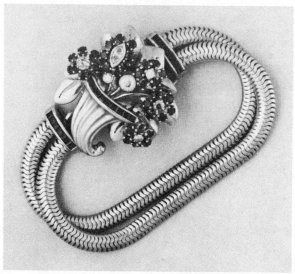

V-103—**Bracelet**—Circa 1945. 14K yellow gold with pink gold conucopia with yellow gold leaves. Centrally set with 1 marquise shaped diamond, 1 old mine yellow diamond, 4 small round diamonds, 1 round yellow diamond and numerous round and calibre cut sapphires and rubies. Missing watch movement. $1,430.00 (A) (Photo courtesy of Sothebys, New York 10-6-83)

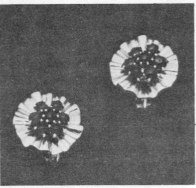

V-104—**Bracelet and Earrings**—Circa 1945. 14K yellow gold hinged bracelet has detachable center set with rubies and diamonds. Matching earclips. Trabent & Hoeffer, Mauboussion. $2,420.00 (Photo courtesy of Sothebys, New York 10-5-83)

V-105—**Money Clip**—Gold with watch. 5.50 cm. x 4 cm. Cartier. Engraved 'Douglas Fairbanks for Alan P.P.W. May 46'. L140 $203.00 (Photo courtesy of Phillips, London 11-24-83)

V-106—**Wristwatch**—Circa 1950. Man's 18K gold square case with 14K link strap. Patek Phillippe & Co. movement #959431. Nickel lever, mono-metallic compensation balance, silvered matte dial applied with gold baton numerals. $1,210.00 (A) (Photo courtesy of Sothebys, New York 4-10-84)

V-107—**Wristwatch**—Circa 1950. Platinum and diamond man's Patek Phillippe & Co. Geneve nickel lever movement, mono-metallic compensation balance, 5 adjustments. Silvered dial applied with calibre and brilliant cut diamond numerals. $1,980.00 (A) (Photo courtesy of Sothebys, New York 4-10-84)

# SECTION II

## "What Is This Metal?"

This is one of the most important questions asked about old jewelry. The metal not only plays a major role in determing value but can also provide clues as to when and where the piece was made.

Almost everyone knows that a gold plated ring is less valuable than one made of Karat gold, but how can the average person tell the difference? What do the numbers and letters stamped on a piece mean? How can silver, white gold, and white metal be identified? Hopefully this section will answer these questions and more.

To properly examine jewelry a magnifying glass of some sort is needed. A jeweler's loupe is a good investment whether you are a collector or a curious owner. A two and one half power loupe is adequate for examinging most markings and is available at jewelry supply stores for less than $2.00. For examining stones a ten (10) power loupe is recommended; a good one can be purchased for less than $35.00. With these aids in hand you are ready to examine the metal.

### Gold

In the United Stated the purity of gold is designated by Karat. Pure gold is 24k, but, because of its softness, it is not suitable for making jewelry. Other metals such as copper, silver, nickel, and zinc are added to gold to strengthen it. What is added and how much is added determine the color and Karat of the gold.

To make this easier to understand let's take an imaginary ring and examine it. The color of the metal is immediately apparent. Gold comes in several colors, but let's pretend that this ring is pink gold. Inside the ring is stamped 10k. What do these things tell us? First, that the gold was mixed with copper, silver, and zinc to make yellow gold. The pink look was achieved by using a larger quantity of copper. The 10k mark assures that 41.67% of the metal is pure gold, and the other 58.33% is copper, silver, and zinc. It also indicates that the piece was made in the United States. (Other countries do not use 10k.) A 14k stamping would mean that the ring contained 58.33% gold and 41.67% other metals. If the ring was marked 18k, it would contain 75% pure gold and 25% other metals.

In Europe gold is stamped according to its fineness. Pure gold is 1000 fine; 18k gold is 75% or 750 fine. Consequently, an 18k ring made in Europe would be stamped 750.

Below is a chart of the most common Karat markings.

| US/Karats | % of gold | Fineness |
|-----------|-----------|----------|
| 24 | 100% | 1000 |
| 22 | 95.83% | 958 |
| 18 | 75% | 750 |
| 15 | 62.50% | 625 |
| 14 | 58.33% | 583 |
| 10 | 41.67% | 417 |
| 9 | 37.50% | 375 |

The 375 at the bottom of the list is the English number for 9k. It will always be found enclosed in a rectangular box with other markings. These are known as hallmarks and are discussed under the silver heading.

## Rolled Gold Plate

Always be sure to look for other letters that might be stamped next to the karat sign. A piece marked 14k R.G.P. is not 14 Karat gold. The R.G.P. stands for rolled gold plate, which is made by applying a layer of gold alloy to a layer of base metal. This "sandwich" is then drawn to the thickness needed for the piece of jewelry. Rolled gold plating was very popular in the 1800's and early 1900's.

## Gold Filled

Other letters that sometimes appear next to the Karat number are G.F. This signifies the piece is gold filled. The name is misleading because the piece is not filled with gold as the name implies, but is made by joining a layer of gold to a base metal as in rolled gold plating. They layer of gold used in gold filled is thicker than the one used in R.G.P., making it more durable and more valuable. Again the numbers tell how much gold and what Karat of gold were used. A piece marked 1/20 12k assures that the alloy is 12 Karat or 50% pure gold and that 1/20 of the total weight of the piece is 12k gold.

## Electroplating

If the piece in question is marked 14k H.G.E., it has been gold plated. The initials stand for Hard Gold Electroplated. It means that the piece is made of base metal that has been plated with a thin coating of gold by an electrical process.

## Other Markings

In the late 1800's many pieces were stamped "solid gold" or advertised as such. These pieces were usually only 6k to 10k gold, but they were gold—not gold filled or rolled gold plate. A law passed in 1906 required the gold content be stamped on jewelry. Before that year many pieces of gold jewelry were unmarked. For ways to determine whether an unmarked piece is gold, rolled gold plated, or gold filled refer to the section "Is it real?".

## PINCHBECK

Pinchbeck is a very old metal rarely encountered today. The name is often misapplied to gold filled or rolled gold plated items. It is not a plate or coating, but a solid metal made by mixing copper and zinc.

The formula, discovered by Christopher Pinchbeck (1670-1732), contained no gold: yet it looked like gold and wore well. The pinchbeck formula was a guarded secret passed down in the family, but other companies developed their own versions. There were so many imitations that Christopher's grandson, Edward Pinchbeck, found it necessary to place this advertisement in the July 11, 1733 edition of the Daily Post:

*To prevent for the future the gross imposition that is daily put upon the publick by a great number of Shop-Keepers, Hawkers, and Pedlers, in and about this town. Notice is hereby given, that the in-*

*genious Mr. Edward Pinchbeck, at the 'Musical Clock' in Fleet Street, does not dispose of one grain of his curious metal, which so nearly resembles Gold in Colour, Smell, and Ductility, to any person whatsoever, nor are the Toys (jewelry and trinkets) made of the said metal, sold by any one person in England except himself; therefore gentlemen are desired to beware of imposters, who frequent Coffee Houses, and expose for Sale, Toys pretended to be made of this metal, which is a most nototious imposition, upon the publick. And Gentlemen and Ladies, may be accommodated by the said Mr. Pinchbeck with the following curious Toys: viz: Sword, Hilts, Hangers, Cane Heads, Whip Handles, for Hunting, Spurs, Equipages, Watch Chains, Tweezers for Men and Women, Snuff-Boxes, Coat Buttons, Shirt Buttons, Knives and Forks, Spoons, Salvers, Buckles for Ladies Breasts, Stock Buckles, Shoe Buckles, Knee Buckles, Bridle Buckles, Stock Clasps, Knee Clasps, Necklaces, Corals, and in particular Watches, plain and chased in so curious a manner as not to be distinguuished by the nicest eye, from the real gold, and which are highly necessary for Gentlemen and Ladies when they travel, with several other fine pieces of workmanship of all sorts made by the best hands. He also makes Repeating and all other sorts of Clocks and Watches particularly Watches of a new invention, the mechanism of which is so simple, and proportion so just, that they come nearer to the truth than others yet made.*

The advertisement referred to necessary items for travel. Quite often copies of favorite pieces were made to wear on "travels". The gold ones were left safely at home. McKeever Persivial in his "Chats on Old Jewelry" states, "In those days when a journey of even a few miles out of Lodon led through roads infested by thieves and highway robbers, careful folk preferred not to tempt these 'gentlemen of the road' by wearing expensive ornaments unless traveling with a good escort; so not only would a traveller with a base metal watch and buckles lose less if robbed, but owing to the freemasonary which existed between innkeepers and postilions and the highwaymen, they were actually less likely to be stopped, as it was not worth while to run risks for such a poor spoil."

With the invention of the electrogilding process in 1840 and the leglization of 9k gold in 1854, the use of Pinchbeck declined and eventually became passe.

Pinchbeck is very collectible, but there are very few pieces available. Part of the fun of jewelry collecting is the "lucky finds." The author "found" the pinchbeck locket pictured on page 30 at an antique show a few months ago. After viewing a few pieces, pinchbeck becomes visually identifiable. Until then take care to buy from a knowledgable dealer.

## Silver

Silver is a precious metal that has always intrigued man. Because of this fascination, regulations have been applied to its use for centuries. After silver is mined, it is refined to .999 pure. Like gold it is too soft to be used in this pure state. Instead it is mixed with other metals for strength.

## Sterling

Sterling silver is .925 fine. This mixture of pure silver and copper has long been regarded for its fine beauty. The word denotes quality of the highest standard. According to Seymore B. Wyler the world "sterling" was coined when King James brought in a group of Germans to refine silver for making coins. Since they were from the East, they became known as Easterlings. When a statute concerning silver was written in 1343, the first two letters were accidentally omitted. Hence the word sterling was first applied to silver.

A lion or leopard stamped into silver signifies sterling. In the United States the word sterling is usually stamped into the piece. All new sterling is marked or punched to signify its credibility.

## Hallmarks

Since the amount of silver involved greatly determines the cost of a piece and the average person could be easily fooled, laws were passed to insure a standard purity. As early as 1335 English law required silversmiths to punch or stamp their mark into any pieces made in their shop. By 1477 a leopards head stamp was required proof that a piece met the accepted silver standards. In 1479 a letter designating the year of manufacture was initiated, making silver even more identifiable. These signs or hallmarks are still used today and provide clues as to when and where a piece was made.

This is a hallmark from brooch II-146 on page 106. The first character, a lion passant, signifies the piece is sterling silver. The anchor is the mint mark for Birmingham, England, and the letter date signifies that it was made in 1889-90. Sometimes, but not always, the maker's mark is included in the hallmark. The type letters and the shape of the box in which the signatures are placed are all important factors when reading a hallmark. Fortunately, there are several good books on hallmarks that include lists of date letters, mint marks, and makers. These provide invaluable aid in dating and indentifying silver.

Items made of sterling get more beautiful as they are used or worn. With use, tiny scratches known as patina develop, giving the silver a warm, soft look. Only gold and platinum are more durable than silver, so do not be afraid to wear it.

**Coin Silver**

Quite often a piece of jewelry or a watch case will be marked coin silver or .900. This means the piece is 90% silver and 10% other metal. At one time this was the standard content of silver coins. Thus the name "coin silver" is synonomous with this percentage of silver content. Often actual coins were melted to make silver items. In fact, this was so prevelant in England that a law was passed in 1696 making the standard for silver items higher (958) in silver content than coins. This did not eliminate the problem. Shrewd silversmiths continued to melt coins and add silver to bring the content up to standard. Since the act did not solve the coin problem and the new "britannia" was softer and less durable, in 1720 the higher standard became optional.

**Silverplate**

A method of silverplating was discovered in 1742 by Thomas Boulsover. While repairing a knife blade, he accidentally fused silver to copper. This accident was the beginning of the Sheffield Plate Industry in England.

In 1840 G.R. Elkington was granted a patent on a process for electroplating silver or gold to a base metal. This process uses electricity to apply a coating of silver to an article made of base metal. Although this coating is usually very thin, pieces more than a hundred years old are sometimes found in amazingly good condition. The most popular base metals were copper and German silver.

## German Silver

The term German Silver is a misnomer. German silver is not silver at all but a combination of nickel, copper, and zinc. A german introduced it to England in the late 1700's. Because its color resembles silver, it made a perfect base for silver-plated items. Hence the name German Silver. To confuse matters even more it is also known as gunmetal or nickel silver.

When a piece is marked E.P.N.S., it is electroplated nickel silver.

## Vermeil

The French definition of vermeil (vair-MAY) is "silver gilt". Items made of sterling silver and coated with gold were favored by French nobility during the reign of Louis XIV and throughout the 18th century. In the early 1800's scientists discovered that the mercury used in the vermeil process was causing the jewelry workers to go blind. The process was banned. Consequently, very little vermeil was made in the nineteenth century.

In 1956 Tiffany's re-introduced vermeil. According to Jospeh Puntell, the Tiffany factory developed a process using a plating of 18-1/2 karat gold covered with a second plating of 22-1/2 karat gold. This new process provided the glowing look of the mercury process without its poisonus side effects.

## Platinum

Platinum, one of the heaviest, most valuable metals known to man, was first discovered in 1557 by Julius Scaligerk, an Italian scientist. In the 1700's Spanish explorers discovered deposits in Peru and called it "plata", their name for silver.

Platinum was used very little until the late 1880's. At that time new developments in jeweler's equipment made it easier to work, and it became popular for mounting diamonds. By the 1920's it was the most popular metal used in jewelry. Platinum's popularity caused white gold to become fashionable. Eighteen karat white gold was advertised as "a look-alike" for the more expensive metal. Platinum's durability made it an excellent choice for the filligree styles of the 20's and 30's.

During World War II the use of platinum for jewelry was restricted by the War Production Board. The metal was needed for a catalyst in munitions' plants. Reluctantly jewelers turned to Palladium, a related metal, as a substitute.

The same ore that yields platinum contains five other metals—iridium, palladium, rhodium, ruthenum, and osmirium. They are known as the platinum group. Of these, platinum, palladium, and rhodium are widely used in jewelry.

**Palladium**

Palladium is one of the six metals in the platinum group. Even though it is harder, lighter, and less expensive than platinum, it has never been as popular.

During World War II, jewelry manufacturers turned to palladium when platinum was restricted. The public could not tell the difference, and palladium was 30% cheaper. Its weight is comparable to 14k gold. After the war full page advertisements were used to promote palladium, but it never gained full acceptance by the general public.

**Rhodium**

Rhodium is another of the six metals in the platinum group. Because of its hardness it is often used as a plating. Quite often a piece will be marked "sterling silver rhodium finished" or "stainless steel rhodium finish". The abbreviated mark for rhodium is "Rh".

# SECTION III

## Is It Real?

This question is most often asked about stones. Because the answer can mean a big difference in value, it is most important that it be correct. The person most qualified to answer this question is a graduate gemologist, a person trained to identify and evaluate stones (usually a Gemological Institute of America graduate).

If you are a collector or a dealer, a good working relationship with a gemologist can be invaluable. Whether you won an extensive collection or just a few pieces that have been handed down in the family, an appraisal by a gemologist with a knowledge of Antique and Period jewelry is needed to insure proper insurance coverage. Most gemologists charge by the job or on an hourly basis. Appraisers who base their fee on a percentage of value, are not recommended.

To insure a good appraisal, look for a gemologist who is a member of ''The International Society of Appraisers'' and lists antique and period jewelry as one of his/her fields of expertise. I.S.A. has a ''Certified Appraiser of Personal Property'' designation. This assures that the appraiser not only has superior knowledge in his/her area of certification but has also completed courses on appraisal theory and ethics.

### Imitation and Synthetic Stones

Genuine stones have been imitated for thousands of years. The Egyptians made glass imitations and endowed them with the same supernatural power as the genuine. Paste, a glass imitation gemstone, was widely used from the thirteenth through the seventeenth centuries. In the eighteenth century Joseph Strass discovered that by adding a high percentage of lead to glass he could increase its brilliance, thus creating more beautiful imitations. By the early nineteenth century a process for making synthetic rubies had been discovered. But it was almost another hundred years before they were commercially feasible for use in jewelry.

Synthetic stones are not imitations. Physically, chemically and optically they are the same as the natural. By the use of heat and

340

pressure man has been able to speed up the process that takes 'Mother' nature thousands of years to produce.

When rubies were first synthesized in the 1800's, they were more expensive than the natural ones. In 1910, August Verneuil came up with the idea of using a smeltering torch that could provide heat equal to half of that produced by the sun. This new process produced stones at a much lower cost. Still they were so highly regarded that jewelers of the 1920's often set them in 18K gold mountings.

Synthetic spinels came on the market in 1926, followed by synthetic emeralds in the early 1940's, and synthetic star sapphires and rubies in 1947.

The process for making synthetic diamonds was perfected in 1955. Today most of the diamonds used for industrial purposes are synthetic.

Gem quality synthetic diamonds have been possible since the 1970's but they are more expensive than the natural ones. Stones such as cubic zirconium (C.Z.'s) and YAG are synthetic stones but they are not synthetic diamonds.

### Doublets and Triplets

Before relatively inexpensive synthetic stones were available, a combination stone called a "doublet" was popular. The jeweler fused a layer of one stone to another, then faceted the stone as if it were one large stone. The most popular doublet was one using garnet and glass. It was used to imitate sapphires, topaz, emeralds, amethyst, rubies and of course, garnets.

A piece of green or blue glass with a red garnet top is intriguing. It takes a trained eye and close inspection to detect. Consequently, pieces of jewelry set with old doublets are quite collectable. Most people are fascinated by them.

The term "triplet" is used to describe a stone that is made up of three parts. This can mean three stones (genuine top and bottom with something else in between), or it can refer to two stones put together with a colored cement that provides the "stone's" color. Because synthetic emeralds are expensive, triplets made of quartz or synthetic spinel joined by emerald green cement are often encountered.

## Tests for Stones

The first test for any stone is visual. Get your 10 power loupe and look at the stone. There are many things to notice. When examining colored stones, look for color zoning. In layman's terms this is a variance of color; usually there is more color or more intense color in some areas of the stone. This "zoning" (especially noticeable in amethyst) is an indication of a natural stone. Synthetic stones usually have more "life" and are evenly colored.

When examining the cut of a stone, notice whether or not there are sharp, precise lines. Natural stones have to be cut to their best advantage and are not always as precise as synthetic ones. Look for signs of layers that could mean a doublet or triplet. Chips and abrasions on the surface of a clear stone are usually an indication that the stone is not a diamond.

Next, look into the stone. Natural stones often have needle-like angular inclusions. Synthetics have curved lines or curved color bandings. Any stone made by the flame fusion process such as glass or synthetics will usually have round gas or air bubbles. (See figures.)

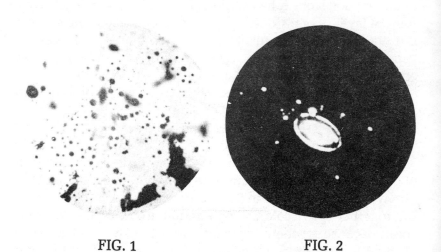

FIG. 1                      FIG. 2

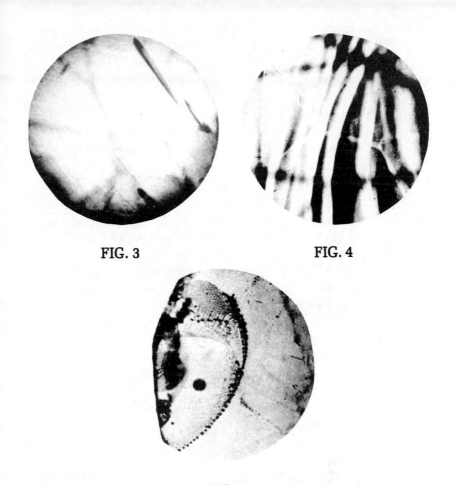

FIG. 3                    FIG. 4

FIG. 5

Figures #1 - 5 are pictures taken under magnification of "glass used as gemstones". Reprinted from the G.I.A. study course on Colored Stones, they are courtesy of the Gemological Institute of America. Figures 1, 2 and 3 show different shaped gas bubbles. Figure 4 shows "swirl marks" and "flow lines". Figure 5 shows groups of "bubbles arranged in a featherlike pattern".

Another more difficult test is one for "refraction". This is done by looking through the stone and focusing on a facet line (where two facets intersect). Slowly tilt the stone back and forth. If one like looks like two or splits apart and comes back together, it is a doubly refractive stone. Peridot, topaz, tourmaline, emerald, quartz, amethyst, citrine, synthetic rutile and zircon are all

343

doubly refracting stones. The last two are highly refractive and can often be identified by this test alone. Diamonds, garnets, spinels and glass do not double refract. Although this test does not give all the answers, its results are well worth the effort to become proficient.

There are many other tests used by the gemologist to determine stones. Synthetics have become so sophisticated that even an expert cannot be sure without the aid of expensive equipment. Today a trained gemologist with a well-equipped laboratory is imperative for proper stone identification.

This not to say that the average person cannot learn to identify and enjoy stones. The best way to gain this knowledge is by becoming visually acquainted with the various stones. Take every opportunity to view and examine them. Antique Shows and Gem and Mineral Shows provide ideal opportunities to handle stones. Most dealers and participants are more than willing to share their knowledge.

**Tests for Diamonds**

If you have a loose clear stone and want to know whether or not it is a diamond there are some simple tests that may help in this determination.

For the first test draw a line on a sheet of white paper. Place the stone (table down) on the line. If the stone is a diamond, the line will not be visible. Any other clear stone will allow the line to show through.

The next test is done by placing the stone on a sheet of white paper and holding a penlight under it. Be sure that the light shines up under the stone. If the stone is a C.Z., YAG, or any other clear stone, the light will outline the stone and also show through the middle. If the done is a diamond, the outline will show through but the middle will remain dark.

Another test is the ''breath test''. If breathing on the stone causes it to ''fog'' this is an indication that the stone in question is *not* a diamond.

All these tests should be performed for the first time using stones that are known. This provides a chance to see the accurate reactions before testing an unknown stone.

An amazingly accurate determination of whether or not a stone is a diamond can be done with a small heat probe instrument.

Diamonds are the most heat conductive of stones. Using this fact the instrument has a small pen-like probe that heats up. When this point is placed on a diamond, the heat is transmitted away from the point, and triggers a beeping sound to signify that it is a diamond. When the probe is placed on any other clear stone the heat is not conducted and no sound is heard. It's a simple fun thing to see. Go to your local jeweler and ask him to demonstrate it.

### Tests for Amber

There are many tests to help determine the authenticity of amber. The Greeks were aware of its static electricity so this was probably the first test. This version of the test was included in the February 1864 Peterson's Magazine:

> Our article on amber and amber combs last year brought out the inquery by whether all combs, or other articles, represented to be amber, are so, or not. We reply that very many things sold as amber are imitations. A lady who has an amber necklace, which belonged to her ancestors, sends us the following as a sure method of testing amber. ''Prepare a fine bit of split straw – piece of split straw an inch long – rub the article briskly with wolen or cotton clothe a few minutes; place it immediately in contact with one end of the straw, (the straw must not lie in the hand, but on a table, or any dry substance). If the beads or comb are real amber, they will lift the end of the straw, and sometimes the point of a very fine needle.''

This test can be done today using bits of tissue paper. The problem is that some of today's plastics also have the same problem.

Another test is done by sticking a hot needle into an inconspicious spot on the amber. If the piece is genuine, it will emit a pine-like odor. According to Marilyn Roos, an amber dealer, this test is not always conclusive because artificial amber made in Russia includes small bits of genuine amber. If the needle should hit any of these pieces, it would test authentic.

The only true test, according to Marilyn, is done with ether. She suggests putting a small amount on a cotton swab and applying it to the piece in question (in an inconspicious place of course). If the piece is genuine, the ether will not affect it. If it is plastic, it will become sticky and the ether will eat into it.

### Gutta Percha

Gutta Percha is one of the easiest plastics to identify. It is black or brownish black in color and very lightweight. When rubbed briskly on a piece of cloth, it emits the very distinctive odor of burnt rubber.

**Ivory**

Unless you are an expert, identifying ivory can be very difficult. A loupe for magnified viewing is a necessity. Elephant ivory has an ''engine turned'' effect when viewed under magnification. Figure 1a shows a piece magnified 15 times. Grain lines, shown in figure 2a (magnified 25x) are found in any true ivory. When ivory is touched with nitric acid, it effervesces; bone, vegetable ivory and plastics do not.

Bone is often used to imitate ivory. Figure 4a shows a transverse section of bone magnified 25 times. A longitudinal section, magnified 50 times is shown in figure 5a. As you can see, it has an entirely different look than that of ivory.

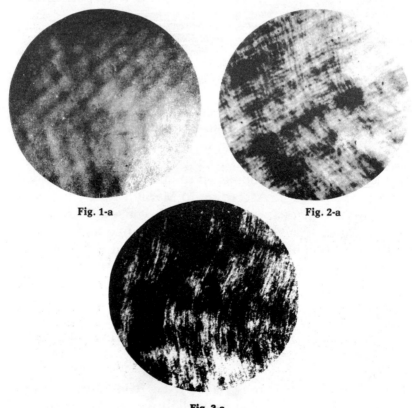

Fig. 1-a                    Fig. 2-a

Fig. 3-a

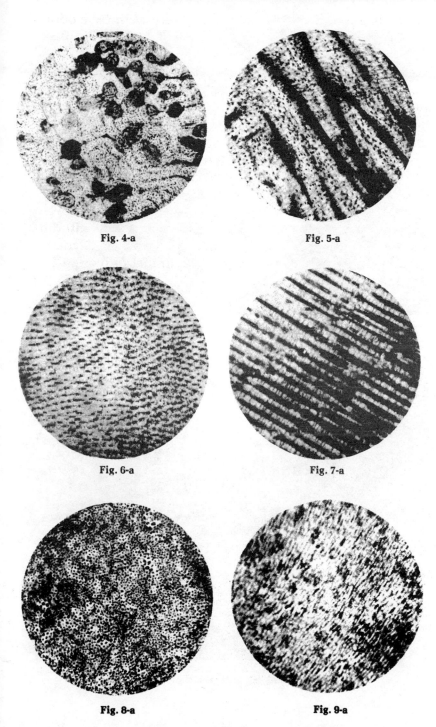

Fig. 4-a

Fig. 5-a

Fig. 6-a

Fig. 7-a

Fig. 8-a

Fig. 9-a

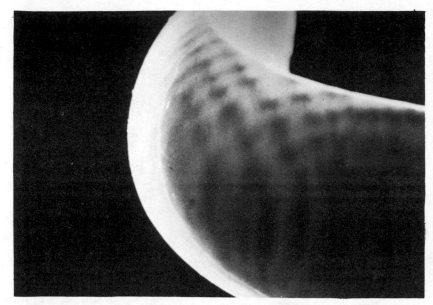

1b. Another view of magnified ivory showing 'engine turned' structure.

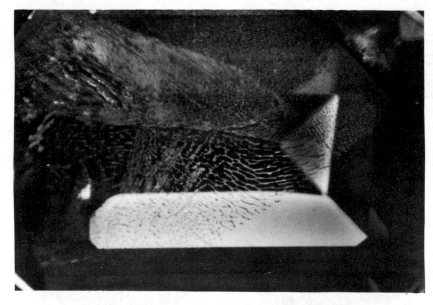

2b. Synthetic ruby magnified to show flux inclusions.

3b. Glass 'stone' magnified to show orange-peel effect and concave facets.

4b. Garnet and glass doublet. Magnified view shows garnet top and trapped gas bubbles under garnet cap.

The so-called vegetable ivorys are fairly easy to identify. When a few drops of sulphuric acid are applied to this type of ivory, it turns a rosy color. True ivory will not be affected by the acid. Figure 6a shows a cross section of corozo nut magnified 25x. A longitudinal view of the vegetable ivory is seen in figure 7a. Figures 8a and 9a show the same views of the doum-palm nut. These pictures are courtesy of the Gemological Institute of America.

## Jet

Bog oak, gutta-percha, onyx and black glass are all often misidentified as jet. Mr. Brian Fall, a volunteer at the museum in Whitby, was kind enough to share his method of identifying jet. He warned me that the test should be done with care so as not to destroy the piece.

Simply rub the piece across a piece of concrete (a sidewalk?). If it leaves a brownish black mark, the piece is jet. If it does not leave a mark it is some other material.

Jet can sometimes be identified by its weight. It has an extremely light-weight feeling, much like the feel of amber. Maybe this accounts for the misnomer "Black Amber" that is often applied to jet.

Jet has sharp, precisely cut lines. Mold lines are an indication of glass.

## Pearls

An imitation pearl can usually be detected by examining the hole through which it is strung. If it is a glass imitation covered with effesce d'orient, a thin film can usually be detected.

Another test for determining whether or not pearls are imitation is done by rubbing them against your teeth. Imitation pearls will feel smooth while cultured or natural pearls will feel "gritty". With a little practice one can become quite proficient at this. This is an easy accurate way to tell the imitation from the cultured.

Cultured pearls are not imitation, and there is no visible difference between them and oriental pearls. Only an expert with the proper equipment (usually x-ray) is qualified to make this judgment. Since the price of cultured pearls is much lower than that of natural ones, always get an expert opinion, in writing, before making a purchase.

## Other Tests

Quite a few materials can be tested by using a few items that you probably already have at home.

First get a pencil with an eraser on the end. Place the "eye-end" of a needle into the end of the eraser. Now all that is needed to complete this "scientific testing unit" is a lighted candle.

After heating the needle over the candle, place the hot point to an inconspicuous place on the piece of jewelry. The odor different materials produce can help you determine it.

Below is a list of several materials and their identifying odors. Always remember to stick the hot needle into an inconspicuous place.

Amber: Pine scent.
Bakelite: Carbolic acid.
Celluloid: Camphor.
Jet: Burning coal.
Tortoise shell: Burning hair.

If you are really interested in learning more about jewelry, learn to use your built in tools. The first tool is your eyes. Notice details. Learn to recognize styles. Visually compare pieces. Expose your eyes to good examples of jewelry by visiting art galleries (notice the jewelry worn in the portraits), going to antique shows and looking through old books.

The hands are another important tool in exploring jewelry. Learn the "feel" of a piece. Touch the finish. Feel the weight. The more you handle jewelry, the more adept you will become at judging it. Surprisingly enough, you may even get to the point when you can determine whether or not a piece is gold just by its "feel".

The most surprising jewelry tool is your teeth. By touching a beaded necklace lightly against my teeth, I can distinguish between glass and plastic. Try it. Get used to the difference in the sound and feel of different substances against your teeth. I will admit this looks a bit strange. I have had people ask "What in the world are you doing?"; but it does work. Again it is something that has to be worked at – an acquired talent – but it is well worth the effort.

## Testing Gold

If a piece has no markings, there may be other clues to help determine the metal. First, examine it closely with a loupe. Look closely at the edges or any place that was likely to rub against things. Many times small patches of base metal are visible at these points. If the base metal is white and the piece is yellow gold, this is fairly easy, but to see brass or copper base metal under yellow is sometimes more difficult. The more accustomed your eyes become to noting subtle differences, the easier it will become. If there are no visible signs of wear, it is possible that the piece is gold. It is also possible that it is not.

There is only one true test for gold, and that is done with acid. Your jeweler can perform this test, and the charge is usually less than ten dollars. But if jewelry is a hobby or if you are a dealer, it would be worth while to invest in a gold testing kit. A good one can be purchased at a jewelry supply store for less than one hundred dollars. This kit will have everything you need to test gold except the most important ingredient – acid. It can be ordered through your pharmacist or purchased pre-mixed at the jewelry supply store.

The first step in testing gold is to find an inconspicious place on the piece of jewelry in which to file a groove or notch. Please take care where the notch is made. Many lovely antique pieces have been ruined by butchers who indiscriminately filed chunks. The groove is to get past any layer of gold in a gold filled piece. Apply a small amount of nitric acid to the groove. If the piece is gold over brass, it will bubble green; if a blueish color appears, the base metal is copper. When the piece is 14K gold or better, the acid keeps its clear water color. If, after a few minutes the spot darkens, it is an indication of 10K gold.

The exact Karat can be determined by using the needles that come with the kit. With these needles a mixture, called Aqua Regis, (one part distilled water, one part nitric acid, and three parts hydrochloric acid) is used. Instructions are included in the test kit.

For those who do not care to invest in a gold test kit, there is a less expensive alternative. Simply purchase glass acid bottles and pre-mixed testing solution for 10, 14, 18 and 22 Karat gold (less than $8.00 a bottle).

Nitric acid is still used to determine if the piece is gold. After the piece has tested gold, make a mark by rubbing the piece on a test stone. If the piece is 14K or better and a 14K solution is used, there will be no reaction. The mark will remain as visible as ever. Proceed by making another mark and using a higher Karat solution until the mark dissolves. If an 18K solution dissolves the mark and the 14K solution does not, the piece is at least 14K.

After testing always rinse the piece with a mixture of baking soda and water to neutralize the acid.

## Testing Silver

Although silver has been hallmarked and stamped for centuries, unmarked pieces are still encountered. If there is reason to believe a piece might be silver, examine it with a loupe. Look carefully at wear points to see if a base metal can be detected. If there are not indications of plating, a more extensive test is necessary.

For the serious collector or dealer, a pre-mixed silver test solution (available from jewelry supply stores for less than $10.00) is highly recommended. It can be an invaluable aid in deciphering silver content.

To test silver properly a notch must be filed (in an inconspicuous place) in the piece being tested. Make sure the notch is deep enough to go through any plate or coating of silver. Apply the pre-mixed solution to the notch and wait a few seconds for the color reaction. If the piece is sterling, the solution will turn a dark red color. On 800 silver it turns brown. If the piece is palladium, there is no reaction. This simple inexpensive test can help make you an expert at evaluating silver content.

## Misnomers

Inaccurate names are often applied to stones. They are usually used to give added importance and more sales appeal. These misnomers sometimes become so commercially accepted that the general public is unaware of what they are actually buying.

The folloiwng is a list of commonly accepted names and what they really are:

| | |
|---|---|
| Alaskan Diamond: | Cornish Diamond: |
| Arizona Diamond: | Goldstone: |
| Arkansas Diamond: | Herkimer Diamond: |
| Arizona Ruby: | Siberian Ruby: |
| Belas Ruby: | Smoky Topaz: |
| Cape Ruby: | Synthetic Aquamarine: |

| | |
|---|---|
| Rock crystal | Rock crystal |
| Rock crystal | An imitation adventurine |
| Rock crystal | Rock crystal |
| Garnet | Tourmaline |
| Spinel | Smoky quartz |
| Garnet | Spinel |

A trade name people often wonder about is "Aurora Borealis". This name is applied to glass that has been coated with a compound to give it an irridescent look.

# SECTION IV

## Makers Marks, Trade Marks and Designer Marks

### MAKERS MARKS, TRADE MARKS AND DESIGNER MARKS

While some of the marks found on jewelry have been written about in the Metals section of this book, there are a number of other marks that are very important to the collector.

These are trade marks, makers marks and designers marks. All three can help date a piece and identify its origin, manufacturer, wholesaler or retailer.

In the United States trademarks became popular in the mid 1800's but there were no laws making any marks compulsory before 1906. Consequently, there are many American pieces with no markings whatsoever.

English pieces with full hallmarks inform us of the date the piece was made, its metal content, the town in which it was assayed and its maker. Unfortunately, many pieces, especially designer ones, were never assayed. Glenais Wild of the Birmingham Museum in Birmingham, England told me this was because many times the makers work was destroyed if for any reason the piece was slightly under specifications. This is also the reason that designers such as Lalique and Fouquet often priced or engraved their marks.

Other markings can also be confused with trade marks. The French used an eagles head as a gold quality mark, an owls head in an oval for imported goods and the head of Mercury with a number of goods to be exported. Until the late 1800's Russia used town marks with the numbers 56, 72 and 92 indicating 14K, 18K and 23K gold content.

Marks used to signify towns were as varied as a hand for Antwerp and a pineapple for Augsburg. Some town marks can be confused with American trade marks if one is not experienced in identifying marks.

This section was added so the reader might become curious about the various marks on a piece of jewelry. Hopefully, it will kindle an interest that will cause the reader to be aware of *any* markings. Markings can help answer the questions: "Who made this piece?; Where was it made?"

This section of short biographical sketches is by no means complete. Some designers and makers are included because of the important part they played in the history of jewelry. Some firms are included because their inexpensive mass-produced pieces have become quote collectable.

The makers and firms are listed in alphabetical order within the Victorian time period. The Art Nouveau and Arts and Crafts are also alphabeticized and separated. The American companies are grouped together at the end of this section.

## Boucheron

This French firm was founded in 1858 by Frederic Boucheron (1830-1902). Over the years some of the best designers of the day were at work in the Boucheron workshops. A London branch of the company was opened on New Bond Street in 1907.

Boucheron is noted today as a designer of luxury and medium priced jewelry.

Mark: BOUCHERON

## John Brogden

John Brogden was an English goldsmith and jeweler working in London from 1842 to 1885. His "archaeological" style pieces were prized for their beautiful filigree and granulation gold work. In 1867 his work earned him a medal at the Paris Exhibition. Two fine examples of his work are in the Victoria & Albert Museum in London.

Mark:

[ JB ]          [ BROGDEN ]

## Castellani

Castellani is one of the most famous names in jewelry of the nineteenth century.

The Castellani story began in 1814 when Fortunato Pio Castellani (1793-1865) started to work in his father's jewelry workshop in Rome. He quickly acquired the status of master goldsmith and opened his own shop on the Via del Corso.

Fortunato Pio's friend, patron and associate, Michelangelo Caetani, Duke of Sermonita (1804-1883), was instrumental in igniting Castellani's interest in "archaelogical" jewelry. He arranged for Castellani to be present (in an advisory capacity) during the excavations of the Reguline Galassi tomb.

Castellani became fascinated with the beautiful Etruscan granulation and he was determined to find the technique used in this goldwork. In Umbria, he found artists using methods similar to the Etruscan work and persuaded them to come and work with him in Rome.

Because of the political situation in Italy, Castellani's shop was closed from 1840 to 1858. During this time Fortunato Pio retired, leaving Casa Castellani in the hands of two of his eight sons, Alessandro (1824-1883) and Augusto (1829-1914).

These sons were extremely interested in archaeological jewelry and enthusiastically continued and expanded upon what their father had begun.

Augusto managed the business and strove to carry on his father's tradition. Later he became the Director of the Capitolini Museum in Rome.

Because of his political involvements, Alessandro was in prison from 1850 to 1858. During his exile from Rome he continued to research and study. Setting up a workshop in Naples, he continued his experiments with granulation. In 1862 he published a pamphlet "Antique Jewelry and its Revival" to accompany the Castallani display at the London Exhibition. This pamphlet was reprinted again in Philadelphia in 1876. Alessandro published a catalogue "Italian Jewellery as worn by the Peasants of Italy, collected by Signor Castellani," in 1868.

Both Augusto and Alessandro were collectors. Augusto's Collegione Castellani was sold to the Louvre in 1860. Alessandro's Estruscan style jewelry was acquired by the British Museum in London and by the Villa Guilea Museum in Rome.

Marks:

See photographs I-92 and II-197 in this book for examples of Castellani's work.

**Child and Child**

This firm of silversmiths and jewelers was established in London in 1880. They were located at 35 Alfred Place, Kensington from 1891 until they discontinued business in 1916.

Known for high quality enamelwork they were patronized by Royalty.

Mark: a stylized sunflower, the stalk flanked by the initials c & c on each side of the stem

**Peter Carl Fabrege (1846-1920)**

Volumes have been written about this Russian goldsmith and jeweler. Hopefully the reader will take the time to learn about this artist by reading some of the books that include photographs of his lavish work. Two of these are: *Carl Fabrege: Goldsmith to the Imperial Court of Russia* by Kenneth Snowman, and *Fabrege and His Contemporaries* by Henry Hawley and published by the Cleveland Museum of Art.

A little booklet *Fabrege* available through the Victoria and Albert Museum in London contains a list of Fabrege's workmasters and their marks. I highly recommend it.

Marks:

# ФАБЕРЖЕ

**Froment-Meurice**

Francois Desere Froment-Meurice was the son of France Froment a French goldsmith who had been in business since 1774.

After the death of his father, his maother married Pierre-Meurice, who was also a goldsmith. Francois Desere went to work in his stepfather's workshop and added Meurice to the Froment name. Francois Desere Froment-Meurice is said to have studied drawing and sculpture. His work shows evidence of this.

In 1839 he exhibited pieces done in the Gothic Revival style for which he is noted. He was often referred to as the ''Cellini'' of the nineteenth century. He was much admired by his contemporaries.

His enamelled Renaissance style pieces are truly treasures.

Emile Froment-Meurice (1837-1913) took over the family business a number of years after his father's death. He displayed jewelry at the Exposition Universelle in Paris in 1867 executed in the styles made famous by his father.

About 1900 he began to experiment with the new Art Nouveau designs.
Both Father and Sons mark: FROMENT MEURICE

## Giuliano

Carlo Guiliano is another outstanding name in nineteenth century jewelry. Born in Naples, it is believed that he met Alessandro Castilini and worked in his shop there. It was probably Alessandro who instigated Guiliano's move to London. It is evident that Giuliano worked for Casa Castilini in London.

From 1867-1874 his work was sold by prestigious firms such as Robert Phillips, Hunt and Roskell, Harry Emanuel and Hancocks. Pieces bearing his mark were sold in fitted cases imprinted with the retail firm's name. Harry Emanuel exhibited some Giuliano pieces at the L'Exposition of 1867 in Paris.

In 1874-75 Carlo set up his own retail shop at 115 Piccadilly. Here in luxurious surroundings he sold his tiny works of art to some of Britians most prominent families.

His sons, Carolo Joseph and Arthur Alphonse, joined him in the business and continued it after his death in 1895.

The firm was relocated in 1912 at #48 Knightsbridge and was closed in 1914.

Marks:

See photographs II-205, II-210, II-211, II-215 and III-155 in this book for examples of Guiliano's work.

## A. W. N. Pugin

Augustus Wilby Northmore Pugin (1812-52) was a multi-talented Englishman who designed silverware, scenery, ironwork, jewelry, dresses and part of the Houses of Parliament.

His writings include *Designs for Gold and Silversmiths* 1836, *The True Principles of Pointed or Christian Architecture* 1841, *The Glossary of Ecclesiastical Ornament an Costume* 1844, and *Floriated Ornament* in 1849.

He was responsible for reviving the art of enameling and for making the Gothic style popular in England.

His famous set of marriage jewelry was exhibited at the Mediaeval Court at the Crystal Palace in 1851.

John Hardman & Co. in Birmingham, England executed most of his designs.
Mark: (AWP monogram)

# ART NOUVEAU
# DESIGNERS AND MANUFACTURERS AND RETAIL FIRMS

### Edward Colonna

Edward Colonna was a German born (1862) decorative designer whose work spanned both the Art Nouveau and Art Deco period.

After finishing his architectural training in Brussels, he came to America (1882) and worked for a company founded by L.C. Tiffany.

While living in Ohio, he wrote a booklet entitled *Essay on Broom Corn*. The booklet of Art Nouveau designs was inspired by the interlaced lines formed by the stalks of corn which were used to make brooms.

In 1898 he traveled to France and designed jewelry for Maison de l'art Nouveau. The book *Modern Design in Jewellery and Fans, 1903* pictures several of his pieces. Gabriel Mourey states in the book "His works have this great charm in my eyes, that they are neither show-case jewels or mere bejoux de parade, things intended solely for display. As a rule, they are quiet and practical."

After Bing's shop closed in 1905, Colonna returned to America.
Mark: COLONNA (stamped)
　　　 SANB (in a diamond, the mark for
　　　 Maison de l'art Nouveau)

### Wilhelm Lucas van Cranch

Wilhelm Lucas van Cranch (1861-1918) was a German painter and jeweler. His Art Nouveau jewelry designs are said to have an "air of decadence."

He won a gold medal in Paris in 1900.
Mark: WLC (in monogram)

### Theodor Fahrner

Theodor Fahrner (1868-1928) was a jewelry manufacturer in Pforzheim, Germany. His mass produced jewelry was usually done in low-carat gold or silver. He used designers from the Artist's colony in Darmstadt. The book *Modern Designers in Jewellery and Fans* pictures two pieces of jewelry executed by this firm. On eof these pieces was designed by J. M. Olbrich.

Mark:

See photograph III-175 in this book for an example of Theodor Fahrner's work.

### Lucien Gaillard

Lucien Gaillard (born 1861) was a French silversmith, jeweler and enameller who inherited a jewelry business in 1892 that had been founded by his grandfather in 1840.

His talents as a silversmith were praised at the 1889 Paris Exposition.

A friend, Rene Lalique is credited with persuading him to try designing jewelry. About 1900 he opened a workshop where he experimented with materials such as horn and ivory. In 1904, he won First Prize for jewellery at the Paris Salon.

Mark: L. GAILLARD (engraved)

### Rene Jules Lalilque

The foremost designer of the Art Nouveau period was Rene Jules Lalique (1860-1945). At an early age he exhibited a talent for art and at age 16 he was apprenticed to Louis Aucoc.

In 1885 he acquired a fully equipped workshop. Here he designed and made jewelry for such firms as Cartier, Boucheron and Aucoc. Much attention was drawn to his work in the 1890's when the illustrious Sarah Bernhardt became his patron.

A series of 145 pieces of jewelry, which took him 17 years to complete, is now housed at the Foundacion Gulbenkian in Lisbon.

Any study of Art Nouveau jewelry is incomplete without a survey of his work.

Mark:  R. LALIQUE
LALIQUE
R.L.

## Liberty & Co.

Liberty and Company in London, England had a most important influence on the Art Nouveau style. Before anyone had ever used the term Art Nouveau, the style was being offered by this company. In fact, the Art Nouveau style was known as ''stile Liberty'' in Italy for quite some time.

A. L. Liberty had always been intrigued by the designs of the Orient. He had been employed by Farmer and Rogers when they purchased part of the Japanese exhibit from the International Exhibition of 1862. When he opened his own shop in 1876, it was devoted exclusively to goods from India, Japan and other parts of the Orient. The aesthetics patronized his shop, and it became a dominant force on the fashion scene.

In 1899 Liberty introduced a new line of jewelry under the name ''Cymric.'' This jewelry was designed by a group of designers connected with the Arts and Crafts movement including Arthur Gaskin, Bernard Cuzner and Archibald Knox. Most of these pieces were manufactured by W. H. Haseler and Son in Birmingham.

Cymric jewelry is described in a Liberty & Co. advertisement as ''an original and important departure in Gold and Silver work. In this development there is a complete breaking away from convention in the matter of design and treatment which is calculated to commend itself to all who appreciate the note distinguishing artistic productions in which individuality of idea and execution is the essence of the work.''

Liberty & Co. jewelry may bear the Haseler mark or one of the Liberty marks.

Marks: LY & CO (in a triple diamond)
CYMRIC (trademark registered with
the Board of Trade in 1901)
W.H.H. (for W. H. Haseler)

See photographs III-163, III-172, III-192 and III-188 in this book for examples of Liberty and Company's work. Photograph III-188 is also the work of William Henry Hassler.

## Murrle, Bennett & Co.

According to Viviene Becker, this firm was strictly a wholesaler of jewelry and not a manufacturer. The firm was founded in London in 1884 by a German (Murrle) and an Englishman (Bennett).

They sold all styles of jewelry including the New Modern designs associated with the Arts and Crafts movement. Most of the pieces were made in Pforzheim, Germany.

Pieces bearing the Murrle, Bennett & Co. mark are much sought after by collectors.

Marks:

## Otto Prutscher

Otto Prutscher (1880-1961) was a pupil of Josef Hoffman in the Wiener Werkslatte. He was an architect and a jewelry designer. His designs were executed by Rozet & Fischmeister, a Viennese jewelry firm.

In the book *Modern Designs in Jewellery and Fans, 1903* W. Fred makes this comment on Prutscher's work: "Otto Prutscher's necklaces and rings are remarkable alike for this beauty and harmonious variety of their coloring. He uses enamel to a great extent and also quite small precious stones. Very uncommon, too, is the way in which he employs meta, though only enough of it to hold the enamel in place. It would appear as if the artist had in his mind a vision of the women who are to wear his work, who are too tender and frail to carry any weight, so that the use of much metal in ornaments for them would be quite unsuitable."

Mark: OP (in a square monogram)

See photograph III-177 in this book for an example of Otto Prutscher's work.

## Louis Comfort Tiffany

Louis Comfort Tiffany (1848-1933), the eldest son of C. L. Tiffany, was a painter, interior decorator, designer, glassmaker and jeweler.

In 1879 he founded Associated Artist, an interior design firm. HIs decorative work reflected his interest in and his love of

Japanese art. In 1889 he associated himself with another exponent of the Oriental Samuel Bing, owner of Maison de l'Art
Nouveau.

Tiffany studios started making jewelry in 1900. When his father
died in 1902, L. C. Tiffany became the manager of the Company's
jewelry workshops.

Marks: Louis C. Tiffany (in italics)
      LCT, Tiffany & Co.

## Philippe Wolfers

Philippe Wolfers (1858-1929) was a Belgian jeweler who was
also trained in art and sculpturing. He designed for his family
firm and enjoyed working with ivory.

He designed a series of Art Nouveau jewelry and marked it
with his special mark to distinguish it from the pieces done for
the family firm.

In the book *Modern Design in Jewellery and Fans, 1903*, F. Khnopff
gives his opinion on Wolfer's work.

> M. WOLFERS *seeks his inspiration in the study of the nature and the forms
> of his marvellous domain, and his vision of things is specially defined in his
> jewels. The detail therein contributes largely to the spirit of the entire work,
> which borrows its character from the decoration itself or from the subject of that
> decoration. He never allows himself to stray into the regions of fancy; at most,
> he permits his imagination to approach the confines of ornamental abstraction.
> Nevertheless, he interprets Nature, but is never dominated by it. He has too
> true, too exact a sense of the decorative principle to conform to the absolute reality
> of the things he admires and reproduces. His art, by virtue of this rule, is thus
> a modified translation of real forms. He has too much taste to introduce into
> the composition of one and the same jewel flowers or animals which have no
> parallel symbol or, at least, some family likeness or significance. He will associate
> swans with water-lilies—the flowers which frame, as it were, the life of those
> grand poetic birds; or he will put the owl or the bat with the poppy—the triple
> evocation of Night and Mystery; or the heron with the eel—symbols of distant,
> melancholy streams. He rightly judges that in art one must endeavor to recon-
> cile everything, both the idea and the materials whereby one tries to make that
> idea live and speak.*

Mark: PW (in a shield with the words 'exemplaire unique')

# ARTS AND CRAFTS
## DESIGNERS AND MANUFACTURERS

The Arts and Crafts movement was a reaction against the dehumanization of man by the machine. It was not a period style but a movement that began in the late 1850's and continued until the 1920's.

Influenced by the writing of John Ruskin (1819-1900) and the philosophy of William Morris (1834-1896) its exponents believed that there should be no distinction between the designer and the craftsman, and that the best art was achieved when artists worked in partnership.

These artists formed Guilds and lived and worked together. Their dreams of bringing art to the common man by executing ordinary items in honest and hand crafted designs were never fulfilled because the expense involved in hand crafting the items made them unaffordable to the very class for which they were intended. Hollbrook Jackson in his book *The Eighteen-Nineties* published in 1913 has this comment about the movement:

> *The outward effect of this search for excellence of quality and utility in art was, however, not so profound as it might have been. This is explained by the fact that the conditions under which Morris and his group worked were so far removed from the conditions of the average economic and industrial life of the time as to appear impractical for general adoption. They demonstrated, it is true, that it was possible to produce useful articles of fine quality and good taste even in an age of debased industry and scamped counterfeit workmanship; but their demonstration proved also that unless something like a revolution happened among wage-earners none but those of ample wordly means could hope to become possessed of the results of such craftsmanship.*

Today many of these pieces are not only collectable—they are also affordable. If you find the style of Arts and Crafts jewelry appealing, I urge you to buy it. I feel sure that good examples are destined to appreciate in value.

## C. R. Ashbee

Charles Robert Ashbee (1863-1942) was the cornerstone of the Arts and Crafts movement. He founded the School and Guild of Handicraft in 1887-88 which served as a "training ground" for young exponents of the movement.

Ashbee was an admirer of Cellini and translated and published Cellini's "treatises" in 1898. A copy of this fascinating work was published by Dover Publications in 1967. It gives an excellent account of how jewelry was made in the sixteenth century.

Ashbee designed most of the jewelry executed by the Guildsmen. He exhibited at the Vienna Seccession Exhibitions number VIII, XV, XVII and XXIV, and with the Arts and Crafts Society from 1888.

Aymer Vallance, writing about British Jewelry in *Modern Design in Jewellery and Fans, 1903*, had this to say about Ashbee's work:

> AMONG pioneers of the artistic jewelry movement, Mr. C. R. Ashbee holds an honourable place. He stood almost alone at the beginning, when he first made known the jewellery designed by him, and produced under his personal direction by the Guild and School of Handicraft in the East End. It was immediately apparent that here was no tentative nor half-hearted caprice, but that a genuine and earnest phase of an ancient craft had been re-established. Every design was carefully thought out, and the work executed with not less careful and consistent technique. In fact, its high merits were far in advance of anything else in the contemporary jewellery or goldsmith's work. The patterns were based on conventionalized forms of nature, favorite among them being the carnation, the rose and the heartsease, or on abstract forms invited by the requirements and conditions of the material—the ductility and lustre of the metal itself. Most of the ornaments were of silver, the surface of which was not worked up to a brilliantly shining burnish, in the prevalent fashion of the day, but dull polished in such wise as to give the charming richness and tone of old silverwork. Mr. Ashbee also adopted the use of jewels, not lavishly or ostentatiously, but just wherever a note of colour would convey the most telling effect, the stones in themselves, e.g. amethysts, amber, and rough pearl, being of no particular value, save purely from the point of view of decoration. Novel and revolutionary as it were, at its first appearance, the principles underlying Mr. Ashbee's jewellery work—viz, that the value of a personal ornament consists not in the commercial value of the materials so much as in the artistic quality of its design and treatment—they became the standard which no artist thenceforward could wisely afford to ignore, and such furthermore that have even in certain quarters become appropriated by the trade in recent times.

Mark: CRA (pricked or scratched)
        GOH ltd (registered 1898)
See photograph III-178 in this book for an example of C. R. Ashbee's work.

## Birmingham Guild of Handicraft
This firm of craft jewelers was founded in 1890.
The Guild became part of Gittins Craftman LTD in 1910. They had a reputation for making good quality hand-made jewelry.
Mark: BGOH (in a square)

## Bernard Cuzner

Bernard Cuzner (1877-1956) was an English silversmith and jeweler. While serving an apprenticeship as a watchmaker he went to night school at the Redditch School of Art. Soon he gave up watchmaking in favor of silversmithing.

Cusner was strongly influenced by Robert Catterson Smith and Arthur Gaskin. Various Liberty & Co. designs have been attributed to him. In 1935 he published an illustrated book of designs entitled *A Silversmith's Manual.*

Cuzner was head of the metalwork department of the Birmingham School of ARt from 1910 until he retired in 1942.
Mark: BC

## Arthur and Georgie Gaskin

Arthur Gaskin was born in Birmingham, England in 1862. In 1883 he was a student at the Birmingham School of Art. Here he met Georgie Evelyn Cave France (1868-1934). Their mutual interest in design, art and illustrating brought them together and on March 21, 1894, they were married.

Arthur was a "born teacher" and was assistant master at the Central School from 1885 until 1903. From 1903-1924 he was Headmaster and teacher at the School of Jewelers and Silversmiths.

Both Georgia and Arthur entered their work in National Competitions. In 1899 they decided to learn to make jewelry. Commenting on the production of this jewelry Georgia wrote in 1929, "In the jewelry I did all the designing and he did all the enamel, and we both executed the work with our assistants."

In the March 1903 issue of The Magazine of Art an article written by Aymer Vallance states:

> public demand for the jewellery is such that strenuous effort is needed by Mrs. Gaskin, who has a gift for divining the individual wants of her clients, to maintain in every case that touch of personality which contributes no little to the attractiveness of her work. I have always thought that jewellery, requiring as it does dainty taste in the designing and delicate manipulation in execution, is an industry specially suited to lady artists, and it is surprising how few comparatively appear to give it a thought. Mrs. Gaskin's achievements ought to show what can be done by anyone possessed of the above qualifications.

This same author had this to say about the Gaskins in "Modern Design in Jewelry and Fans," 1903:

*Mr. Gaskin came to the conclusion that it was of little benefit for a draughtsman to make drawings on paper to be carried out by someone else; studio and workshop must be one, designer identical with craftsman. It is not very many years since Mr. Gaskin, ably seconded by his wife, started with humble, nay, almost rudimentary apparatus, to make jewelery with his own hands; but the result has proved how much taste and steadfast endurance can accomplish. Their designs are so numerous and so varied — rarely is any single one repeated, except to order — that it is hardly possible to find any description to apply at all. But it may be noted that, whereas a large number have been characterized by a light and graceful treatment of twisted wire, almost like filigree, the two pendants here illustrated seem to indicate rather a new departure on the part of Mr. Gaskin, with their plates of chased metal, and pendants attached by rings, a method not in any sense copied from, yet in some sort recalling the beautiful fashion with which connoisseurs are familure in Norwegian and Swedish peasant jewelry.*

Mark:    A.J.G

G

See photographs III-165 and III-197 for examples of Gaskin's work.

### C. H. Horner

C. H. Horner is a collectable name in English jewelry. He designed his own pieces and his factory produced them from start to finish. This vast array of items included pendants, brooches, chains and hat pins. Most pieces were done in silver and embellished with enamel. The winged scarab and insect motif were frequently used.

Horner pieces are available at London Street Markets and are reasonably priced.

Mark: C. H. (Chester assay)

### Fred I. Partridge

Fred I. Partridge was an English metalworker and jeweler who worked from about 1900 until 1908.

In 1902 he went to work with C. R. Ashbee and the Guild of Handicraft. Partridge was influenced by the work of Lalique and his work reflects this interest.

Partridge married May Hart, a Birmingham trained enameller, in 1906. They set up a business on Dean Street in Soho. From this location they supplied pieces for firms such as Liberty & Co.

A piece by May Hart Partridge in this book on page --, photograph III-149. It is signed by May and dated 1911.

Mark: PARTRIDGE

## Edgar Simpson

Edgar Simpson was an English designer who worked from about 1896 until 1910. He ws one of the original designers at the Artificers Guild when it was founded in 1901. Eventually he became their chief designer.

A good example of what his contemporaries thought about his work can be gleaned from his excertp from an article by Aymer Vallance published in "Modern Design in Jewelry and Fans," 1903:

> MR. EDGAR SIMPSON, of Nottingham, is an artist of great gifts, as his drawings and, still more, the specimens of his actual handiwork here illustrated fully testify. Many excellent designs lose vigor and character in the process of execution from the original sketch; but Mr. Simpson, on the contrary, manages to give his designs additional charm by the exquisite finish with which he works them out in metal. Particularly happy is this artist's rendering of dolphins and other marine creatures; as in the circular pendant where the swirling motion of water is conveyed by elegant curving lines of silver, with a pearl, to represent an air bubble, issuing from the fish's mouth.

Mark: an Artificers Guild with EDWARD SPENCER DEL in a circle

See photograph III-160 in this book for an example of Edgar Simpson's work.

## Henry Wilson

Henry Wilson (1864-1934) was an English sculptor, architect, metalworker and jeweler. He established a workshop in 1890 and joined the Art Workers Guild in 1892. He taught metalworking at the Central High School of Arts and Crafts from 1896 to about 1901.

Wilson exhibited with the Arts and Crafts Society from 1889 and became its President in 1915. His book on design and techniques entitled "Silverwork and Jewellery" was published in 1903.

A Hair Ornament attributed to Henry Wilson was sold by Phillips Blenstock House, London on July 7, 1983 for $1,958. This description was furnished by Phillips: "A good Arts and Crafts gold, silver, plique-a-jour and opal hair ornament attributed to Henry Wilson on stylistic grounds, the crescent-shaped top inset with three circular plique-a-jour plaques decorated in pink, green and turquoise with tulips, flanked by gold florets and silver leaves, with an oval opal cabachon below and tortoiseshell tines to the comb, 17 cm long."

Mark: H.W. (in a monogram)

See photograph III-168 in this book for an example of Henry Wilson's work.

# The American Arts and Crafts Revival

In Chicago the Arts and Crafts Movement was well received by those who shared its philosophy of social and cultural reforms.

After a visit in the 1880's to C. R. Ashbee's Guild in London, Jane Addams became an advocate of the Arts and Crafts Movement. She was instrumental in fostering the movement in America. When Ashbee came to the United States in 1900, he lectured at the Chicago Art Institute and stayed at the Hull House, a settlement run by Jane Addams. The Chicago Arts and Crafts Society was founded there in 1897.

For more information about the Arts and Crafts revival in America I urge you to read "Chicago Metal-Smiths" by Sharon Darling, published by the Chicago Historical Society in 1977. It offers valuable insight to the movement and its exponents. Many of the designers and manufacturers listed in this book are sure to become even more collectable. The book offers excellent photographs of the makers marks.

## The Kalo Shop

Clara Black named the shop she founded in 1900 "Kalo," a Greek word meaning beautiful. At first the shop produced leather items and woven goods but when Clara married George S. Welles, a metalworker in 1905, her interested turned to metalwork and jewelry.

All the items produced by the Kalo shop were hand made. The couple set up a school and workshop known as "The Kalo Art-Craft Community" in their Chicago residence.

Jewelry bearing the Kalo stamp is much sought after by collectors. Since jewelry constituted about half of the company's total sales, pieces are still available at reasonable prices. Mark: KALO

## Florence Koehler

Florence Koehler (1861-1944) was a jewelery designer and craftswoman who lived and worked in Chicago. She was one of the leaders of the Arts and Crafts revival in America and one of the founders of the Chicago Arts and Crafts Society.

Sharon S. Darling's "Chicago Metal-Smiths" lists her as Mrs. F. H. Koehler and states that she was "mentioned as a successful local metalworker and jewelery maker in an article by Harriet Monroe 'An Experiment in Jewelry' " (House Beautful, July 1900).

# ART DECO RETAIL FIRMS

## ART DECO

The Art Deco period style was reflected in the jewelry made by leading jewelry firms such as Bocheron, Cartier, Chaumet, La Cloche, Mauboissin and Van Cleef & Aprels. Some important designers of the period were George Fouquet, Gerard Sandoz, Jean Despres and Raymond Templier.

### Cartier

This firm was founded in 1847 when Louis Francois Cartier opened a small shop in Paris. In 1898 the company relocated to 13 Rue de la Paix.

A London branch was opened in 1902 followed by the New York branch in 1903 or 1912.

Cartiers is credited with making the first wristwatch in 1904. The firm executed some of the finest examples of Art Deco jewelry.

Marks: LFC (in a diamond shaped shield)
      AC (with a hatchet)

See photographs III-79, III-89, III-159, IV-207, IV-209, IV-227, IV-229, IV-231, IV-232, IV-249, IV-257, IV-265, IV-266 and V-91 in this book for examples of Cartier's work.

### Chaumet & Cie

This French firm was founded in 1780 by Erienne Nitot. The company was commissioned to make the Emperor's coronation crown and sword after Nitot assisted an accident victim who turned out to be the First Counsul Napoleon Bonaparte. They also executed the wedding jewelry for Marie Louise in 1810. In 1875 they opened a showroom in London.

Their Art Deco pieces were most sophisticated.

### George Jensen

George Jensen (1866-1935) was a Danish goldsmith and silversmith who opened a shop bearing his name in 1904. He designed, made and sold jewelry and silverware.

His distinctive style is still evident in the work produced by the firm today.

Marks: Jensen; GJ

### La Cloche

La Cloche was both a manufacturer and retailer of Art Deco jewelry. Founded in Madrid in 1875, the Paris branch was opened in 1898. The firm was known for its high fashion style executed in the finest materials and embellished with colored gems and diamonds.

### Van Cleef & Arpels

This French firm was founded in 1906. It is credited with creating the first 'minaudiere.' In 1930 this name was trademarked by them.

Their main office is still in Paris but they have branches in London and New York.

# COLLECTABLE
# AMERICAN MARKS

### Black, Starr & Frost Co. New York

This firm of goldsmiths and jewelers was established in New York in 1810 and known as "Marquand & Co." In 1839 the company's name was changed to "Ball, Thomkins and Black;" and in 1851 it was changed to "Ball, Black & Co."

The name "Black, Starr & Frost" was with the company from 1876 until it merged with the Gorham Corporation in 1929.

Their customers were prestigious and pieces from their stock were often illustrated in fashion magazines of the day.

Marks:  See photograph IV-198 in this book for an example of Black, Star & Frost Company's work.

B S & F
Black Starr
Black, Starr & Frost Ltd.

## Gorham Corporation Inc. Providence, R.I.

This company, founded by Jabez Gorham in 1815, is included in this section because of some jewelry it produced in the late nineteenth and early twentieth century. This jewelry was designed by a group of artists under the direction of William C. Codman and executed by a group of silversmiths selected by Edward Holbrook. The pieces were marketed under the name MARTELE and are quite collectable.

They were usually made of silver, silver gilt or copper. The few pieces with stones were set with the colorless ones most popular during the Art Nouveau period.

Mark:

## Wm. B. Kerr & Co.

This firm of goldsmiths, silversmiths and jewelers was founded in Newark, New Jersey in 1855 by William B. Kerr.

The company mass produced pieces in the neo-Renaissance style and the Art Nouveau style.

The Gorham Corporation purchased the company in 1906.

Today pieces bearing the Kerr trademark are prized by collectors.

Marks:

## C. L. Tiffany

In 1853, C. L. Tiffany founded Tiffany & Co. Prior to that year he had been in partnership with J. B. Young (1837) and J. L. Ellis (1850).

Pieces bearing the Tiffany name can best be dated by following the progression of moves by the company:

1853-54:     217 Broadway
1854-1870:   550 Broadway
1870:        Union St. and 15th St.
1868:        London Branch opened.

Tiffany & Co. exhibited at the Exposition Universelle in Paris 1867, and at the Philadelphia Centennial Exposition of 1876. In 1878 and 1889 they won gold medals in Paris.

Special marks were added to Tiffany & Co.'s usual markings for pieces made for the World's Columbian Exposition in Chicago in 1893, the Exposition Universelle in Paris in 1900 and the Pan-American Exposition in Buffalo in 1901. These are shown below.

Marks:

1898 | 1900 | 1901
World's Columbian Exposition Chicago. | Exposistion Universelle, Paris. | Pan American Exposition, Buffalo.

See photographs II-202, III-92, III-93, III-153, III-156, IV-235, V-96 and V-97 in this book for examples of Tiffany and Company's work.

## Unger Brother

This firm of silversmiths and jewelers has a very collectable trademark.

Unger Brothers began making jewelry in 1878. Eugene and Frederick Unger opened a shop at #18 Crawford St. in Newark, New Jersey in 1881.

P. O. Dickinson, the company's chief designer, was issued a series of patents for Art Nouveau jewelry design in 1903. The Company mass produced these designs in silver and silver gilt from 1904 until 1910. In 1914 they discontinued the manufacturer of jewelry.

Marks:

(Old Mark.)  (Old Mark.)  (1904)

## Wayne Silver Co.

This firm was founded in Honesdale, Pennsylvania in 1895. They are described as making "fancy and useful articles of silver, not plated." Records indicate that they discontinued business after the turn of the century.

Marks:

## Whiting & Davis Co. Inc.

This company was founded in 1876 in Plainville, Massachusetts. In 1907 C. A. Whiting became owner. Shortly after this, the first chainmail mesh machine was developed and Whiting & Davis became the world's largest manufacturer of mesh products.

Many fine examples of their early bags have survived. These are eagerly sought after by collectors because of their beauty and durability. New bags manufactured by this company are sold in many major department stores.

The company also produces a line of antique and museum reproduction jewelry.

Marks:

# GLOSSARY

## A

**Algrette** — Jewels mounted in a shape resembling, feathers or a feather motif.

**A-Jour Setting** — An open work setting in which the bottom portion of the stone can be seen. Also a setting in which the metal has open work.

**Albert Chain** — A watch chain for a man or a woman with a bar at one end and a swivel to hold a watch at the other.

**Alma Chain** — A chain with broad ribbed links.

## B

**Baguette** — A stone cut in the shape of a narrow rectangle.

**Banded Agate** — Agate which has bands of lighter and darker colors. It can by onyx (black/white), cornelian (orangish red/white), or sardonyx (brown/white).

**Bangle** — A rigid bracelet often tubular and hinged.

**Basse-Taille** — An enamelling technique in which a transluscent enamelling is applied to an engraved metal surface.

**Baton** — A stone cut in the shape of a long narrow rectangle.

**Beauty Pins** — Pins popular from the mid 1800's until after the turn of the century. Usually under 2" long with rounded ends.

**Belcher Mounting** — A claw type ring mounting on which there were many variations. Popular from the 1870's thru 1920's.

**Benoiton Chain** — A chain worn suspended from the top of the head that encircled the head and dropped down onto the bosom.

**Bezel** — A metal rim which holds the stone in a ring, a cameo in its mounting or a crystal on a watch.

**Black Amber** — A misnomer for jet.

**Bloomed Gold** — A textured finish on gold that is created by immersing in acid to give it a matte pitted effect.

**Bog Oak** — Wood preserved in the bogs of Ireland and used to make jewelry during the Victorian era.

**Bohemian Garnet** — A dark red pyrope garnet.

**Brilliant Cut** — A cut that returns the greatest amount of white light to the eye. It usually has 57 or 58 facets. Usually used for diamonds or other transparent stones.

**Briolettes** — A tear drop shaped cut covered with facets.

**Brooch** — An ornamental piece of jewelry which has a pin back for affixing it to clothing or hats. Usually larger in scale than the ones referred to as "pins".

**Brooch-Watch** — A watch with a brooch affixed so it is worn as one would wear a brooch.

**Bulla** — A round ornamental motif found in ancient jewelry.

## C

**Cabochon** — A stone cut in round oval shape in which the top is convex shaped (not faceted).

**Cairngorm** — Yellow brown to smokey yellow quartz named after the mountain range in which it is found in Scotland.

**Calibre Cut** — Small stones cut in the shape of squares, rectangles or oblongs used to embellish jewelry.

**Cameo** — A layered stone in which a design is engraved on the top layer and the remainder is carved away to reveal the next layer, leaving the design in relief. Also done in shell, coral and lava.

**Cameo Habille** — A type of cameo in which the carved head is adorned with a necklace, earrings or head ornament set with small stones.

**Cannetille** — A type of metal decoration named after the type of embroidery made with fine twisted gold or silver thread. It is done using thin wires to make a filligree pattern. Used frequently in England in 1840.

**Carat** — A unit of weight for gemstones. Since 1913 one metric carat is one fifth of a gram or 200 milligrams.

**Carbuncle** — Today used to refer to a garnet cut in cabochon. In the middle ages it referred to any cabochon cut red stone.

**Cartouche** — An ornamental tablet used in decoration or to be engraved, usually symmetrical.

**Celluloid** — One of the first plastics. A compound of camphor and guncotton. Highly flammable.

**Champlive** — An enamelling technique in which enamel is put into areas engraved or carved into the metal.

**Channel Setting** — A type of setting in which stones of the same size are held in place by a continuous strip of metal at the top and bottom literally creating a channel for the stones.

**Chasing** — The technique of embellishing metal by hand using hammers and punches to make indentations – thus raising the design.

**Chatelaine** — A metal clasp or hook worn at the waist from which hang a variety of useful items suspended by chains.

**Chaton** — The central or main ornament of a ring.

**Cipher** — A monogram of letters intertwined.

**Claw Setting** — A style of ring setting in which the stone is held by a series of vertically projecting prongs.

**Clip** — A piece of jewelry resembling a brooch but instead of having a pin stem to fasten into clothing it has a hinged clip that hooks over and into the fabric. Very popular from the 1920's - 40's. Sometimes made as a brooch that incorporated a double clip. It could be worn as a brooch or disassembled and used as a pair of clips.

**Cloisonne** — An enamelling technique in which the enamel is placed into little preformed compartments or cells built on to the metal.

**Collet Setting** — A ring setting in which the stone is held by a circular band of metal.

**Coronet Setting** — A round claw setting in a crown like design.

**Cravat Pin** — The same as a tie pin.

**Creole Earrings** — A hoop style in which the metal is thicker and wider at the bottom than at the top.

**Croix a la Jeanette** — A piece in the form of a heart from which a cross is suspended. A form of French Peasant Jewelry. Circa 1835.

**Cross-Over** — A style of ring, bracelet or brooch in which the stone set decorative portions overlap and lie alongside each other.

**Crown Setting** — An open setting resembling a crown.

**Cultured Pearl** — A type of pearl induced and stimulated by man to grow inside a mollusk.

**Curb Chain** — A chain in which the oval flattened links are twisted so that they lie flat.

**Cushion Cut** — A square or rectangular shape with rounded corners. Also called "antique cut".

**Cut Steel Jewelry** — Jewelry made of steel studs which are faceted. Popular from the 1760's until the late 19th century.

**Cymric** — A trade name used by Liberty & Co. for articles sold by them which were designed and manufactured by English firms. The name was adoped in 1899.

## D

**Designer** — A person who designs jewelry. Occasionally they were also makers of jewelry.

**Damascene** — the art of incrusting metals with other metals.

378

**Demi-Parure** — A matching set of jewelry consisting of only a few pieces such as a necklace with matching earrings or a bracelet with matching brooch.

**Demi Hunter** — A watch with a lid over the face in which there is a circular hole in the middle to expose the hands of the watch.

**Dog Collar** — A type of necklace consisting of rows of beads or a wide band worn snugly around the neck.

**Doublet** — An assembled stone consisting of two materials, usually garnet and glass.

## E

**Edwardian Jewelry** — Jewelry made during the reign of Edward VII, 1901-1910, that does not fall into the "Art Nouveau" or "Arts and Crafts Movement" category.

**Electro-Plating** — The process of covering metal with a coating of another metal by using electrical current.

**Electrum** — A pale yellow alloy made by mixing 20% gold and 80% silver.

**Enamel** — A glass-like material used in powder or flux form and fired on to metal.

**Engine-Turning** —Decoration with engraved lines produced on a special lathe.

**Engraving** — A technique by which a design is put into a metal surface using incised lines.

**Eternity Ring** — A ring with stones set all the way around. Symbolizing the "never ending" circle of eternity.

## F

**Fede Ring** — An engagement ring which features two hands "clasped in troth".

**Ferronniere** — A chain that encircles the forehead as portrayed in Leonardo da Vince's "La Bell Torronniere". A 16th century adornment, it was revived during the Victorian era.

**Filligree** — Ornamental designs made by using plain twisted or plaited wire.

**Fob** — A decorative ornament suspended by a chain usually worn with a watch.

**Foil** — A think layer or coating used on the back of stones to improve their color and brilliance.

**French Jet** — It is neither French nor Jet, instead this term usually refers to black glass.

# G

**Gilloche** — Engraved decoration of geometric design achieved by engine turning. Usually used as a base for translucent enamel.

**Girandole** — Brooch or earring style in which 3 pendant stones hang from a large central stone.

**Gunmetal** — An alloy of 90% copper and 10% tin that was very popular in the 1890's.

**Gutta-Percha** — A hard rubber material made from the sap of a Malayan tree. Discovered in the 1840's, it was used for making jewelry, statuary and even furniture.

**Gypsy Setting** — A type of setting in which the stone is set down flush in the mounting.

# H

**Hairwork Jewelry** — Jewelry made using hair worked on a table or jewelry that incorporates hair and was worked on a pallette.

**Hallmark** — A group of markings used on silver and gold in England since 1300 to designate the fineness of the metal, the town in which it was assayed, and the name of the maker.

**Holbeinesque** — A style of jewelry popular in England in the 1870's. Its inspiration was from the design of Hans Holbein the Younger.

**Hunting Case** — A watch that has a lid covering the face. A case spring is activated by pushing on the crown causing the lid to pop open.

exchange rate of the dollar was about $1.45 to the pound.

An important fact to keep in mind when observing auction prices is that approximately 70% of those buying at auction are

# I

**Incise** — A line cut or engraved in a material.

**Intaglio** — A design cut below the surface of a stone. The opposite of a cameo.

**Intarsia** — The use of stones to make a picture by cutting them out and inlaying them flushly into a background stone.

# J

**Jabot Pin** — A type of stick pin worn on the front of ladies blouses.

**Jet** — A very light weight black or brownish black material which is a variety of the coal family.

## K

**Karat** — Pure gold is 24 karats. The karat of gold alloy is determined by the percentage of pure gold. For instance 18K gold is 750 parts pure gold and 250 parts other metal or 18 parts pure gold and 6 parts other metal.

## L

**Lava Jewelry** — Jewelry made of the lava from Mt. Vesuvius. Usually carved into cameos or intaglios and sold as souvenirs of the "grand tour".

**Lavaliere** — A light scaled necklace usually consisting of a pendant or pendants suspended from a chain. In the 1890-1910 era it usually had a baroque pearl appendage. The word is probably derived from the Dutchess de la Valliere, a mistress of Louis XIV.

**Line Bracelet** — A flexible bracelet composed of stones of one size or graduating in size, set in a single line.

**Luckenbooth Brooches** — So called because they were sold in street stalls (Luckenbooths) near St. Giles Kirk in Edinburg. The motif usually consisted of one or two hearts occasionally surrounded by a crown. When the motif included the initial "M" the brooch was referred to as a Queen Mary Brooch.

## M

**Marcasite** — A misnomer that is now commonly accepted trade name for pyrite. Popular from the 18th century onwards.

**Marquise** — A boat shaped cut used for diamonds and other gem stones. Also called a "navette" shape.

**Memento Mori** — "Remember you must die." Grim motifs such as coffins, skeletons, etc. Worn as a reminder of ones mortality.

**Millegrain** — A setting in which the metal holding the stone is composed of tiny grains or beads.

**Mizpah Ring** — A popular ring of the 19th century consisting of a band with the word Mispah engraved across the top. "May the Lord watch between me and thee while we are absent from the other."

**Mosaic** — A piece of jewelry in which the pattern is formed by the inlaying if various colored stones or glass. Two types of mosaic work are Roman and Florentine.

**Mourning Jewelry** — Jewelry worn "in memory of" by friends and relatives of the deceased. Often sums of money were set aside in one's will to have pieces made to be distributed to mourners attending the funeral.

**Muff Chain** — A long chain worn around the neck and passed through the muff to keep it secure.

# N

**Necklace Lengths** — Choker 15 inches, Princess 18 inches, Matinee 22 inches, Opera 30 inches, Rope 60 inches long.

**Nickle Silver** — A combination of copper, nickle, zinc and sometimes small amounts of tin, lead or other metals.

**Neillo** — A decorative technique in which the metal is scooped out (in the same manner as champleve) and the recessed area is filled with a mixture of metallic blue black finish. The technique dates back to the Bronze Age. Good examples of this work can be found in the Siamese Jewelry of the 1950's in this book.

# O

**Old Mine Cut** — An old style of cutting a diamond in which the girdle outline is squarish, the crown is high and the table is small. It has 32 crown facets plus a table, and 24 pavillion facets plus a culet.

# P

**Paste Jewelry** — Jewelry which is set with glass imitation gems. Very popular in the 18th century, it provides us with many good examples of the jewelry from that time period.

**Parure** — A complete matching set of jewelry usually consisting of a necklace, earrings, brooch and bracelet.

**Pate de Verre** — An ancient process in which glass is ground to powder, colored, placed in a mold, and fired. It was revived in the 19th century and used to make many pieces of Art Nouveau jewelry.

**Pave Setting** — A style of setting in which the stones are set as close together as possible, presenting a cobblestone effect.

**Pebble Jewelry** — Scottish jewelry (usually silver) set with stones native to Scotland. Very popular during the Victorian era.

**Pendeloque** — A faceted drop shaped stone (similar to a briolette) that has a table.

**Pietra Dura** — (Hard stone). Flat slices of chalcedony, agate, jasper and lapis luzuli used in Florentine mosaic jewelry.

**Pinchbeck** — An alloy of copper and zinc invented by Christopher Pinchbeck in the 1720's that looked like gold. It was used for making jewelry, watches and accessories. This term is very misused today. Some dealers refer to any piece that is not gold as "pinchbeck".

**Pique** — A technique of decorating tortoise shell by inlaying it with pieces of gold and silver. Popular from the mid 17th century until Edwardian time.

**Platinum** — A rare heavy, silvery white metallic element which is alloyed with other metals and used to make fine pieces of jewelry.

**Plique-A-Jour** — An enamelling technique that produces a "stained glass effect" because the enamel is held in a metal frame without any backing. An ancient technique, it was revived and used extensively by Art Nouveau designers.

**Poincon** — A French term for the mark on French silver similar to the English Hallmark.

**Posy Ring** — A finger ring with an engraved motto (often rhymed) on the inner side.

## R

**Regard Ring** — A finger ring set with 6 stones of which the first letter is each spell REGARD. The stones most commonly used were: Ruby, Emerald, Garnet, Amethyst, Ruby and Diamond.

**Repousse Work** — A decorative technique of raising a pattern on metal by beating, punching or hammering from the reverse side. Often called embossing.

**Rhinestone** — Originally rock crystal found along the banks of the Rhine river. Today, a misnomer for colorless glass used in costume jewelry.

**Rhodium** — A white metallic element that is part of the platinum group. Because of its hard reflective finish it is often used as a plating for jewelry.

**Riviere** — A style of necklace containing individually set stones of the same size or graduating in size that are set in a row without any other ornamentation.

**Rose Cut** — A cutting style in which there are 24 triangular facets meeting at the top with a point. The base is always flat. Diamonds cut this way are usually cut from macles.

**Ruolz** — A gilded or silvered metal named after the inventor of the process who was a French chemist.

## S

**Sautoir** — A long neck chain that extended beyond a woman's waist. Usually terminating in a pendant or tassel.

**Signet Bangle** — A hinged tubular bracelet with a central plaque for engraving. Very popular in the 1890-1910 time period.

**Signet Ring** — A ring with a central plaque on which ones initials were engraved. Sometimes a seal or crest was used.

**Scarf Pin** — A straight pin approximately 2½ inches long with a decorative head. It was used between 1880-1915 to hold the ties in place. It is the same as a tie pin.

**Seed Pearl** — A small pearl weighing less than ¼ grain.

**Shank** — The circle of metal that attaches to the head of a ring and encircles the finger.

**Star Setting** — A popular setting in the 1890's in which the stone is placed in an engraved star and secured by a small grain of metal at the base of each point.

**Stomacher** — A large triangular piece of jewelry worn on the bodice and extending below the waistline. An 18th century style that was revived during the Edwardian period.

**Swivel** — A fitting used to attach a watch to a chain. It has an enlongated spring opening for attaching the watch. The swivel allows the watch to hang properly.

**Synthetic** — A man-made material with the same physical, chemical and optical properties as the natural. Not to be confused with imitation.

## T

**Taille D Epargne** — An enamelling technique in which engraved depressions are filled with opaque enamel.

**Tiffany Setting** — A round six prong mounting with a flare from the base to the top.

**Trademark** — The mark registered with the U.S. Patent Office that identifies a wholesaler or retailer.

## V

**Vermeil** — Guilded silver. Sterling silver with a gold plating.

## W

**White Gold** — An alloy of gold, nickle and zinc developed in 1912 to imitate the popular platinum.

**White Metal** — A base metal of tin, antimony and copper used in the manufacture of costume jewelry. It is usually electroplated.

# SELECTED BIBLIOGRAPHY

## I. Art and Style

*Barelli*, Renoto. Art Nouveau, Fulthan, Middlesex, Hamlyn House, 1969.

*Batterberry*, Michael, Twentieth Century Art, New York, McGraw—Hill Book Co.

*Battersly*, Martin, Art Nouveau, Middlesex, Hamlyn House, 1969.

*Buel*, J.W., The Magic City, St. Louis-Philadelphia: Historical Pub. Co., 1894.

*Grief*, Martin, Depression Modern, New York, Universe Books, 1975.

. Treasures of Tutankhamun, New York, The Metropolitan Museum of Art, 1976.

*Warren*, Geoffrey, All Color Book of Art Nouveau, London, Octopus Books Limited, 1972.

## II. Catalogues

*Benjamin Allen & Co.*, Wholesale Jewelers Catalogue, Chicago: 1947.

*The Brecker Book 1947*, Wholesale Catalogue, Chicago, Austin N. Clark, 1946.

*Criterion Illustrated Wholesale Catalogue*, Chicago, Rahde-Spencer Co., 1929.

*The Crystal Palace Exhibition Illustrated Catalogue*—London 1851, "The Art Journal Special Issue New York, Dover Publications Inc., 1970.

*Henn & Haynes, Jewelry & Opticians*, Gift Suggestions 1916 Chillicothe, Ohio, New York, The United Jewelers Inc., 1916.

*Marshall Field & Co. 1896 Illustrated Catalogue* Edited by Joseph J. Schroeder, Jr., Chicago, Follett Publishing Co., 1970.

*R. Chester Frost & Co. 1896 Illustrated Catalogue*, Chicago, Illinois, Manufacturing Jewelers, 1896.

*Montgomery, Ward & Co., Fall & Winter 1928-29 Catalogue* #109 Kansas City: Montgomery Ward & Co., 1928.

*Montgomery, Ward & Co. Fall & Winter 1931-32 Catalogue* #115 Kansas City: Montgomery Ward & Co., 1931.

*Montgomery, Ward & co. Spring & Summer 1946* Kansas City: Montgomery Ward & Co., 1946.

*Montgomery, Ward & Co., Fall & Winter 1958-59* Kansas City: Montgomery Ward & Co., 1958.

*C.B. Norton Illustrated Jewelry Catalogue* Kansas City: 1923.

*C.B. Norton 1924—Illustrated Jewelry Catalogue* Kansas City, Mo.: 1924.

*The Ring Mounting Salesman* Issued by Graffe & Stanik. Chicago, Ill.: 1920.

*Sears, Roebuck & Co. Fall & Winter 1933-34* Kansas City: Sears, Roebuck & Co., 1933.

*Sears, Roebuck & Co. Fall & Winter 1935-36*

*Sears, Roebuck & Co. Fall & Winter 1936-37* Copyright by Sears Roebuck & Co., 1936.

*J.R. Wood & Sons Jewelry & Diamonds Catalogues* New York: 1927.

*Otto Young & Co. 1888, Chicago, Illinois* Chicago: J.L. Regan Printing Co., 1888.

## III. Fashions

Carter, Earnestine. *The Changing World of Fashion* New York: G.P. Putman's Sons, 1977.

Gold, Annalee. *75 Years of Fashion* New York: Fairchild Publications Inc., 1975.

    *Fifty Years of Fashion* New York: Fairchild Publication Inc., Based on material that appeared originally in Women's Wear Daily.

## IV. General Antiques

    *Three Centuries of American Antiques* By the editors of American Heritage. New York: Bonanza Books, 1979.

    *The Conoissures Complete Period Guide* Edited by Ralph Edwards and L.B. Ramsey New York: Bonanza Books, 1968.

Bishop, Robert and Patricia Coblentz. *The World of Antiques, Art and Architecture in Victorian America* New York: E.P. Dutton, 1979.

Depperd, Carl W. *Victorian, The Cinderella of Antiques* New York: Doubleday & Co., 1950.

Lavine, Sigmund A. *Handmade in America* New York: Dodd, Mead & Co., 1966.

McClinton, Katharine Morrison. *Antiques Past and Present* New York: Branhall House, 1971.

Mebane, John. *Treasure at Home* New Jersey: A.S. Barnes & Co. Inc., 1964.

Norbury, James. *The World of Victoriana* New York: Hambyn House, 1972. A beautiful book filled with interesting information.

Peter, Mary. *Collecting Victoriana* New York: Frederich A. Praeger Pub., 1968.

Pevsnev, Nicholaus. *High Victorian Design* London: Architecural Press, 1951.

Shull, Thelma. *Victorian Antiques* Vermont: Charles E. Tuttle Co., 1963.

## V. Jewelry

Armstrong, Mary, *Victorian Jewelry* New York: McMillian Publishing Co., 1976. A beautiful book about jewelry.

Bauer, J. and A, *A Book of Jewels* Prague: Artia, 1966.

Benda, Klement. *Ornament and Jewellery* Prague: Svoboda, 1967. Archeological finds from Eastern Europe.

Bradford, Ernle. *English Victorian Jewellery* New York: Robert M. McBride & Co. Inc., 1957.

Bradford, Ernle. *Four Centuries of European Jewellery* Great Britian: Spring Books, 1967.

Burgess, Frederich W. *Antique Jewelry and Trinkets* New York: Tudor Publishing Co., 1919.

Curran, Mona. *A Treasury of Jewels and Gems* New York: Emerson Books Inc., 1962.

Curran, Mona. *Collecting Antique Jewellery* New York: Emerson Books, 1964.

Evans, Joan. *A History of Jewellery 1100-1870* Boston, Mass.: Boston Book and Art Publications, 1970.

Gene, Charlotte. *Victorian Jewelry Design* Chicago: Henery Regnery Co., 1973.

Goldemberg, Rose Leeman. *Antique Jewelry, A Practical and Passionate Guide* New York: Crown Publishers, 1976.

Flower, Margaret. *Victorian Jewellery* New York: Duell, Sloan and Pearce, 1951.

Fregnac, Claude. *Jewellery From The Renaissance to Art Nouveau* London: Octopus Books, 1973.

Hornung, Clarence P. *Antique and Jewelry Designs* New York: George Braziller, 1968.

Jessup, Ronald. *Anglo-Saxon Jewellry* United Kingdom: Shire Publishers Ltd., 1974.

Kuzel, Vladislav. *A Book of Jewelry* Prague: Artia, 1962.

Giltay-Nijsoon L. *Jewelry* New York: Universe Books, 1964.

Percival, MacIver. *Chats on Old Jewellery and Trinkets* New York: Frederich A. Stokes Co., 1902.

Peter, Mary. *Collecting Victorian Jewellery* New York: Emerson Books, Inc., 1971.

Sataloff, Joseph and Alison Richards. *The Pleasures of Jewelry & Gemstones* London: Octopus Books, 1975. A beautiful informative book.

Schumann, Walter. *Gemstones of the World* New York: Sterling Publishing Co., 1979. A great new book on gems.

Smith, H. Clifford. *Jewellery* New York: G. P. Putnams & Co., 1908.

*Jewelry Ancient to Modern* New York: Viking Press in cooperation with the Walters Art Gallery, Baltilmore, 1979.

## VI. Magazines

Adrian, "Setting Styles Through the Stars," *Ladies Home Journal* Feb. 1933, pgs. 10-11.

Bliven, Bruce. "Flapper Jane," *The New Republic* Dec. 9, 1925, pgs. 65-67.

Case, Tina Bailie, "Fashion Primer for Winter," *Independent Women* Nov., 1937, pgs., 348-50.

Hampton, Edgar Lloyd, "A 1200 Mile Style Parade," *Nations's Business* April 1937, pg. 78.

Hageland, Ruth. *Country Gentleman* Sept., 1934.

Koues, Helen. "The Reflector of the Times," Good Housekeeping May, 1935, pgs. 62-63.

Lewis, Mary. "Culottes for Action," *Collier's Magazine* May 9, 1942, pg. 50.

Mollay, Anne Shirley. "Jewels for the Yuletide," *Country Life* Dec., 1926, pgs. 88-90.

Ray, Marci Beynon. "The Jewel for Every Occasion", *The Delinator* April, 1928, pg. 35.

Read, Helen Appleton. "The Exposition in Paris," *International Studies* Nov., 1925, pg. 93.

Robinson, Selma. "Glowing Compliments," *Saturday Evening Post* Sept. 29, 1934, pg. 26.

Samberg, Ronben. "Costume Jewelry," *Fortune Magazine* Dec., 1946, pg. 140.

"The Neo-Modern School," *The Delinator* Oct., 1936, pg. 32.

"Crazy over Jewelry, *Collier's Magazine* Dec. 15, 1943, pg. 93.

*American Magazine* March, 1948, pg. 118.

*Business Week,* Sept. 10, 1938, Sept. 5, 1942, Feb. 2, 1943, April 17, 1943, Sept. 2, 1944.

*Colliers Magazine,* July 26, 1947, pg. 34.

*The Delinator,* Oct. 1936.

*Fortune Magazine,* Jan., 1937, May, 1946, Dec., 1946.

*Frank Lesless Illustrated Newspaper,* Jan. 5, 1878 through Nov. 23, 1878.

*Godey's Lady's Book,* Philadelphia, January-December, 1850, January-June, 1859; New York, July-December, 1896.

*Gleasons Pictoreal Drawingroom Companion,* Oct. 8, 1853.

*Good Housekeeping,* May, 1939.

**Harper's Magazine,** New York: Harper & Brothers, January-December, 1876, July, 1877.

*Life Magazine,* June 27, 1949, pg. 93, April 21, 1952, April 26, 1954, pg. 129, Sept. 10, 1956, pg. 49.

*The Literary Digest,* Nov. 21, 1925, Jan. 16, 1926.

*Look Magazine,* May 31, 1955.

*Newsweek,* Aug. 1, 1955, May 5, 1958.

*Time Magazine,* Sept. 8, 1941, pg. 64, April 13, 1942, pg. 18.

*The Young Ladies Journal,* January-December, 1887.

## VII. Metals

Bradbury, Frederich. *Bradburys Book of Hallmarks* Sheffield, England: J.W. Northend Ltd., 1928.

Wyler, Seymour B. *The Book of Old Silver* New York: Crown Publishing Inc., 1937.

# VIII. Personalities

Bently, Nichola, *Edwardian Album* New York: Viking Press, 1974.

Pearsall, Ronald. *Edwardian Life and Leasure* New York: St. Martin's Press, 1973.

Purtell, Joseph. *The Tiffany Touch* New York: Random House Inc.. 1971. A good book on the famous Tiffany's.

Strachey, Lytton. *Queen Victoria* New York: Harcourt, Brace & Co., 1921.

# IX. The Times

*The Fabulous Century* by the editors of Time-Life Books. Vols. 1-VI. New York: Time Inc., 1969.

*The Centennial Portfolio; A Souvenir of the International Exibition in Phil.* Philadelphia: T. Hunter, 1876.

*Life History of the United States* Vols. 1-12. New York: Time Inc., 1964.

Brunhammer, Yvonne. *The Nineteen Twenties Style* New York: Paul Hamlyn, 1969.

Dickens, Charles. *David Copperfield* New York: Simon & Schuster, 1959.

Jenkins, Alan. *The Twenties* New York: Universe Books, 1974.

Jenkins, Alan. *The Thirties* New York: Stein & Day Publishers, 1976.

Partridge, Bellamy, and Otto Bettmann. *As We Were 1850-1900* New York: McGraw-Hill Book Co., Inc., 1946.

Randel, William Pierce. *Centennial American Life in 1876* New York: Chilton Book Co., 1969. A most informative book.

## NOTES

[1] *The Crystal Palace Exhibitilon Illustrated Catalogue* London 1851, The Art. Journal Special Issue; New York; Dover Pub. 1970 pg. 127.

[2] *Godey's Lady's Book.* June 1855, pg. 501.

[3] *The Centennial Portfollio; A Souvenir of the International Exposition in Philadelphia* Philadelphia: T. Hunter, 1876, no page number.

[4] *Ibid.*

[5] *Ibid.*

[6] Patridge, Bellamy, and Otto Bettmann. *As We Were.* New York: McGraw Hill Book Co., 1969, pg. 140.

[7] *McCalls Magazine,* May, 1909.

[8] Buel, J.W. *The Magic City,* St. Louis, Philadelphia: Historical Publishing Co., 1894, pg. 2.

[9]*Ibid.*, no page number.

[10] *The Columbian Exposition Album.* Chicago: rand, McNally & Co., 893.

[11]Burl, J.W. *op. cit.*, no page number.

[12]Jenkins, Alan. *The Twenties.* New York: Universal Books, 1974, pg. 66.

[13]Adrian. "Styles Through the Star," *Ladies Home Journal* February 1933, pg. 10.

[14]Read, Helen Appleton. "The Exposition in Paris," *International Studio* Nov., 1925, pg. 95.

[15]*Business Week*, Sept. 5, 1942, pg. 64.

[16]*Ibid.*

[17]*Business Week Magazine*, Feb. 27, 1943, pg. 51.

[18]*Newsweek*, May 5, 1958, pg. 98.